PRAISE FOR *LEADERSHIP FOR SUSTA*

Rooted in experience and encouragement of what can be achieved, *Leadership for Sustainability* provides school leaders with an inspiring 'greenprint' for embedding sustainability throughout school communities. Every school should have access to this book to support their vital role at the centre of education for sustainability, so that every young person is equipped for a healthier, happier and fairer future.

Dr Elizabeth Rushton, Associate Professor of Education, UCL Institute of Education

Leadership for Sustainability is not a neutral book. At each turn, Dixon's personal values and purpose shine through his words, and he is unafraid to challenge the status quo and big names. He elegantly describes what it really means to be a leader with sustainability as one of your values, as much as the operational process by which you might accomplish the aim of moving your school estate to net zero. The provocations and reflections in each chapter help to frame the discussions, and form the starting point for your own journey towards leadership for sustainability, if you have courage enough to grasp them. This is a provocative and challenging book for traditional leadership models.

Dr David Preece, Head of Geography, Teach First

This thought-provoking book is both timely and relevant to addressing issues related to sustainability in schools and global issues linked to COP26. Dixon uses the five Cs of sustainability – captaincy, curriculum, campus, community and connections – as chapter headings to underpin the understanding of why sustainability is important, which I found useful, along with the recommendations for leaders at the end of each chapter.

Although this book is primarily geared towards primary settings, there are definite links to secondary schools and extracurricular eco-councils too. In particular, Dixon ensures that the definition of sustainability is unpicked and misconceptions addressed, along with clear links to the United Nations Sustainable Development Goals, and highlights the importance of sustainability as a core geography concept. The book's appendices also present a wide range of policies and strategies which could be implemented in schools to raise awareness of sustainability.

Helen Pipe, Head of Geography, Hartshill Academy (Midland Academies Trust)

Leadership for Sustainability develops the reader's understanding of green issues and sustainability and sites them within the context of school leadership, learning, emotional intelligence, curriculum innovation and school improvement. The focus on transformational leadership and linking the local to the global, supported by grounded examples from the author's own practice and that of others, makes possible the planning and actions needed in order to implement a whole-school sustainability agenda that is more than just a tokenistic gesture. The book offers concrete ideas to develop a school culture in which the sustainability agenda is supported by, and supports, a learning culture focused on equity and inclusion.

The radical changes needed to create a greener school are embedded in examples of deliberate and explicit acts of transformation that link together school staff, students, families and the community as equal partners. As David says, 'sustainability is literally life, the universe and everything' – and fortunately for school leaders he offers a clear contextual exploration of the issues and a road map that will allow each school to plan its own journey while seeing itself as part of the global challenge to save the planet one school at a time.

Chris Straker, Director, consultant and trainer, Restorative Thinking Ltd

It is clear that students are concerned about a future, their future, in a world of altered climate and constrained resources. Survey after survey tells us this and yet we move glacially, if at all, towards solutions that might give them confidence. As educators, our priority is to make the abstract, distant and global into something that is real, now and local. If we are making learning visible, we need to make sustainability visible.

This is what David Dixon has done in writing *Leadership for Sustainability*.

He has given schools a way forward – a method of taking control at a local level and delivering, for students and their community, a practical way of making a difference. He also realises that the best protagonists are created in primary schools. (I've seen first-hand how effective smaller environmentalists can be!) Yes, we need systemic change, but we also need to get everyone on board to support such measures. The best way is to start at home – and this book is an excellent place to begin that journey.

Dr Paul S. Ganderton, Principal Consultant, Paul Ganderton Consulting, educator and environmental scientist

LEADERSHIP for SUSTAINABILITY

SAVING THE PLANET
ONE SCHOOL AT A TIME

SCHOOL

DAVID DIXON

independent
thinking press

First published by

Independent Thinking Press
Crown Buildings, Bancyfelin, Carmarthen, Wales, SA33 5ND, UK
www.independentthinkingpress.com

and

Independent Thinking Press
PO Box 2223, Williston, VT 05495, USA
www.crownhousepublishing.com

Independent Thinking Press is an imprint of Crown House Publishing Ltd.

© David Dixon, 2022

The right of David Dixon to be identified as the author of this work has been asserted by him in accordance with the Copyright, Designs and Patents Act 1988.

First published 2022.

Cover images © achraf asfraoui and Vector Tradition – stock.adobe.com.
Globe image © Vector Tradition – stock.adobe.com.

The content of this publication has not been approved by the United Nations and does not reflect the views of the United Nations or its officials or Member States.

Quotes from Government documents used in this publication have been approved under an Open Government Licence. Please visit www.nationalarchives.gov.uk/doc/open-government-licence/.

Pages 7–8: extract from Bill Scott's blog © Bill Scott, 2019 from What ELSA said to Ofsted. *University of Bath* [blog] (16 April). Available at: https://blogs.bath.ac.uk/edswahs/2019/04/16/what-elsa-said-to-ofsted. Used with kind permission. Page 9: cartoon by Simone Lia © Guardian News & Media Ltd, 2022. Available at: https://www.theguardian.com/culture/ng-nteractive/2016/may/08/simone-lia-on-urban-development. Used with permission. Page 48: Figure 2.5 © United Nations (UN), 1987 from *Report of the World Commission on Environment and Development: Our Common Future* [Brundtland Report]. Oxford: Oxford University Press. Available at: https://sustainabledevelopment.un.org/content/documents/5987ourcommon-future.pdf. Used with kind permission. Pages 61–62: extracts from Green, J. (2015). *The Environmental Curriculum: Opportunities for Environmental Education across the National Curriculum – Early Years Foundation Stage and Primary.* Wolverhampton: University of Wolverhampton and National Environmental Education Association. Available at: https://naee.org.uk/wp-content/uploads/2015/06/NAEE_The_Environmental_Curriculum.pdf. Used with kind permission. Page 69: The Song of the Nightshade Fairy by Cicely Mary Barker © The Estate of Cicely Mary Barker, 1925. Used with permission. Page 76: Figure 3.3 © Oxfam, 2015 from *Global Citizenship in the Classroom: A Guide for Teachers* – second table on p. 5 is adapted by the publisher with the permission of Oxfam, Oxfam House, John Smith Drive, Cowley, Oxford, OX4 2JY, UK (www.oxfam.org.uk). Oxfam does not necessarily endorse any text or activities that accompany the materials, nor has it approved the adapted text. Used with kind permission. Page 99: Figure 3.5 © Jane Genovese. www.learningfundamentals.com.au. Used with kind permission. Page 104: quote from LEEF website © LEEF, 2022. Used with kind permission. Page 110: photographs © estate of Victor Miller. Used with kind permission. Page 112: Figure 4.1 adapted from © John Whitelegg. Used with kind permission. Page 121: Figure 4.5 © Sarah Lazarovic. Used with kind permission. Page 158: Figure 5.2 Crown Copyright and Open Government License from A Guide to the Wellbeing of Future Generations Act. Available at: https://gov.wales/sites/default/files/publications/2019-06/easy-read-a-guide-to-the-wellbeing-of-future-generations-act.pdf. Page 169: Figure 5.4 adapted from the original from Greening Actions Available at: http://www.greening-campaign.org. Used with kind permission. Page 172: Figure 5.5 © Graham Burnett. Used with kind permission. Page 175: quote © Starhawk (2016). Why diversity is important in permaculture. *International Permaculture*, 90 (winter): 7–9. Page 195: quote © The Resurgence Trust from S. Kumar, 2011 from: We are all leaders. *Resurgence*, 264. Available at: https://www.resurgence.org/magazine/article3272-we-are-all-leaders.html. This article was first published in *Resurgence*, Issue 264, January/February 2011. All rights to this article are reserved to The Resurgence Trust. To buy a copy of the magazine, read further articles or find out about the Trust, visit www.resurgence.org. Page 203 © Sarah Lazarovic. Used with kind permission.

Independent Thinking Press has no responsibility for the persistence or accuracy of URLs for external or third-party websites referred to in this publication, and does not guarantee that any content on such websites is, or will remain, accurate or appropriate.

British Library Cataloguing-in-Publication Data
A catalogue entry for this book is available from the British Library.

Print ISBN 978-178135401-8
Mobi ISBN 978-178135405-6
ePub ISBN 978-178135406-3
ePDF ISBN 978-178135407-0

LCCN 2021949279

Printed and bound in the UK by
Charlesworth Press, Wakefield, West Yorkshire

The problem is that we still lack the culture needed to confront this crisis. We lack leadership capable of striking out on new paths and meeting the needs of the present with concern for all and without prejudice towards coming generations ... human beings contrive to feed their self-destructive vices: trying not to see them, trying not to acknowledge them, delaying the important decisions and pretending that nothing will happen. Pope Francis (2015, pp. 39, 43)

I dedicate this book to my partner, Zaria Greenhill, for her unrelenting support. Also, to my children, Sequoia and Robb, who are a constant reminder that the planet needs to be future-proofed.

FOREWORD BY LORD KNIGHT
OF WEYMOUTH

In my three years as minister of state for schools in England, it was a regular irritation that I was constantly fending off people who wanted to add yet another thing into the curriculum. It felt like the answer to every social problem was to teach about it in schools. But, occasionally, something comes along that needs time and space. For me, embedding sustainability into our school curriculum is a no-brainer.

International surveys of young people consistently tell us that they have little confidence that they can influence climate change (Schleicher, 2021). Research also shows growing levels of climate anxiety among children (Reuters, 2020); they feel ill-equipped to change what is otherwise a bleak future in a rapidly depleting environment.

When I talk to teachers and school leaders, they would like to be able to include more education for sustainability in the timetable. Some manage to use their curriculum freedoms, and other flexibilities, to go beyond the straitjacket of accountability and deliver on this aspiration. But they are exceptional leaders.

A few years ago, I was at an event in Leeds to discuss education change. I met Mark Moorhouse, the then head teacher at Matthew Moss High School in Rochdale. He talked about some of the innovations he had led in his school. Asked how he found the time and space given the constraints of league tables and inspections, he replied that he looked for where the rules did not apply. He realised that the rules only applied during the school day, and so added a sixth voluntary day for self-directed learning. Within the school day he used his other freedoms and flexibility to continue the innovation.

It takes unusual courage as school leaders to keep asking 'Where does it say I can't do that?' We can't wait for all leaders to be as imaginative as Mark. The need for education for sustainability is urgent. It needs to be at scale and to touch every child. That is why I have been working on a top-down solution. In recent months I have been working with a range of education and environmental organisations to try to get sustainability and climate change education mandated in schools in England. I have introduced a private members bill into the UK parliament to try to achieve this by changing the law on the aims of the national curriculum. I also want to follow Italy's lead and transform citizenship into sustainable citizenship.

While I have been encouraged by cross-party support for this measure, I have been disappointed by the government's response. Education ministers do not support this curriculum change and argue that schools can do more if they want to build on the basics required by the national curriculum.

I will keep pressuring ministers with my colleagues in parliament and beyond. However, given that they are not persuaded at the very time when they are hosting COP26 in the UK, I do not see ministers giving way in a hurry. We therefore need other options to meet the demands of pupils, teachers and school leaders to better prepare them to live sustainable lives that afford the possibility of a successful future. Perhaps it is time for a bottom-up solution.

Leadership for Sustainability is the right book at the right time. What most head teachers and principals want is inspiration and practical advice regarding how to embed sustainability in their schools. David Dixon draws on his own experience as a school leader to show what is possible now.

This book challenges leaders to use their powers over the curriculum to change what and how young people learn. The author shows the potential to not only move the school estate to carbon zero but also to realise the learning from that shift. Finally, in the spirit of sustainability, he shows the critical role schools play in leading behaviour change across their communities.

The path David Dixon offers is exciting. It is not a narrow path; he sets out an approach that allows for the different context of each school in its diverse setting. My excitement is due to the fact that leaders now have a reference tool to help them build their own intrinsic motivation to do the right thing for their whole school communities. Rather than waiting to be told by ministers and parliamentarians, this book frees up schools to get on with it. I hope they read and act. We can't afford to wait.

Lord Knight of Weymouth

FOREWORD BY PAUL VARE

There are two reasons why this book is both important and original, so I am delighted to have been given the opportunity to highlight them. One cliché that I won't trot out is the claim that the book is timely. For sure, its publication comes hot on the heels of the COP26 climate change conference held here in the UK and coincides with the Department for Education's launch of a new sustainability and climate change education strategy for England, but even the publishers would admit that such timing is fortuitous. This book will always be timely, not simply because the themes it addresses have been with us for decades and become more urgent with each passing year; but because there was never a time when they were not critical to our current and future well-being.

Getting back to those two points; firstly, this work is important because it distils years of research and experience. Those of us who have been working in this field for decades will recognise the concerns raised so eloquently and may be familiar with many of David's sources of inspiration. But, here, they are brought together in a way that makes them accessible to the next generation of professionals with whom we now entrust our young people. Naturally, teachers and education leaders will want to make their own discoveries – and mistakes – but there is a depth and richness to this Noah's ark of material that provides the perfect resource bank to inform future voyages of discovery.

The second point I would highlight is the book's originality. The great contribution that it makes is the author's perspective itself. As a head teacher who has put these ideas into action over many years, David speaks with an authority that few authors on this topic possess. This is not simply a repository of useful tools; it is also a manual offering practical ways of working with these ideas, with real pupils in real schools.

Ultimately, this book is about leadership; that is, it illuminates a way forward through what might seem an impenetrable web of complex overlapping issues.

Despite years of treaties and conventions, the carbon load of our atmosphere still rises, inequalities between peoples grow, species loss continues apace and irreplaceable habitats are lost. It may feel like it is all too late; for business as usual, it certainly is. That makes it all the more critical that our unsustainable system of human development changes now. The radical transformation that is required cannot be an overnight phenomenon, and neither will it take a single recognisable form. The system will change because all of us – who, after all, constitute the system – are changing ourselves in myriad unforeseen ways. To prepare our young people for this transformation, rather than for a world that cannot be sustained, education must change too. This is the message conveyed in the book's subtitle. The change may be radical but it will happen one school at a time, and this book suggests how.

In his introduction, David describes his own shame in taxing the Earth with his past lifestyle, but that is as far as the guilt-trip goes. While this work reflects years of learning, it is forward-looking and positive in its outlook. The author may no longer be leading a school, but be in no doubt – in the following pages he continues to lead the way.

Paul Vare

ACKNOWLEDGEMENTS

I owe a debt of gratitude to the colleagues I worked with at Bowbridge Primary and Mulgrave Primary who supported the sustainability mission and vision and literally worked above and beyond the call of duty – in particular, Eileen Reddish, Carol Wilkinson, Dave Webster, Leander Jex, Sanjiv Chapman, Sara Abbas and Dermot Hughes. Thanks also to the chairs of governors of the respective schools, Sue Trentini and Roger Hibbitt, for being such valuable critical friends and allowing us space to plough new furrows.

A special mention should be given to Chris Gilchrist, formerly of Newark and Sherwood Energy Agency, who we worked with on several exciting projects, enabling our work to have a European dimension while helping us to address local fuel poverty.

Thanks to Ian Gilbert of Independent Thinking for suggesting the book in the first place and for his subsequent support. I would also like to give special thanks to Lord Jim Knight and Dr Paul Vare for their generous support and insightful forewords.

Thanks to David Bowman, Beverley Randell and all at Crown House Publishing who stuck with me through thick and thin, particularly Louise Penny for her patience and diligence during the editing process (and, in later stages, Emma Tuck).

Thinking way back, I should acknowledge the considerable influence of my grandmother, Harriet Dixon (Nana). She taught me sustainable values through thrift, gardening, cycle rides, community interaction and, above all, authenticity and kindness.

Finally, I am eternally grateful to Geoff Bowen, a lecturer at Ilkley College, for showing my student self the vital importance of environmental education locally and globally and how it ensures 'learning for life' on many levels.

CONTENTS

CONTENTS

GLOSSARY OF ACRONYMS

ACEs   adverse childhood experiences

CO2e   carbon dioxide equivalent

CPD   continuing professional development

Defra   Department for Environment, Food and Rural Affairs

DfE   Department for Education

DfES   Department for Education and Skills

DfID   Department for International Development

ECEfS   early childhood education for sustainability

ESD   education for sustainable development

ELSA   English Learning and Sustainability Alliance

EYFS   early years foundation stage

G7   Group of Seven

GCDA   Greenwich Co-operative Development Agency

GDP   gross domestic product

GENE   Global Education Network Europe

GLP   Global Learning Programme

INSET   in-service training

kWh   kilowatt hour

LEEF   London Environmental Educators Forum

NAEE   National Association for Environmental Education

NGO	non-governmental organisation
PSHE	personal, social, health and economic (education)
PTA	parent–teacher association
RSE	relationships and sex education
SDGs	Sustainable Development Goals
SEAL	social and emotional aspects of learning
SEEd	Sustainability and Environmental Education
SELCE	South East London Community Energy
SMSC	spiritual, moral, social and cultural
SNAG	school nutrition action group
UN	United Nations
UNESCO	United Nations Educational Scientific and Cultural Organisation
UNICEF	United Nations Children's Fund
WEIRD	Western, Educated, Industrialised, Rich and Democratic
WRAP	Waste Resources Action Programme
WWF	World Wide Fund for Nature

INTRODUCTION

> Today catastrophe is well on its way, it is losing no time at all, but education seems still unable to get started, has indeed not even readjusted itself to start. The race may, after all, prove a walk-over for disaster.
>
> **H. G. Wells (1942, p. 63)**

When I relinquished primary school headship after leading two schools (three if you count an amalgamation) over 20 years, it was tempting to think that I deserved to sit back, potter in the garden and do some part-time school improvement consultancy to pay for extended out-of-season holidays. I am, after all, a middle-class baby boomer (those born between 1946 and 1964) who, like some of my peers, had it all in terms of homeownership, relatively high disposable income and an index-linked pension. Wasn't I therefore 'entitled' to an easier life after a stressful time in schools in very challenging circumstances?

The reason why I chose to sweat over a hot laptop to produce this book can be found in the realisation that I'm entitled to nothing. Why? Because my life to date has likely taken much more out of planet Earth's biosphere than has been replenished. This is starkly illustrated by Earth Overshoot Day.[1] This 'marks the date when humanity's demand for ecological resources and services in a given year exceeds what Earth can regenerate in that year'.[2]

I think of my numerous foreign holidays by plane and the hundreds of thousands of miles I've driven. This is compounded by my consumption of processed food with high carbon and water footprints, living in energy-thirsty houses and lazily using cheap products procured from ethically dubious sources. I also wince about

---

1 To determine the date of Earth Overshoot Day, Global Footprint Network combines environmental data from many sources to assess humanity's resource situation. See https://www.footprintnetwork.org.
2 See https://www.overshootday.org.

the amount of single-use plastic I've consumed and how many cheap electronic devices and articles of clothing I've discarded without thought for how they were manufactured or disposed of. All this is nothing compared to bringing up two children in one of the most prosperous areas of the world: children themselves requiring vast planetary resources.[3] I've also benefitted from countless outdoor pursuits and aesthetic pleasures derived from the natural world, with some like skiing causing much damage.[4]

I'm as guilty of obliviousness, self-justification, obfuscation and denial of my personal responsibilities towards our planet as the next person.[5] Like many, I've also put my environmental concerns into a box marked 'to be dealt with later' while carrying on regardless. I'm one of the people benefitting from a WEIRD society – Western, Educated, Industrialised, Rich and Democratic (Henrich, 2021) – that instigated Enlightenment thinking, selfish individualism and associated superiority complexes.[6] Like many others in 'developed' nations, I've felt a misplaced sense of entitlement to my spoils, as if this was the natural way of things.

Having had a background in environmental education, I was aware earlier than most of today's headline environmental problems. This led me to put sustainability increasingly at the heart of my work, while endeavouring to pursue a low-impact lifestyle. But, as you can see from my past accumulation of overconsumption, I'm not preaching from an ivory tower of smug virtue. I sometimes did my best, but hindsight has shown me that it wasn't good enough. Suddenly, the distant deadlines for action of my youth have come uncomfortably close, along with a sinking feeling that some have passed. So, it's all too apparent that the social and

---

3   On average, in developed nations, having a child creates 58.6 tonnes of carbon dioxide equivalent (CO2e) per year and meat eating 800 kg of CO2e per year. See Wynes and Nicholas (2017) for other things we do which cause high emissions.
4   For the detrimental impact of skiing, see Beaudry (2019).
5   Denial is a fascinating area of psychology. To illustrate this in relation to this subject matter, see the account of a community whose glacier was rapidly melting, but didn't want to address climate change in Kari Marie Norgaard's (2011) book *Living in Denial*.
6   The Enlightenment (sometimes referred to as the Age of Reason) emerged in Europe in the late 17th century and was the basis for the rapid developments in science, technology, economics and industry that have delivered the many material benefits we see today. The 'rational' thinking and belief in 'objective facts' behind it also increased the questioning of long-held religious and other traditional cultural beliefs, including regarding how societies should be run. New artistic forms also emerged during this time and later – both because of the Enlightenment (for example, realistic paintings depicting anatomical accuracy, science themes and everyday life) and as a reaction against it (such as Romanticism in the late 18th and early 19th century; the Arts and Crafts movement in the later part of the 19th and the early 20th century; and, in the early 20th century, Dadaism). Its modernist philosophy promoted the notion of continual linear progress and this greatly accelerated unsustainable human existence by magnifying our exploitative tendencies and the rift between ourselves and nature. It made people forget that we are part of a finite and precious world.

economic activities which are depleting planetary resources at an alarming rate need to change course as we enter the uncertainties of the geological Anthropocene epoch. National Geographic says: 'the current epoch is called the Holocene, which began 11,700 years ago after the last major ice age'.[7] This is being rapidly superseded by the Anthropocene Epoch, triggered by profound changes to the planet's biosphere caused by human activity. This shows that, like asteroid strikes and volcanic eruptions, humans are radically and detrimentally changing the biochemical make-up of the planet. It should be noted that not all humans are culpable as there are many billions who live well within planetary limits (unfortunately, in abject poverty due to exploitation and/or neglect by the people who live well beyond those limits).

Another strong motivation for writing this book is raw fear, enhanced by having a young daughter, who is 6 years old at the time of writing and might well be alive at the end of the century. Way before this, by the time she's an adult, environmental tipping points may well have been reached (some say that they already have) and I literally fear for her life and her generation, let alone those coming later. She may inherit some material advantage from my estate, but this will literally be worth nothing if civilisation crumbles due to the biosphere being unable to bear the burdens human beings place upon it.

Despite mending many of my damaging ways, I still owe the planet a substantial debt. So, if you see this book as a guilt trip, I suppose it is. At least I'm not in denial!

SIMPLE ARITHMETIC

Saving the planet one school at a time might seem an extravagant claim. But imagine if every school *really was* a sustainable school in the widest sense, as I will outline in Chapter 1. The difference this would make to education and wider society would be inestimable – although let's try. My calculation goes as follows: one sustainable head teacher with a school roll of, say, 500 pupils, with 50 staff, would not only have the potential to influence those 550 individuals, but also their families, extended families and friends, which could take the figure up to several thousand. If the school had a high profile in this field, with the way social media works, it could reach many more, perhaps tens of thousands. If all the schools in

7   See https://www.nationalgeographic.org/encyclopedia/anthropocene.

3

England did the same, through six degrees of separation, we're talking about a reach of millions across the country and beyond.

But who are the planet savers needed to lead sustainable schools? In Chapter 2, I characterise leaders for sustainability as guardians of the long-term future who can inspire others to join them by providing opportunities for co-creating new solutions. They model types of thinking and behaviour which encourage everyone in the school to unleash their minds to avoid blind acceptance of what is 'normal' (much of the present normal being a planet wrecker). These leaders are upbeat and solution-focused through holistic means, offering a bright future for everyone. They have a strong moral compass – being values-led – and display high levels of empathy and courage. Above all, they are authentic rather than mass-produced cardboard cut-outs. These leaders think outside of the box, while recognising that the box, in the form of the present education sector, can't be ignored. They break away from unnecessary conformity and subtly game the system for the benefit of all. It's all about wanting everyone to thrive and flourish (Critchley, 2019) rather than just survive.[8] I emphasise that education leaders don't need to be trapped by the accountability imposed by a national education service and that, rather than being a peripheral issue, having a sustainability ethos is really the only sensible option on many levels. A sustainability mindset can throw off the chains of compliance laid down by others for reasons of power and/or outdated processes and traditions.

AGE OF STUPID?

Most baby boomers and many in succeeding generations have been living in cloud cuckoo land by perpetuating a myth that we should expect indefinite economic growth on a finite planet. Consequently, graphs illustrating the rise of greenhouse gases and species extinction show exponential trends. When cells in the body grow like this we call it cancer! And it's not as if greening the present economy or waiting for various techno-fixes or large-scale geoengineering will necessarily be our ultimate salvation (although aspects of these will be needed).[9] Just as

---

8   In Valerie Hannon's (2017) thought-provoking book *Thrive* she argues that in order for more of us to really thrive, we need more disruptor leaders – especially in education – who challenge dominant damaging paradigms in schools and society generally.

9   See https://www.geoengineeringwatch.org.

importantly, we need a change of priorities within a change in our very culture. Schools should be at the vanguard of this change. Films such as Al Gore's *An Inconvenient Truth* and its sequel spell out in graphic detail the factual overview of our plight.[10] For me though, the 2009 film *The Age of Stupid* has more of an emotional impact. It's set in the environmentally ravaged year 2055 and centres on an old man who looks through archive film of our time and wonders why not enough was done to alleviate climate change. Thought-provoking and scary!

Our current stupid Western societal approach is also bound up with neoliberalism, which although in most forms advocates governance with rigid structures of laws, rules and regulations (unlike neoconservatism) promotes the idea that other issues (including climate change etc.) should be sorted out by market forces which harness the power of individual choice and technical innovation. Perhaps it could be our saviour if we had more time to play with![11]

Most schools have tinges of green, but they're not really sustainable in the same way that wider society isn't. Schools with sustainability at their core can overcome this by becoming part of the zero-waste circular economy. This helps to bring consumption down to within the planet's ability to replenish and avoid overshoot. This is in contrast to the 'take–make–use–dump' linear model, escalated by the Industrial Revolution and based on the consumption of fossil fuels. A circular economy works in harmony with the biosphere, and if happiness isn't dependent on the consumption of ever more stuff, why should schools subscribe to the old unsustainable narrative? The practical ways of working towards this circularity feature in Chapters 3, 4 and 5. In particular, Chapter 4 shows how school buildings and grounds (officially referred to as 'the school estate'), when linked to the curriculum, can deliver fantastic learning opportunities through adding to biodiversity and showing in microcosm how a circular economy can work in reality.

---

10 The scientific facts presented by Gore are largely irrefutable and should have scared us into change. Why haven't they? Once again, complex psychology is at large.

11 See George Monbiot's (2016) account of neoliberalism, and also David Harvey's (2005) book *A Brief History of Neoliberalism*. Both are quite a revelation and shocking in their way.

PERFECT HARMONY

Look out for the subject of harmony as it's a strand which runs throughout the book. Harmonious ecosystems work to their optimum, as do harmonious schools.[12] This is a challenge to achieve, but more than worth it.

Unfortunately, we are beset by a variety of linearities, many of which contribute to unsustainability. In Chapter 2, I highlight the problems with WEIRD linear/rational thinking in contrast to more rewarding ecological systems approaches. The novelist Hilary Mantel said, 'I don't dwell on time's arrow so much. I'm looking for what's cyclical' (The Guardian, 2020). Perhaps we should all do this a bit more.

In this light, Chapter 3 discusses decarbonising the curriculum by going through the similar and linked process of decolonising the curriculum. Both these elements can be seen as a reaction against the exploitative culture and structures of power that have dominated our society from time immemorial, through the mercenary exploitation of the biosphere and human resources for the advantage of the few at the expense of the many. This is very obvious when looking at the dark satanic mills of the 19th century and the dirty industry equivalents today, but due to complex and hidden supply chains, is not so obvious unless blatant examples are flagged up by the media. Most people who are comfortably above the breadline are happy with, or at least tolerate, our present economic system because it's assumed that it's the natural way of things. You don't have to look too far down the social stratification from me and you to see that this is crooked thinking, and it gets ever more crooked when applied to so-called 'developing' countries who suffer from our present and historic excesses (back to WEIRD psychology again!). This is why it's so important for schools to encourage young people to become critical thinkers, rather than just accept received wisdom.

It's significant that questioning the status quo regarding our use of the biosphere and lithosphere is becoming more mainstream, giving us cause for hope. Crimes against humanity in the form of genocide are being extended to ecocide (Higgins, 2015) as litigation has begun across the world to prosecute individuals and corporations for damaging the natural world on which we all depend. The rights of the planet are at last coming to the fore. Leaders for sustainability are part of this paradigm change.

....

12 Seek out The Prince of Wales, Tony Juniper and Ian Skelly's (2010) beautifully illustrated book, *Harmony: A New Way of Looking at the World.* The photographs alone are worth it.

GOING WITH THE FLOW

To address our planetary challenges, there's a clamour for change from learners of all ages. For example, economics students at universities are rejecting classical and neoclassical economics in favour of sustainability-based 'new economics'. At the other end of the education spectrum, primary school children and their parents lobby for more local climate change action. Too often the response, if any, from education providers can be dismissive, too tokenistic or not joined up. Nonetheless, education leaders at all levels should be galvanised by the following three bodies of research from which I've taken excerpts (the full reports are well worth reading):

1   42% of young people aged 10–18 say they have learnt a little or hardly anything or nothing about the environment at school; 68% want to learn more about the environment and climate change; 49% would like to be more involved in projects or activities that help the environment; and 86% thought all schools and colleges should help pupils to do things to help the environment (Green Schools Project and NUS, 2019, p. 3–4).

2   70% of teachers think that the education system needs radical change for the times we live in; 69% think there should be more teaching about climate change in UK schools; and 75% feel they haven't received adequate training to educate students about climate change.[13]

3   77% of the general public said that learning about climate change should be part of the school curriculum.[14]

I feel it's rather shaming that many school leaders sit back and watch children and students taking the lead. Are they too compliant, risk-averse, cowed by The System or just too happy with the status quo? Ofsted, the school inspection body in England, is equally obtuse. For example, the English Learning and Sustainability Alliance (ELSA) lobbied Ofsted with the following suggestions and requests. That inspectors:

● encourage reporting and look for evidence of learning for sustainability and suggest whole school approaches to it;

---

13 See https://d25d2506sfb94s.cloudfront.net/cumulus_uploads/document/i6swtiz9ta/YG-Archive-02012020-OxfamClimateCrisis.pdf.
14 See https://yougov.co.uk/topics/education/survey-results/daily/2020/01/22/d1cab/1.

- look for integrated approaches to curriculum, behaviour and attitudes and personal development;
- use the interview time with students to see how their education matches with their concerns about the future and the world.

Furthermore, that Ofsted:

- suggests CPD for whole school approaches';
- 'quality of education' judgements include educating for a socially responsible and sustainable world and link with Defra's 25 Year Environment Plan (and Bill) and DfID's Connecting Classrooms through Global Learning and, so that SDG4 is reported on in a holistic way. Scott (2019)

To date, Ofsted has taken no notice of these recommendations.

The desire to live sustainably is also much more apparent across the general population. For example, the Climate Assembly UK, which is a branch of the Citizenship Assembly, came up with 25 recommendations in order of priority. Number one was: 'Informing and educating everyone (the public, industry, individuals and government).' Within the top 10 was the desire for 'A joined-up approach across the system and all levels of society' and 'Local community engagement' (Climate Assembly UK, 2020, p. 12). Members of this assembly were recruited at random from across different demographics, and this gives yet another mandate for a leader for sustainability in a school.

FISH, FORFEITURE AND FROGS

Chapter 5 shows how leaders for sustainability have an in-depth knowledge of their catchment areas and the wider world, past and present. This provides added insight into the causes of many of our unsustainable tendencies, allowing an escape from the following syndromes. Although they can be viewed as clichés, I've found them to be useful points of reference.

'Shifting baseline syndrome' is a phrase first coined by Pauly (1995). He was an ecologist looking at fisheries and came to the conclusion that his peers tended to judge the health of fish stocks by comparing them with how they were at the start of their careers, rather than investigating further back through historical records. As a result, their findings didn't fully take account of the decline over time because the baseline was set too recently. McClenachan (2009) showed this by studying photographs of trophy fish caught off the coast of Florida. In the 1950s they were longer than a tall man. By the 2000s their average length was less than 30 cm. This concept has been used in many other ecological studies and also by writers such as Robert Macfarlane, when highlighting how children and adults today tend to know much less about the natural world and so value it less. They don't realise that it has diminished over time because they have no points of comparison (see also Soga and Gaston, 2018).

Source: © Guardian News & Media Ltd, 2022

It's good to see that an increasing number of younger people are overcoming shifting baseline syndrome in light of the climate emergency. They *do* realise what they're losing and wish to do something about it – often to the shame of their elders – as exemplified by Greta Thunberg's campaigns.

'Corporate memory loss' is a related concept. Gardener and Bainbridge (2006) found examples of this when experienced personnel left a company without fully passing on their knowledge to those remaining or new people coming in. This sometimes led to drops in health and safety standards and the malfunctioning of certain administrative systems. They said that there was nothing new in this; it had always occurred, particularly in periods of rapid change. To illustrate this, they quoted Santayana (1905): 'Progress, far from consisting in change, depends upon retentiveness. Those who cannot remember the past are condemned to repeat it' (Gardener and Bainbridge, 2006, p. 1). Change can also be mistaken for progress if we always think that bigger is better and that upgrades are beneficial. In the context of sustainability, this book argues that education should be part of a process of cultural change, enrichment and adaptation, rather than just promoting a narrow definition of 'progress'. This includes developing the wisdom to know what to retain, what to resist and what to adopt, otherwise our ability to cope is always in catch-up mode due to the 'rapidification' caused by technological advances.[15]

'Boiled frog syndrome' describes how if a frog is thrown into boiling water, it'll jump out immediately. If, however, it's placed into tepid water and the heat is gradually turned up, it'll be less likely to notice and will end up being compliantly boiled. This is a metaphor for any situation that is unacceptable, but which if introduced incrementally and surreptitiously will become the accepted norm. In my opinion, this is what has happened to many education leaders in England. They've been 'boiled', by being assimilated into a system which, although they might periodically grumble about it, generally assures compliance with its demands. This has led to a narrowing of the curriculum and the plummeting mental health of pupils and staff. Despite prevailing challenges, education should aim to help achieve the greater good for everyone in terms of physical safety, mental well-being and social justice. These can't exist on a sick planet and, conversely, a healthy planet needs well people in all senses. Well-being is also linked to school improvement (Rees, 2017), which is why it features prominently throughout this book.

I was depressed to hear a principal of a sixth-form college bemoaning the loss of exams due to the COVID-19 crisis. I paraphrase him here: 'These students have been in full-time education since the age of 4 and at the age of 18, at the *culmination of their schooling*, have been robbed of the chance of a university place and successful career.' He was displaying the classic signs of boiled frog syndrome. Is it really the case that a young person's time in school is all about the build-up to the exams they take between the ages of 16 and 18? Is the end product above the process? Shouldn't education be as much about 'drawing out' a child's originality (to return to the original etymological meaning) as 'putting in' and examining the way they retain this? Shouldn't education be a process of synthesis between

---

15 In his second encyclical, *Laudato Si*, Pope Francis (2015, p. 15) refers to an acceleration in the pace of life and work ('rapidification'), which causes anxiety to individuals, places strain on communities, and harms the environment.

educators and learners which produces a new and better culture? At the moment, it appears that we spend far too much time weighing the pig rather than feeding it!

TALK IS CHEAP

There are myriad writers on education leadership, ranging from eminent academics to cultish gurus. I reference some of these, although I keep returning to the practical things we did in my own schools to embed sustainability and the effects these had. I not only aim to show the art of the possible, but also how we as leaders have a rich potential to deviate from the norm without jeopardising our positions or those of our colleagues. We can enhance what can be done on the ground to embed sustainability in the widest sense. It's difficult to provide hard and fast templates for this because each school is unique, but I suggest ways of operating which can be tailored to any situation. To provide context, I offer the five Cs of sustainability:

- **Captaincy.** Through an in-depth study of leaders in a wide variety of primary schools that achieved Eco-Schools Green Flag status, I distil what a leader for sustainability really looks like, how they operate and why their traits deserve a distinct and special leadership category more in keeping with facing up to current challenges. I give examples of whole-school approaches through systems thinking and planning frameworks for those who wish to embed sustainability, rather than see it as a bolt-on. Captains of sustainability lead from the front where necessary, but more often use distributive and servant methods of leadership to empower everyone for the greater good.

- **Curriculum.** Education for sustainable development (ESD) is explored and I give lots of practical examples of how it can enhance teaching and learning through cross-curricular approaches, while also enabling schools to tick the 'standards agenda' boxes. The value of learning via head, heart and hands is central to this process and exemplified in forest school practices. The thorny problem of sustainability bias is tackled. How can we enable children to deal with issues impartially, while also wishing them to live more sustainably?[16]

16 See Tilbury (1997) for examples of using a head, heart, hands approach to help learn about environmental problems.

- **Campus.** A school's buildings and grounds can be utilised to bring down a school's overall carbon and other footprints and improve biodiversity, while enriching the ESD curriculum. This is where schools can showcase sustainability in tangible forms, such as low-impact procurement and skilful waste and energy management. This can be highly influential for those who use them day to day or who come across them as physical or online visitors. Reduce, recycle, reuse, repair and repurpose feature prominently. I also show that behaviour change is often more important than grand eco-technology when it comes to sustainability, and another reason to strongly link campus with curriculum.

- **Community.** Any school community should be an asset rather than a 'problem', and sustainability can be the catalyst for community enrichment which then provides a positive feedback loop into the children's experience of education and their capacity to learn. I show how this manifests in improved community cohesion and better mental health for all school stakeholders. Early intervention programmes are also shown to benefit from a sustainability approach, taking the Every Child Matters agenda into a new dimension in terms of physical, mental and social well-being.

- **Connections.** 'Linked thinking' are the watchwords here. This is where leaders for sustainability subtly weave together all the elements within each of the other Cs and make relevant connections between them. I provide additional examples of how making connections can improve overall 'wisdom' (individually and collectively) through additional insights into the complexities of the modern world and how schools can play a pivotal role in securing a sustainable future.[17]

---

17 The linear format of most books, be they fact or fiction, can also be a barrier to holistic thought. Throughout the book, I show how links between areas of knowledge and concepts are just as important as the knowledge and concepts themselves. Having an ecological perspective encourages people to eschew computational and linear thinking and 'silver bullet' solutions. This is why I highlight the interconnectedness of issues: not just to appreciate the complexity of things but to encourage the search for joined-up initiatives. The 'think global, act local' adage is a vital part of this and another important strand of the narrative.

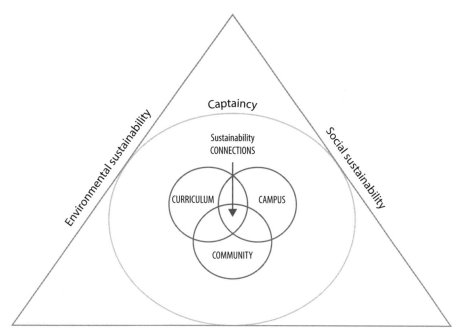

Figure I.1: Main elements of the book

Education leaders are well placed to cause butterfly effects that initiate even greater waves which can disrupt the destructive status quo.[18] This requires a certain kind of moral fibre, itself a product of a certain set of values, which most have within themselves if they care to fully use it. This incorporates a sixth C, namely courage, featured in the concluding chapter.

To help leaders make informed judgements about sustainability, I recommend interdisciplinary and multidisciplinary approaches throughout the book. This is where much of our education and schooling lets us down because it tends to be non-joined-up and siloed by subject, and this gets worse as children get older. Sustainability is a natural vehicle for developing a type of fully integrated learning

---

18 The butterfly effect was popularised by climatologist Edward N. Lorenz in 1963 and became a central concept in chaos theory. It described how even a tiny event can trigger knock-on effects that continue to amplify it, such as the flap of a butterfly wing eventually leading to a tornado on the other side of the world. The added message is that we meddle with nature at our peril.

ecology for the benefit of all. This also keys into the conventional school improvement agenda. Sustainable schools can deliver success as measured by test results and inspections through benevolent rather than coercive means and without that success being the be-all and end-all of a school's existence.

The leadership for sustainability recommendations on page 15 and at the end of each chapter are there to encourage further thought and discussion among school stakeholders.

APPENDICES

At first, I was loath to include model sustainability policies because there's always a temptation for someone to do a copy-and-paste job, rather than develop them organically as sustainability becomes embedded. However, on second thoughts I deemed it useful to add them so that anyone new to this area wasn't starting from scratch. The appendices contain examples of sustainability policies and planning formats which need to spring from strategic development.

Some schools have a separate 'sustainability policy'. This can be a good starting point, although I preferred to incorporate our sustainability ethos within the mission statement (see Appendix 1). This fed into the school improvement plan and from there into separate operational policies, such as those covering ethical procurement (Appendix 2), fair trade (Appendix 3) and energy (Appendix 4). A highly significant policy – food and catering – features in Appendix 5. This is a prime example of an area that can gain greatly from a curriculum, campus and community approach. In Appendix 6, a sample subject curriculum policy shows how ESD can be embedded, in this case within design and technology. Appendix 7 is an illustration of how a harmonised approach can be taken when several partners wish to raise the profile of learning in a community. This is based upon a real-life example which is described in Chapter 5.

A learning charter (Appendix 8) came about because we wanted a succinct methodological overview to which stakeholders (and inspectors) could refer. It also reiterates the importance of 'soft' outcomes – as opposed to the 'hard', easily measurable variety – and illustrates how sustainability can be the driver for a 'learning entitlement' for all and a practical guide to fulfilling a school's mission.

I have included a curriculum statement (Appendix 9) based on one developed at my head teacher friend Naheeda Maharasingam's school (such a statement is obligatory in England and has to appear on the school's website). She wanted to highlight how her school's curriculum needed to be culturally relevant as well as responding to the learning needs of each child. It also aimed to create critically aware, active learners, not passive receivers of knowledge. Once again, sustainability underpinned the statement.

Naturally enough, in our school, each curriculum policy featured sustainability (see again Appendix 6), and this fed into the teachers' planning. Appendix 10 shows the integrated subject overview guidance, which helped teachers to fill out their own medium-term plan (Appendix 11). We didn't have to reinvent the wheel on this; it just required us to weave in ESD once there was a good understanding of what it looked like in the curriculum.

It's important to view all of these policies as pieces of a sustainability jigsaw, rather than as stand-alone, which is why there are cross-references between them. They are also designed to be used constantly as reference points for practical actions, not consigned to a dusty shelf once written. Leaders for sustainability need to walk the talk!

LEADERSHIP FOR SUSTAINABILITY RECOMMENDATIONS

- Escape shifting baseline and boiled frog syndrome by stepping back and taking a fresh look at your school's situation and how it operates in the context of external factors. Assess how much influence you really have over your situation, rather than what others imply or tell you. Question your school's present 'normal'. Make a point of accessing information and people from beyond your echo chamber. Try to be open-minded about ideas and concepts which might seem alien but might inspire new thinking.

- Escape fatalism and cynicism in relation to your situation. Remember how you felt at the start of your career when it's likely more things seemed possible.

- Recognise that school leaders are in a fantastic position to help the cause of sustainability as part of the same educative process which influences the lives and life chances of the thousands of children who pass through their schools and the tens of thousands, or more, who may be influenced through various butterfly effects.

- If you haven't thought too much about neoliberalism, I'd recommend finding out more about it. Once I did, it explained a lot about the state of our current society and how to cope with it as a school leader.

Chapter 1

SUSTAINABILITY STEERS

The world is not indefinitely large. We simply can't hurl ourselves at it with the abandon of the past 10,000 years.

Colin Tudge (1996, p. 342)

This chapter outlines the scope of sustainability as applied in this book. Sometimes sustainability can be restricted to quite narrow and distinct areas centred around the conservation of nature and recycling. As important as these are, I want to go beyond this 'greenism' to show that sustainability is literally life, the universe and everything!

Sustainability can be a slippery concept due to being multi- and cross-disciplined and concealed within other labels. It's often misconstrued because it invariably crops up in single issues (our use of plastics being a case in point), which omits relevant links to other issues and the overarching problems with our economic system. For example, much of the plastic in the UK is made from gas imported from the environmentally damaging fracking industry in the United States. This means that we shouldn't just worry about plastic in our rivers and oceans.[1] Why do we use so much plastic in the first place?

There's much room for debate over causes, effects, connections and remedies for various environmental, social and economic problems. In some ways this is a strength because it lends itself to participatory approaches to identifying and dealing with complexity, but it's also a weakness if those participating lack basic ecological knowledge and/or have vested interests and are intent on

---

1 For an account of fracked gas and plastic, see Moyes (2020).

greenwashing.[2] It's also a weakness if people don't participate because they're not able to and are excluded, or because they are happy with the present business-as-usual scenario or, at the very least, can tolerate the status quo without too much question. After all, business as usual is much easier to understand and quantify in terms of gross domestic product (GDP) than by using more complex measures, such as the Genuine Progress Indicator and various well-being indices.[3] It may well be a case of 'the Devil playing the best tunes', because too many of us are caught up in the turmoil surrounding producing and consuming. Being sustainable requires more in-depth thinking and this can be just too tiresome, thus fuelling justification and/or denial of the status quo.

PROTECTING GAIA

There are natural feelings of 'biophilia' (love of life or living systems, as described by Wilson (1990)), which are prompting some of us to pursue paths based upon a sustainability ethos. James Lovelock's (2000 [1979]) concept of Gaia links to this, in that he propounded a theory which says that the Earth is like a complete living organism made up of billions of interconnecting living and non-living parts, some of which are you and me and which together create and sustain life.

From this, Lovelock maintains that evolution has left us in a privileged position because the Earth had nurtured creatures who have contributed to the well-being of the whole environment and thus themselves. However, he says: 'I never realised just how destructive we were, or that we had so grievously damaged the Earth that Gaia now threatens us with the ultimate punishment of extinction' (Lovelock,

---

2   Beware greenwash. Many organisations trumpet their green credentials when, in fact, compared to the damage they cause to the biosphere, they are infinitesimal. The phrase was probably first coined by Jay Westerveld in a 1986 essay regarding the United States' hotel industry's practice of asking guests to indicate which towels they hadn't used to help 'save the environment'. This was actually a ploy to save money on laundry, as the hotels did little else to be sustainable (see Watson, 2016).

3   The Genuine Progress Indicator is one of an increasing variety of measures which gauge many other factors of human existence, not accounted for in measures of GDP. A version developed in the United States uses over 250 social, economic and environmental factors to determine human progress or regression. These include levels of pollution, amount of voluntary activity and rates of crime (see https://gnhusa.org/genuine-progress-indicator). An example of a well-being index can be seen at http://global-perspectives.org.uk/volume-three/infographics. See also Raser-Rowland and Grubb's (2016) book *The Art of Frugal Hedonism*. They advocate 'recalibrating senses' and creating a 'new normal' to rethink values in terms other than material consumption.

2007, pp. 188–189). I tell children that it's not a matter of 'saving the planet', it's about the 'planet saving us'.

BIOSPHERE BLUES

When talking about the biosphere, I'm referring to the thin strip of the Earth's surface which can support life in any shape or form. Although estimates vary depending on whether you count single cellular life in the atmosphere, it's about 20 km thick from the deepest ocean trench to the top of Mount Everest (obviously, humans can only thrive in a much thinner portion of this). I demonstrate this to children by placing some cling film around a globe. This layer is what we're inadvertently destroying. The thinness shows its preciousness and its vulnerability.

The fact that humans can survive on all continents is testament to our cleverness in manipulating our environment to maintain a suitable microclimate by wearing optimal clothes, building houses and utilising external energy sources for heating or cooling. Developing agriculture and many other technologies has also consolidated our superiority over all other species. This is our success, but also our undoing, because in its current form – despite renewables and other 'green' technologies – we are still wreaking havoc on the biosphere. It isn't sustainable.

DEFINING SUSTAINABILITY

A simple dictionary definition of sustainability is: 'the ability to be maintained at a certain rate or level'.[4] Other words that spring from a thesaurus relating to being 'sustainable' include: 'trustworthy', 'reliable', 'dependable', 'good', 'valid', 'legitimate', 'warranted', 'well founded', 'justified', 'just', 'sound', 'reasonable' and 'sensible'.[5] For the purposes of this book, defining sustainability revolves around two questions: first, how long are we talking about, and, second, what are we applying it to? When confronted with difficult times, my late mother always said,

---

4   Oxford University Press, sustainability, *Lexico.com* (2021). Available at: https://www.lexico.com/definition/sustainability.
5   Oxford University Press, sustainable, *Lexico.com* (2021). Available at: https://www.lexico.com/definition/sustainable.

'nothing lasts forever'. This is demonstrably true when you consider that in millions of years the Earth will be consumed by the sun as it becomes a red giant beginning its death throes. So, definitions of sustainability are always relative to the period of time to which they refer.

If we were traditional economists, we might talk about keeping inflation at a sustainable rate of 2% per annum. When talking about sustainable leadership, we might be putting in place a system to ensure succession planning by nurturing people through mentoring and training, so they can fill leadership roles as other staff members leave. When applied in the context of this book, we are thinking in terms of preserving the planet's ability to function in such a way as to ensure the continuing existence of life – including ours – in perpetuity, and for this life to be worth living. This means there is an interlacing of environmental, social and economic elements and the need to discuss philosophically what perpetuity and quality of life mean. Again, it's not just about being 'green'.

Stripped back to the basics, sustainability can be seen through the following model.

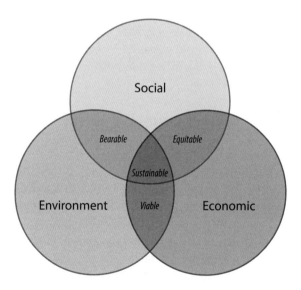

Figure 1.1: Basic model of sustainability

Notice that sustainability resides in the central area which is above and beyond the 'viable' environment/economic, 'equitable' economic/social and 'bearable' social/ environment overlaps. This is important because it emphasises why sustainability over the long term is hard to achieve (even if we agree on a definition). For example, in the case of clothing manufacturing, an industry might achieve equitable social and economic conditions for the producers, but fail to fully address the environmental consequences of sourcing the raw materials and the manufacturing process. Cotton might be grown using farming methods which fail to protect the soil and surrounding ecosystem by using harmful pesticides and herbicides.[6] Manufacturing methods might include hazardous dyes and other chemicals which leach into soil and rivers. Sooner or later, the environmental damage would have a detrimental impact on the social and economic fabric of the community. The children's book *The Lorax* by Dr. Seuss illustrates this better than many an academic tome by highlighting the wanton destruction of the natural world for monetary gain.

BREAKING DOWN AND JOINING UP

Another way of gaining a basic understanding of sustainability is through the three pillars model (see Figure 1.2). This model is in contrast to Figure 1.1, which emphasises the links between the three elements.

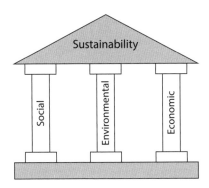

Figure 1.2: Three pillars of sustainability

6   See pages 128–130 for more on this.

It's useful to have an understanding of each of these pillars and, as described earlier, just as important to see where they link and where the causes and effects lie.

This shows how important it is to judge how long an action or behaviour can continue without causing problems. If the judgement is that it may be okay over the next few decades, but will jeopardise aspects of life for future generations, then it's patently unsustainable. As Meadows et al. (1992) put it: 'A sustainable society is one that can persist over generations, one that is far-seeing enough, flexible enough and wise enough not to undermine either its physical or social systems of support.' By many measures, we can hardly claim much of this wisdom and this is where education can be instrumental in redressing the balance.

GENERATION GAME

People blithely talk about the need to 'leave a world fit for our children and grandchildren'. The United Nations (UN) World Commission on Environment and Development – better known as the Brundtland Commission – said that ecological sustainability must ensure it 'meets the needs of the present without compromising the ability of future generations to meet their own needs' (UN, 1987, p. 16). How many future generations was not defined. In this context, looking to the needs of our grandchildren is really very short term as it only thinks about two future generations, who might already be on the planet (depending on your vintage). Perhaps we should see this from another perspective, as expressed by the well-known saying: 'the world is not given by [our] fathers, but borrowed from [our] children' (Berry, 1971, p. 26). The famous naturalist Jane Goodall takes this further by saying: 'We have not borrowed our children's future – we have stolen it and we're still stealing it' (Cooper, 2017).

Scientists shouldn't have a monopoly on explaining the consequences of unsustainable lifestyles to the rest of us. Indigenous people, particularly in the Arctic regions, bear direct witness to their effects and can add their own unique perspectives on what we are losing and how we can change our ways (more on this in Chapter 3). I think we should be as forward-thinking as the Iroquois First Nations Americans. Harland (2018, p. 6) describes this perspective as spanning 14 generations – seven before and seven after, with us in the middle. We need to use the wisdom of our ancestors to help forge a sustainable future in perpetuity.

Harland is writing from a 'permaculture' perspective. This approach to sustainability can extend to all areas of life. For example, permaculture would say that the ultimate goal of farming isn't to produce crops but to nurture the soil. If this is done, crops will be forthcoming for the indefinite future. Similarly, in a school, you could say that leadership should make sure that all human beings are nurtured to ensure a measurable yield of learning. Permaculture will be discussed in more detail in Chapter 5.

MEASURING AND DRAWING LINES

Most people know intuitively that material wealth above a certain level yields diminishing returns of happiness,[7] and that often the best things in life are free, such as having access to unsullied nature or the love and companionship of other human beings. Yet generally these things aren't commodified, and the overall economic system doesn't 'value' them sufficiently. GDP doesn't take into account the purveyance of love or voluntary acts of human kindness, it only measures monetary transactions. So, I add to GDP if I buy and drive a car, but I don't if I give my time to help the local charity shop. GDP likes arms sales and reconstruction after war, but not peace talks that make weapons irrelevant. It likes pollution because of the economic activity involved in clearing it up. If GDP were a person, we'd say they were amoral, if not downright immoral.

However, GDP isn't a human being; it's merely a human *construct* that appears to have taken on a life of its own, but it's portrayed as indomitable and itself a law of nature as defined by classical economics. The system it creates and supports isn't inhuman, but *unhuman*. Despite escalating environmental depletions and associated social and economic damage, most politicians and the media encourage us to worry about GDP if it isn't rising. There's a weird cognitive dissonance going on here, because it's often the same agencies flagging up the doomsday scenario of environmental breakdown. Yet it's still a mistake to commodify 'natural capital' with a wholly monetary value because this is an inadequate measure. What price do we put on a sunset or the sight of a whale?[8]

7   This is backed up by academics such as Layard and Ward (2020), also featured in Chapter 5.
8   The UK government's Department for Environment and Rural Affairs (Defra) produced guidance on valuing nature and conceded that 'It is also recognised that a natural capital approach does not always require monetary valuation' (Defra, 2020, Section 1.2). This document still sees nature as mainly an exploitable 'service' for humans though.

As a leader, even if you have a clear idea about what sustainability is, when it comes to creating a sustainable school there is an additional challenge: namely, where do you draw a line between the sustainability of your own educational establishment and that of the outside world? How you answer this question depends upon how far you go down the sustainability road. It can be challenging to get your head around the issues, but they are, after all, based in our everyday existence. All it takes is a bit more detailed knowledge, benevolent values, new perspectives, joined-up thinking and sometimes a leap of faith. Also, it's worth realising that a school *is* a part of the outside world, so whatever a school leader does will make a difference beyond the perimeter fence.

EMBODIMENT OF CONFUSION

The embodied carbon issue is worth a special mention here because many people don't realise its significance. Embodied carbon is all the CO_2 – and/or greenhouse gas equivalent (CO_2e) – that accumulates when a product is created, from the extraction and processing of raw materials to manufacture, packaging, transportation to a consumer, then disposal. This means that although, on paper, a country like the UK has a much-reduced carbon footprint because most of its mining, carbon-excreting energy production and heavy industry and manufacturing has disappeared, the carbon this would have produced is displaced (outsourced) to those countries from which it imports goods. If this is taken into account, the UK's carbon footprint – although reducing – is still very high because the carbon is embodied in the stuff. This can also be labelled as 'Scope 3 emissions' (described in more detail in Chapter 4). These emissions accounted for about 358,000,000 tonnes per annum (including international aviation) in 2017 (Harvey, 2020). Compared to Russia, China, the United States, India and Japan, the UK imports the most carbon per capita (Office for National Statistics, 2019). This means that we should always look at consumption-based data rather than territorial data.[9] It's also worth knowing that methane is about 30 times worse than the equivalent volume of CO_2 for causing greenhouse effects. Food waste, poor soil management, gas pipe leakages and melting permafrost are the chief human-made causes.[10]

9 For more information on the carbon footprint of countries, see: http://globalcarbonatlas.org/en/ CO2-emissions.
10 For more information on methane, see Voiland (2016).

People get fixated on reducing CO2e footprints. As important as this is, it can mask the issue of biodiversity loss (which is closely related). The Science Academies of the Group of Seven (G7) nations stresses the need for greater awareness of how supply chains and consumption have a diverse impact on the natural world, and hence its capacity to soak up excess carbon and renew the biosphere resources that are needed to sustain life.[11] The production of palm oil at the expense of the rainforest is a classic example of this. As is commercial forestry, which is sterile and can deplete soils and diminish their capacity to sequester carbon.[12] A school's procurement policy needs to take this into account (see Chapter 4).

In a related point, Brahic (2021, pp. 3–4) points out that 'the bio-diversity crisis poses as great a risk to human societies as climate change. Yet it has a fraction of the public profile'. She thinks this is partly due to the difficulty of quantifying it and pinning down the causes and effects within and across ecosystems, which are even more complex than those which drive the climate. The role of insects in pollinating food crops (about 35% of these crops rely on insect pollination, according to the Natural Resources Conservation Service[13]) and as the base layer of food chains and webs is a case in point. A sustainable school prioritises nature study (natural history) and also tries to increase biodiversity in the school grounds (see Chapters 3 and 4).

So, this is my take on sustainability, which I hope will give context to the rest of the narrative.

LEADERSHIP FOR SUSTAINABILITY RECOMMENDATIONS

- Check what colleagues think sustainability really is and compare their responses to the discussion here. A sustainable school needs clarity on this matter.

---

11 See https://www.interacademies.org/sites/default/files/2021-04/DES7289_2_S7%20 Statement_Biodiversity.pdf.

12 For a useful non-technical overview of the value of good soil management (including reduced water consumption) linked to the Sustainable Development Goals (SDGs – to be described later), see https:// www.natureandmore.com/en/sustainable-development-goals-and-the-link-to-organic.

13 See https://www.nrcs.usda.gov/wps/portal/nrcs/main/national/plantsanimals/pollinate.

- Don't expect full consensus on any aspect of sustainability, but, by the same token, don't be afraid to put forward bold plans just because some people don't get it. Seeing is believing.

- We need a scientific and a wider cultural perspective on sustainability. Make sure you tap into everyone's knowledge to get balance. When running training for teachers and leaders, I've found that there are many misconceptions, or a lack of understanding, about some of the science, especially in primary schools where most staff tend to have arts backgrounds. Similarly, aspects of social and economic phenomena aren't recognised as being part of the sustainability picture, and people with pure science backgrounds can miss this, especially in secondary schools and above.

Chapter 2

CAPTAINCY

The deepest form of role constraint is the fact that the individual's own true self, if still alive, must watch helplessly while the role self lives.

Charles Reich (1970, p. 121)

LEADERSHIP: HORSES FOR SUSTAINABILITY COURSES

It took me six years of part-time study to complete a doctoral course in education leadership. Within that time, we were exposed to and asked to critique countless leadership styles, strategies and management techniques. This was very valuable, not least because it showed that there was no one-size-fits-all approach when it comes to leading a school (six years to realise the obvious!). During this time, my research into leadership for sustainability revealed it as a legitimate category in its own right, with the potential to improve schools across all areas rather than just in 'eco-matters'. Like other portfolio leadership styles, it could deliver easily measurable added value and – just as importantly – enjoyment, fulfilment and better well-being, not just for children but for all stakeholders.

Apart from sharing the results of my studies and thoughts since, in this chapter I describe some effective applications of this leadership approach in terms of real-life situations. They're context specific, but I hope you will find them useful as an insight into what might be possible elsewhere.

FLYING THE GREEN FLAG

I studied a cohort of 10 head teachers who led Green Flag Eco-Schools – Green Flag being the highest grade of an internationally recognised accreditation for sustainability in schools.[1] My study went into great depth through visits, questionnaires, interviews, scrutiny of curricula and analysis of documentation. My research emerged from the question, 'Why do a small minority of leaders wish to put sustainability at the heart of their schools' ethos?' I found great similarities among my participants, despite their schools being in very different circumstances – ranging from small and deeply rural to large and inner-city. This showed that the values of the head teacher held the key to the school's sustainability ethos. I put together a new model which I called (not very originally) 'green leader'. I regret this now because the G-word can be off-putting to the uninitiated and conjure up images of hippiedom or eco-fanaticism, not deemed worthy of serious consideration by the mainstream.

All but one of the leaders had strong links to the natural world before the age of 18, and they confirmed that this sort of childhood had influenced their desire to embed ESD in their schools. The majority had considerable professional training in areas which gave them a wide-ranging and deep knowledge of natural systems and how these relate to social systems, including permaculture (for more on the leadership implications of this, see Chapter 5). Most of them also had experience and/or training which afforded them a wide perspective of education at a national level. Some were in regional or national networks which reinforced this perspective. These networks dealt with educational initiatives in general, as well as those related to ESD. This meant that they were outward- rather than inward-looking and were keen to discuss the philosophy of education, rather than forever being bogged down in the minutiae of operational management. They were also keen to promote their ESD work more widely. For example, one suburban school had a farm which the children helped to run, and they received frequent visits from other school leaders as well as local and national politicians. From this you could see that they were truly 'inside out' leaders who were far from being parochial and were keen to broadcast their work, not as an ego trip, but to spread their 'inside' school practice more widely 'outside' for the common good. (More on this on page 34.)

---

1   For an overview of the criteria, see: https://www.eco-schools.org.uk.

A church school ethos featured in half of the schools and seemed to be influential in the development of ESD, in that it emphasised the importance of caring for oneself and one's family, school and community. Two of the head teachers explicitly stated their desire to integrate sustainability with the Christian ethos of their schools. I've come across other leaders since who have linked a sustainability ethos with other major religions (most of which have a strong strand of sustainability teachings).

Most of the head teachers were single-minded and had the urge to drive sustainability within their school and beyond. They were certainly far more transformational than transactional. Two of them referred to this as a 'mission' (one of these wasn't from a church school), and another said that it was his 'vocation'. One said that 'you need evangelists' to spread the word about sustainability and that her own 'drive' had been needed to promote it. This smacks of red-caped, superhero leadership, although this isn't meant as a criticism. It reinforces the point that although distributed leadership can be a useful school strategy and an indicator of a horizontal power structure, you still need an instigator and a holder of the vision and mission to embed ESD – or any change, for that matter. From this, you can detect 'charismatic' and 'hero' tendencies, in that the personal characteristics of the ringleader define and drive a particular ethos, while they model attributes such as resilience and risk-taking.

The leaders I studied were successful in the conventional sense, meaning that the powers that be largely left them to their own devices. You can see how this sort of leadership is diametrically opposed to 'designer leadership' – a set framework of leadership which aspiring leaders are taught to adopt by certain kinds of professional development, closely linked to managerialist approaches.

Fig. 2.1: Green leader model

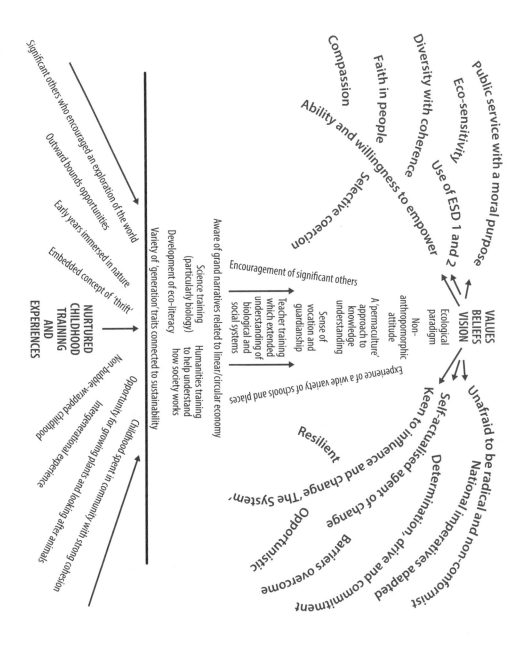

GREEN LEADERS: ROOT AND BRANCH

I conceptualised the green leader model as a tree to provide an organic representation of the lives of my participants (see Figure 2.1).

A tree exemplifies ecological systems. The school leaders' childhood roots were the source of the energy which carried them through into adulthood and defined their values, beliefs and behaviours across their whole lives, not just their professional lives. Some had been influenced by working-class grandparents who had lived through post-Second World War austerity and who themselves had sustainability values, which showed up in thrifty and low-waste lifestyles and in their commitment to their communities. The head teachers actively sought higher education which not only offered deep understanding of social and biological systems, but also the opportunity to enter into a vocation dedicated to public service with a strong moral purpose. Once in positions of influence, this was given free rein, and – despite external constraints – they were eager to create sustainable schools through a connected ecosystem made up of the curriculum, campus and community. They weren't afraid to be radical and non-conformist, while at the same time empowering others to help the sustainability cause, flagging it up locally and nationally, so that others might take it on. They were keen to allow children to have a voice to debate environmental issues and, where necessary, to take actions to improve matters at the level of campus and community or to lobby politicians for positive change.

Although they showed great faith in people and distributed their leadership, they weren't averse to using 'selective coercion' to get their own way. In this respect, they could be described as 'green Machiavellians'.[2] They were astute at 'gaming' the system to sideline the bits they didn't believe in and were can-do when they came up against barriers – nimble and spontaneous rather than cautious and slow. Setbacks didn't diminish their optimistic attitude, their drive or their commitment to sustainability. If they had a gut feeling about something, they would tend to trust it rather than wait for 'objective' information. They realised that schools and

---

2 Hanson and Middleton (2000) devised a 'green Machiavellian' leadership model which, although quite ruthless and dictatorial in some respects, was redeemed by the sustainability values of the leader and did in fact include collaborative strategies as befitting Machiavelli himself, who I feel has had a bad press.

their communities are complex places with lots of 'wicked problems',[3] and didn't shy away from this by seeking simplistic silver-bullet solutions. They displayed ecological thinking – inspired by what Orr (2005) describes as nature-inspired ecological literacy – and applied it to all aspects of school life, not just to the realms of sustainability.

Above all, the leaders I studied had a global perspective and an appreciation of what this meant for their role (local to global and back again). Being a world-centric guardian sounds like a very daunting role, and is not for the faint-hearted, but if you are to be a school leader, then this shouldn't be ducked. After all, a world-centric perspective is embodied by the Universal Declaration of Human Rights, which needs to be operated at all levels of society.[4]

BARRIERS AND BURDENS

The head teachers in my study encountered many barriers when pushing back the frontiers of sustainability in their schools. In particular, a lack of:

- Leadership time needed to fully implement sustainability due to national and local imperatives and associated bureaucracy.

- Finance to alter school infrastructure to ensure that the campus was running at low waste and was also able to utilise microgeneration using renewables (this was made even more difficult by antiquated buildings or the poor design of newer builds).

- Suitable ESD training for teachers and support staff (invariably, early career teachers had little of this).

- Sustainability training for site staff and budget managers.

Although these barriers were considerable, they weren't insurmountable. The head teachers sought special grants for sustainability projects (such as developing nature areas or installing microgeneration technologies), accessed continuing

---

3   Wicked problems are persistent and complex and sometimes not fully solvable – see Jones (2015) and https://www.interaction-design.org/literature/topics/wicked-problems. See also Mike Bottery's (2016) account of this in the context of leadership for sustainability in his book *Educational Leadership for a More Sustainable World*. This is one of the few books to look at this sort of leadership from an academic perspective.
4   See https://www.un.org/en/about-us/universal-declaration-of-human-rights.

professional development (CPD) for staff through organisations such as World Wide Fund for Nature (WWF)-UK and ensured that they networked with other like-minded schools and organisations to further enrich the curriculum. To achieve this, they often had to work double time by making grant applications and/or liaising with non-governmental organisations (NGOs), parents and community groups that might help the cause. Using astute delegation also helped all this and I certainly found it particularly beneficial to empower middle leaders and support staff, such as the school business manager and the site manager (more on this in Chapters 4 and 5). They also had a 'can-do' rather than a 'why it can't be done' mentality and were willing to take risks, using the maxim: better to apologise than to ask for permission.

As well as facilitating the learning of others, these leaders were also unashamed learners themselves and seemed to retain a curiosity about the world as a whole, rather than seeing themselves as being in a fixed state of superior knowingness. This meant they were receptive to new knowledge and ideas and would adapt their practice accordingly.

SHADES OF GREEN

All the head teachers in my study were highly reflective and critical of their sustainability practice and saw it as a work in progress. From my in-school observations and in-depth conversations with the leaders, I could see that, despite all having a Green Flag, they were on a continuum of greenness, defined by their own knowledge and background, how long they had been in post and the history of the school they'd inherited. It appeared that those who had the strongest moral imperative to embed sustainability were those who lived it in their personal lives. One 'objective' indicator of this was calculating their respective personal carbon footprints. Those with the lowest tended to lead schools with the most integrated and meaningful sustainability approaches and smallest operational carbon footprints. This pointed to some of them 'walking the talk' more than others, and suggested that an ESD ethos was deeply embedded in their non-work lives. These leaders also fitted the generative[5] and servant descriptions of leadership[6] that embody the leader for sustainability model to a tee, emphasising that there are few, if any, self-serving or ego-driven elements which might befall a Machiavellian or hero leader who is using coercive, transactional and managerialist means. These values-based models emanate from within individuals and aren't sanctioned by an external force.

Leaders for sustainability personify how leadership operates across the school. They seem to have less of a rigid dichotomy between 'the person' and 'the role'. They are *authentic* from their core, hence the wish to transform their values and beliefs into tangible sustainability reality. This leader uses their personality not as some ego-driven imperative but to live and model sustainability in its widest sense. This is 'being the change', rather than implementing change at the behest of others or for self-gratification and external reward.

Ryan (2008) described a sort of school leader who is 'inside out', and this fits the leadership for sustainability model. They have strong values and beliefs, laced with passion, energy, communication/networking skills and the organisational abilities to put them into operation. Overall, these leaders 'take a close look at the needs of their children and establish a clear moral purpose' (Ryan, 2008, p. 8). He also says that such leaders 'never entertain self-doubt' (Ryan, 2008, p. 6). I wish I could say the same! Although Ryan places emphasis on developing others and collaborative working, there is more than a hint of Machiavellianism or, at the very least, the hero head. But why should this be a criticism? Leaders need to lead and to break new ground, rather than merely manage, but, crucially, they need to do so for the right reasons. In the context of this book, I'm advocating that it is 'right' to embed sustainability, but this often requires deviation from the norm. So, to follow the logic, for this deviation to happen, we need deviant leaders, or mavericks, who are strong enough to steer a school along a different path (more on mavericks later). After all, leaders need to lead! I've couched this in terms of the six Ps in Figure 2.2. Notice how dynamic and non-linear such a leader needs to be, without being hierarchical or too dictatorial.

. . . .

5   Generative leadership is based upon strongly held values and a moral purpose that recognises and embraces complexity, rather than being afraid of it and forever trying to implement improvements through reductive means. Klimek et al. (2008, p. 29) see schools as 'living systems' and suggest that generative leaders should focus on identity (sense-making capacity that everyone understands), information (which is free-flowing and transparent) and relationships (rich and authentic at all levels, without rigid hierarchy).

6   The phrase was attributed to Robert K. Greenleaf, an AT&T executive, who wrote: 'The servant-leader *is* servant first ... The best test, and difficult to administer, is: do those served grow as persons?' (Greenleaf, 2002 [1977], p. 27).

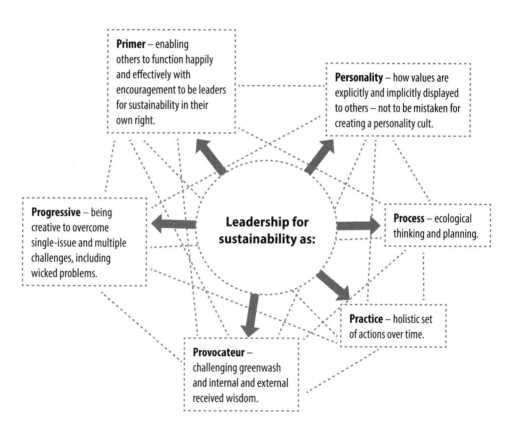

Figure 2.2: Matrix showing authentic leadership for sustainability in action

This also fits the notion of quiet leadership, meaning a leader doesn't seek the limelight, but acts with vision, courage and sometimes sacrifice to make the world a better place (Badaracco, 2002, p. 9).

MIND YOUR LEADERSHIP LANGUAGE

The development of a school sustainability culture is greatly assisted if leaders understand how their use of language determines the school's working relationships with all stakeholders and how their plans are formulated and turned into actions. I once did a semiotic analysis of words which had crept into education from industry. These included: targets, impact, timelines, production, total quality management, human resources, milestones, benchmarks, risk assessments, performance, outcomes, 360 analysis, intervention, value added, cost-benefit analysis, process, deep dives ... Many of these words are associated with summative and mechanistic objective measurement, as if children were on a linear production line administered by a series of uniformly trained teachers and support staff overseen by a manager.[7] They need to be used with discretion by a leader for sustainability, whose lexicon would be better served with: kindness, collegiality, progress with humanity, patience, serving, individuality, culture, respect, gentleness, growth, nurture, enablement, empowerment, celebration, sharing, cooperation, collaboration, fairness, enjoyment, empathy, fulfilment ... which give suitably different messages about the ways in which people are treated and educated rather than just schooled and administered.

I'm *not* saying that mechanistic = completely bad, and ecological = completely good (although the mechanistic is very much a product of the WEIRD paradigm described in the introduction). What I *am* saying is that an overemphasis on, and overuse of, the former at the expense of the latter can be the death knell for a sustainability ethos. When buying a wind turbine, I would use lots of mechanistic thinking to make sure I got the correct model, with optimal performance and at the best price for my budget. The formal part of my maths and science education would be essential for this, as would my faith in the manufacturing system which produced it in terms of quality control, delivery and installation. I would also need to know that the turbine company had specialist expert personnel and that the

---

7   See Sterling (2004, pp. 58–59) for more on mechanistic vs ecological paradigms.

parts were sufficiently standardised to make them easy to replace. Crucially, it would have been my world view, based upon ecological thinking, that prompted me to buy a wind turbine in the first place. This means that my intrinsic values and sense of individual responsibility led to these actions. Incidentally, my values would also extend to checking out the ethical side of the purchase to determine whether the materials were from the least damaging source, what would be the overall carbon footprint and whether the associated workers are treated fairly.

SYSTEMS AND STRUCTURES

There's also a link between systems thinking and ecological understanding through various types of joined-up thinking. Having said that, it's important to see the distinctions. For example, systems thinking might produce a rota or a set procedure as well as a way of understanding group dynamics or the motives of an individual. To aid creative and holistic solutions, ecological understanding needs to err on the side of natural ecology, which embraces complexity and welcomes the resilience born of diversity. This is how coral reefs function. This perspective also recognises that if one thing alters, invariably, there are neutral, positive and negative knock-on effects – and certainly not all anticipated (these are the butterfly effects we discussed). A strong yet flexible ecological system can also overcome the shock of 'Black Swans' (described in Chapter 5) and wicked problems. But schools still need a fair amount of 'conventional' systems thinking, with its quota of mechanistic thinking that produces linear action plans, procedures and so on. It's just a matter of getting the balance right.

To show part of this systems thinking process, Figure 2.3 is a mapping exercise that we undertook in our London school when we wanted to scope out how to gain the first Eco-Schools accreditation level of Bronze. By doing this, we were acknowledging and embracing the complexity rather than looking for simplistic solutions. Following this exercise, we were better placed to prioritise actions and resources to include 'conventional' action plans. However, the evaluations of these were always undertaken in relation to the whole. We weren't slaves to linear plans, and we weren't afraid to radically alter or jettison them if things weren't working out.

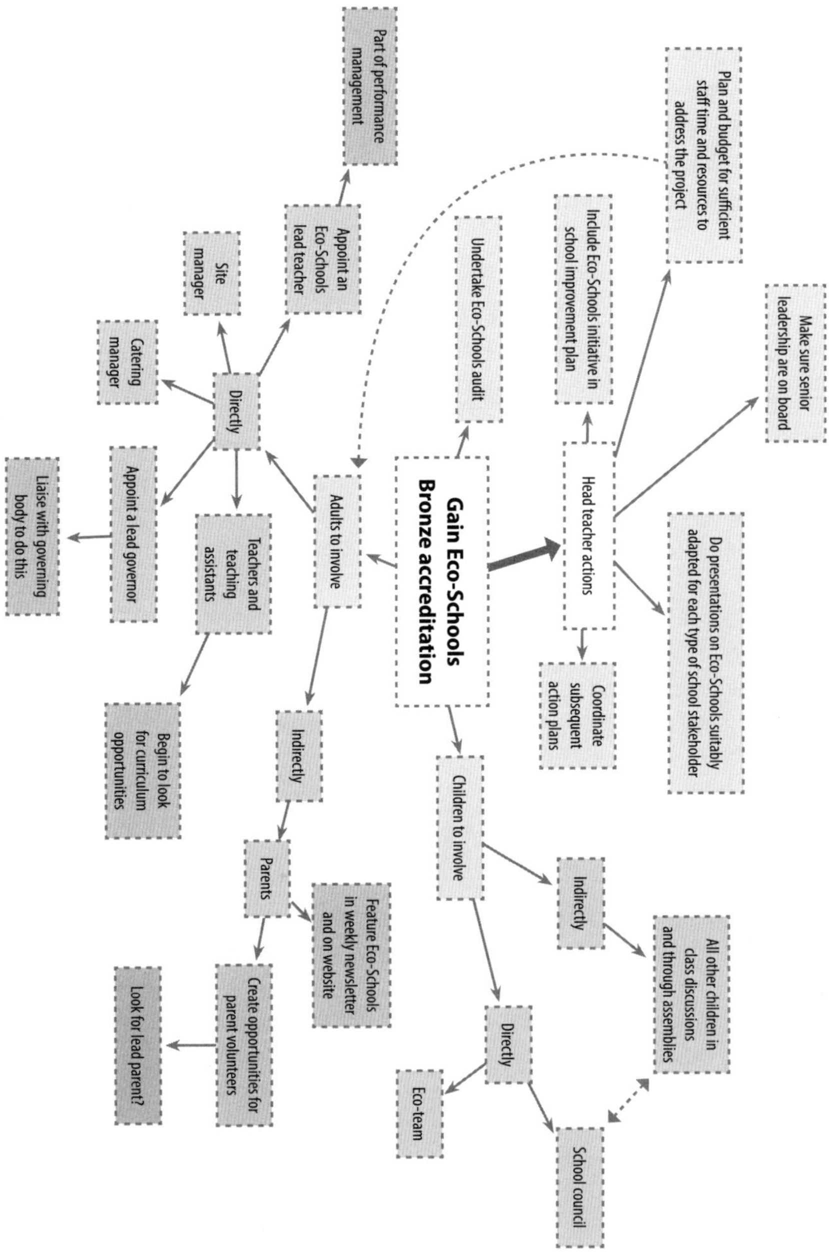

Figure 2.3: Example of a school improvement mapping exercise

Gain Eco-Schools Bronze accreditation

Head teacher actions
- Plan and budget for sufficient staff time and resources to address the project
- Make sure senior leadership are on board
- Do presentations on Eco-Schools suitably adapted for each type of school stakeholder
- Coordinate subsequent action plans

Undertake Eco-Schools audit

Include Eco-Schools initiative in school improvement plan

Adults to involve
- Directly
  - Appoint an Eco-Schools lead teacher — Part of performance management
  - Site manager
  - Catering manager
  - Appoint a lead governor — Liaise with governing body to do this
  - Teachers and teaching assistants — Begin to look for curriculum opportunities
- Indirectly
  - Parents
    - Feature Eco-Schools in weekly newsletter and on website
    - Create opportunities for parent volunteers — Look for lead parent?

Children to involve
- Indirectly
  - All other children in class discussions and through assemblies
- Directly
  - Eco-team
  - School council

By seeing the big picture we could look for links and complementary areas. This meant that, despite the complexity, in the end the number of planned actions were lessened and sometimes made more straightforward. It also made clear which areas of the overall plan were most relevant to various individuals and groups. This type of mapping exercise suits collaboration, encouraging creative thought and co-creation before the actions are pinned down. Having a vision and a purpose should be the starting point and driver for the overall schema. Your planning and action will encompass your sustainability ethos and your imagination.

The proponents of systems thinking, such as Fullan (2004), have always advocated that it should be flexible and provide a wide variety of perspectives and techniques for leaders to utilise. It mimics ecological systems in that it contains diversity – a diversity of expertise and ideas. Diversity in nature provides resilience, longevity and strength. Think how much more resilient a natural rainforest is when compared to monoculture farming. Systems thinking resonates with a green outlook.

Ecological systems thinking can take this further and help to identify and make sense of very complex causes and effects on learners (positive and negative) and help leaders to be proactive in making all aspects of school life worthwhile. Realising the significance and complexity of the hidden curriculum is of particular relevance to this.[8] There are many interpretations of this phenomenon, but I see it as all those things children experience above and beyond the delivered subject curriculum, including the learners' perceptions of what they encounter and various kinds of interactions outside the classroom (including behind the bike sheds!). This reflects the criticisms of Illich (1995) and the 'de-schoolers', who thought that schools were deeply damaging simply by being schools. Having home-educated my teenage son I know all about this! This theme is picked up again in Chapters 4 and 5. Identifying where the curriculum needs to be decolonised also fits this agenda (discussed further in Chapter 3). To get a handle on some of these issues, we used an assessment tool which measures pupils' attitudes to self and school.[9]

8   Newberry et al. (2013) provide a useful overview of the hidden curriculum, which emphasises the effect of emotional responses triggered by circumstances and includes the way unintended prejudice can badly affect an individual's or group's capacity to learn.

9   See https://www.gl-assessment.co.uk/assessments/pass.

MEETING OF MINDS

As we have seen, horizontal leadership associated with leadership for sustainability requires authentic conversations in which everyone feels valued and able to contribute without fear or favour. These need quite strict rules of engagement, which are developed by the group, otherwise meetings can be interminable. They certainly shouldn't be ruled by committee or an end in themselves with no action points. Circle meetings are a useful format for achieving this and link to Nancy Kline's principles of creating a thinking environment.[10] This requires quite a lot of coaching, as professional educators are not always renowned for suspending judgement, careful listening or speaking with clear intention, especially after a hard day in the classroom. But if people are physically comfortable (they may need tea and cake), the meetings aren't overlong and are conducted using circle time principles, they can be a lot more productive and satisfying, rather than being perceived as yet another occupational hazard.

It also helps if circle meetings are distinct from briefings, which merely involve the dissemination of routine information (dates for events, new health and safety arrangements, etc.). Much of this information can be gleaned from emails or the school intranet platform. This means that circle meetings afford participants the time and structure to create new knowledge and understanding – essential requisites for learning organisations. Circle time formats for children are similar and share the aims of inclusivity and respect for everyone in the group.[11] I wish we'd used circle techniques far more in the schools I've led, as I'm sure they would have sped up the development of an authentic distributed leadership culture.

I'm advocating leadership which is not just a managerial mechanism for achieving narrow, external performance targets, although it needs to achieve these as well to retain credibility with the less enlightened bean counters who can and do eject people from the system for failing to reach summative targets. This type of leadership is about encouraging meta-learning and critical thinking by educators and learners. It's also about seeing education as a series of motivational, investigative, creative, integrated and social activities, not just narrow, subject-orientated, individualistic activities, dictated by formulaic teaching and knowledge-heavy

10 See https://leanin.org/circle-resources/how-to-make-your-circle-meetings-a-success.
11 See https://www.circle-time.co.uk.

syllabuses. The thinking behind this is well established and has been debated for many decades in terms of progressive vs traditional education methodology.[12]

HEART OF GLASS

Leaders for sustainability can circumvent the argument between traditional and progressive systems of education by offering a different model based on sustainability, which can satisfy both, although in reality it adheres more to the progressive when it comes to school ethos and leadership styles (see Figure 2.4). I developed this working model to show staff and inspectors the rationale behind my sustainability drive. It shows how a learning paradigm approach has the potential to break the glass ceiling of attainment for all learners. A leader could operate this model without a sustainability focus – for example, the key ethos might be creativity, in particular through the arts (and I've seen many successful schools with this focus). But one of my central arguments is that this would ignore the added agency sustainability has to improve a school across the board while keeping the accountability wolves from the door *and* helping to save the planet. Incidentally, a sustainability focus can also deliver marvellous creativity, as Chapter 3 illustrates.

---

12 The 1967 Plowden Report shows how this debate is little changed. It's also at the heart of the Cambridge Review of Primary Education (Alexander (ed.), 2010), entitled *Children, Their World, Their Education* and also known as the Alexander Report, which is worth a look because it contains many examples of good primary practice, many of which link to sustainability. For a powerful account of the discrediting of progressive education in the 1970s, which resonates today, read Gretton and Jackson's (1976) *William Tyndale: Collapse of a School – or a System?*

Attainment ceiling

Actions	Characteristics	Actions
Teaching to the test using standard syllabus created by others. Regular test practice. Standardised and formulaic teaching. Child performance, progress and targets judged mostly by test data. Data shared with parents to gain their support with extra homework or tuition outside school. A few cultural events celebrated (e.g. Black History Month, Christmas, Diwali).	Staff are directed to 'appropriate training'. Rapid improvement in test scores, but little change in overall attainment (i.e. capacity and enthusiasm to learn). Creativity sidelined. Learners prone to anxiety. Seemingly 'child-centred', but using limited criteria (i.e. that which is easily measured). Temporary improvement, unless there are accompanying long-term strategies. The curriculum is very narrow and omits important aspects of science, arts, PE, PSHE, critical thinking and global learning. Pupils seen as passive recipients of teaching. School does not see itself as a community hub (i.e. there to actively contribute to community sustainability).	Shared commitment to raising standards. Effective monitoring and evaluation. Challenging school targets. Related teacher and year group targets. Well-focused improvement activities. Effective performance management. Effective tracking of progress. Effective teaching to deliver targets. Subject strategies well implemented. Booster classes. ESD is present, but does not have high profile, apart from some 'green events' such as litter picking, recycling or gardening.

	Characteristics	**No limits to learning!** Actions	Characteristics
	Sustained improvement to test scores for all abilities.	Pupils are taught metacognition	Emotional intelligence is promoted for all.
	Staff can be burnt out due to demands for ongoing pupil progress data and the reliance on this for performance-related pay.	Teachers have highly developed knowledge of how pupils learn.	Joy of learning is a central ethos of the school.
		Pupils understand their preferred learning styles.	Teachers enjoy teaching and seek new skills and competencies.
	Pupils can suffer burnout and become demotivated learners by the end of primary school.	Promotion of pupils' involvement in their own assessment and learning.	Despite high expectations, 'quick fixes' are not expected.
	Pupil and staff welfare seen in terms of bolt-on interventions.	Staff see themselves as learners.	Holistic and generative leadership is employed.
	Staff have limited choice in training options linked to performance management.	Promotion of pupil independence *and* collaboration.	PSHE is a cross-curricular issue.
		Teachers formulate their own curriculum to suit their learnings, taking into account the context of the community.	The physical and emotional environment is very conducive to learning.
	Parents further mobilised for fundraising and to volunteer in classrooms.	Cross-curricular links are embedded and fully understood due to good subject knowledge.	Pupils' cultural backgrounds valued unconditionally.
			Teaching seen as an art as well as a science. Performance management recognises this.
		Workload of teachers and support staff constantly reviewed.	Happy atmosphere throughout the school.

Attainment ceiling

Actions	Characteristics	Actions	
	School uses cultural events and the promotion of British values to tick boxes for external inspection.		
	Performance management is used as a control mechanism.		
	Parents are only valued for their utility.		
	No room for ESD or other non-statutory parts of the curriculum.		
TACTICS (Short-termist: school dictated to by outside influences and initiatives)		STRATEGIES (Longer-termist: some autonomy achieved by improving easily measurable standards)	

Managerialist
Mechanistic thinking
Organisation of learning   ←

Figure 2.4: Using ESD for school improvement

	Characteristics	No limits to learning!	
		Actions	Characteristics
	ESD is a peripheral issue in the curriculum. It may also be seen in eco-teams and Eco-Schools accreditation.	Qualitative data valued (i.e. linked to pupil welfare).	Creativity, arts and sports are valued and promoted.
		Parents and families seen as partners in learning.	Open-door policy for parents.
	ESD is a peripheral issue in the curriculum. It may also be seen in eco-teams and Eco-Schools accreditation.	ESD ethos embedded as a driver for school improvement in terms of curriculum, leadership and the general operation of the school.	ESD is a reference point (i.e. all stakeholders question whether the school operates sustainably in terms of the environmental, social and economic elements of its curriculum, campus and community).
			Regular field trips – day and residential – to urban and country settings.
			Social justice, nature studies and global learning are central features.
		LEARNING PARADIGM (Very autonomous, yet outward looking. Always adapting for the short-, medium- and long-term needs of the school, linked to improving sustainability in wider society)	
⟶	**Holistic leadership** **Ecological thinking** **Learning organisation**		

The model can be viewed in two ways. It could represent the journey of a school in trouble, which needs to boost test results using short-term tactics. Once this was achieved, it could develop longer-term strategies and avoid constant external scrutiny. Eventually, it could adopt a learning paradigm, encompassing the philosophy of a learning organisation. A veritable journey from hell to nirvana! Perhaps, more realistically, it can represent the state of a single school whose leadership needs to employ tactics, strategies and a learning paradigm in varying degrees, due to the need for accountability within the wider education system. This leaves ample room for a school to steer its own course, on which leadership values are translated from ethos into practical actions. I've highlighted the ESD aspects to show how they complement the move from narrow mechanistic methods to emancipatory learning.

The potentially damaging mental health effects of some of the strategies can be ameliorated by those of the learning paradigm. For example, if the emotional resilience of the staff and pupils is good, then they will be less susceptible to the pressures of testing. Our aim was always to work towards a situation where many of the tactics and strategies wouldn't be needed, due to the development of highly skilled teachers, better motivated learners and a less intrusive and managerialist leadership style. This creates a virtuous circle where testing is not so high stakes.

POLICY TO PRACTICE

It's all well and good if a leader has a strong personal commitment to sustainability and the moral imperative to embed it, but where does that leave school stakeholders? If a school hasn't encountered this sort of approach before, a leader, much like a progressive football manager, might end up losing the dressing room. To overcome this danger, it's imperative to take the time to co-create the overall vision, mission and related policies *with* school stakeholders, so they don't think that things are being done *to* them. Not only can this process bolster distributed leadership, but it spreads the ownership and understanding of sustainability and other important themes across the school. To me, a vision is all about where you want the school to be tomorrow, while the mission is about what is happening today. In effect, the vision feeds the mission in a continuous process. As more of the vision is achieved and incorporated into the mission, further blue-sky thinking can be instigated. This is why sustainability, like all aspects of school improvement, is a journey rather than a destination.

There is no right or wrong answer to this. An internet search of 'school sustainability policies' reveals many different approaches. Here's an introduction to one I've put together from an amalgam of examples:

Our school aims to be a fully functioning sustainable school through an integrated approach to the curriculum (what children learn), campus (buildings and grounds) and community (parents and other local people). This will include increasing the site biodiversity, cutting carbon footprints and promoting social justice for all. We also want to be outward-looking, provide a local to global perspective for all school stakeholders, and show others how sustainability works in practical ways to influence their behaviour and link with like-minded others to discover new ideas and practices.

READY, STEADY, GREEN?

One useful way of launching a whole-school sustainability initiative from scratch is to hold an event, inviting all staff and stakeholders (including parents and governors). It's vitally important to establish what sustainability entails because, as shown previously (and I apologise for labouring the point), it's much more than being green. This can be done through an overview by the head teacher, a consultant or as a facilitated group exercise before embarking on the practical applications. When I've done this in schools, I establish groups to each represent one aspect of sustainability in a school, and get them to define what it really means and how it links to the other aspects. The link is shown by a string exercise, in which one person from each group travels to all the others, holding a very long piece of string, and has to give three strong reasons why their areas of sustainability are linked. If these are accepted, the string is gripped by the receiving group and the person moves on to the others in turn (in any order). By the end there is a vast string matrix – an interchange of ideas and, literally, joined-up thinking. The dissemination at the end consolidates the learning, leaving people better placed to conduct an audit of what aspects of sustainability are already covered, the extent of this and how existing practice can be extended and/or new practice established.

Without these sorts of processes (which have time and resource implications), schools can easily miss important aspects – such as areas of social justice or ecological considerations – or, worse still, drift into a state of tokenism and greenwash. From this, a central vision needs to be established, which – in tandem with a good working knowledge of what sustainability covers – will determine what eventually happens in practical terms. Once again, I recommend a facilitated exercise to enable a co-created vision to emerge. Stakeholders and staff, in mixed groups, can then start to map out how this vision might play out in the curriculum, campus and community, linked to the UN Sustainable Development Goals (SDGs) (see Figure 2.5).

Figure 2.5: UN SDGs

Source: **UN, used with permission**[13]

----

13 See https://www.un.org/sustainabledevelopment. The content of this publication has not been approved by the United Nations and does not reflect the views of the United Nations or its officials or Member States.

The SDGs are:

---

the blueprint to achieve a better and more sustainable future for all. They address the global challenges we face, including poverty, inequality, climate change, environmental degradation, peace and justice.[14]

Within each of the 17 goals there are 169 targets, and the UN details how they can be achieved (hard-pressed school leaders don't need to read all the targets!). Despite being in separate categories, they are interrelated and often integrated. They also take it as read that you can't have a healthy and happy human population without having a healthy and sustainable biosphere (i.e. there is no rigid dichotomy between the human and the natural world). The dire state of health is not confined to poor nations. In the UK, this was highlighted by Marmot et al. (2020), whose review linked poor health to poverty and a type of malnutrition not immediately associated with hunger, namely obesity (although many children in the UK do go hungry). Chapter 3 shows examples of how schools can cover the SDGs in a practical sense. Chapter 4 gives more detail on this and how schools can help families and children be better fed.

We can also look at the SDGs within 10 categories called 'Doorways to Sustainability', which I helped to develop with the National College for School Leadership in 2007/2008, and which I and others have adapted since.

The links between the doorways and the SDGs can be summarised as:

1   **Buildings and grounds (school estate):** choice of building technologies and equipment with low environmental impact. School grounds developed to help children learn about the natural world and sustainable living (SDGs 1, 2, 3, 11, 12, 13, 15, 17).

2   **Energy and water:** reducing carbon and water footprints through more efficient use and where possible creating microgeneration and water capture systems (SDGs 6, 7, 11, 12, 13, 17).

3   **Travel and traffic:** finding less polluting alternatives to vehicle travel by cutting deliveries, accessing local produce and encouraging children to walk, scoot or cycle to school (SDGs 11, 12).

....

14 See https://www.un.org/sustainabledevelopment/sustainable-development-goals.

4 **Purchasing and waste:** using ethical goods and services locally sourced where possible and reducing, recycling, reusing and repurposing goods as much as possible (SDGs 11, 12, 13, 16, 17).

5 **Food and drink:** eating and drinking healthily, growing and preparing your own food on site and sourcing food and drink locally wherever possible (SDGs 1, 2, 3, 11, 12, 13).

6 **Inclusion and participation:** respecting human rights, freedoms, cultures and creative expression. Respecting the rights of nature (avoiding ecocide) and challenging prejudice and injustice (SDGs 3, 5, 10, 11).

7 **Local well-being:** making your school a community hub for learning and actively contributing to positive change to help the quality of life of local people. Helping people to value the good as well as changing the bad (SDGs 11, 16, 17).

8 **Global dimension:** developing understanding of global issues and realising how we are connected to and influence every aspect of human and non-human life on the planet as individuals and collectively. Think global, act local (SDGs 1, 2, 3, 6, 10, 11, 12, 13, 14, 15, 17).

9 **Biodiversity:** learning how the web of life works and how this links to ecological understanding and thinking. Appreciation of how badly damaged the planet has become due to certain human activities and how this can be rectified (SDGs 5, 11, 12, 13, 15).

10 **Aesthetic and spiritual appreciation of nature:** developing ways to commune with nature and admire its beauty and complexity at micro and macro levels. Providing people with opportunities to be mindful and to contribute their own artistic interpretations which celebrate life on Earth (SDGs 4, 5).

Figure 2.6 shows how all this can come together in a framework to help school stakeholders to use the doorways and SDGs to co-create a fully functioning sustainable school across the curriculum, campus and community.

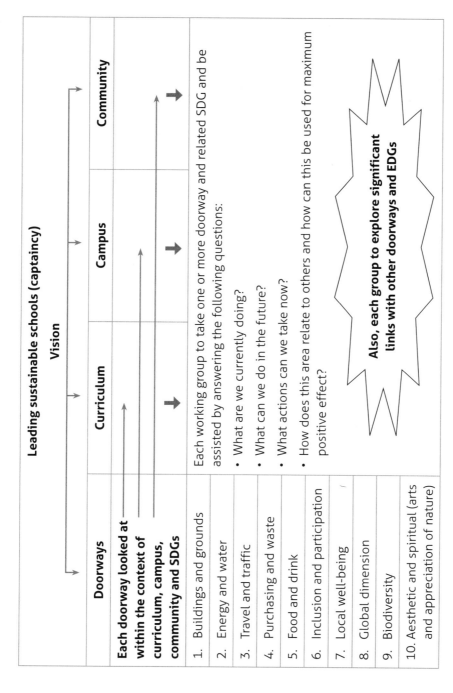

Leading sustainable schools (captaincy)

Vision

Doorways	Curriculum	Campus	Community
Each doorway looked at within the context of curriculum, campus, community and SDGs			
1. Buildings and grounds	Each working group to take one or more doorway and related SDG and be assisted by answering the following questions:		
2. Energy and water	• What are we currently doing?		
3. Travel and traffic	• What can we do in the future?		
4. Purchasing and waste	• What actions can we take now?		
5. Food and drink	• How does this area relate to others and how can this be used for maximum positive effect?		
6. Inclusion and participation			
7. Local well-being			
8. Global dimension	**Also, each group to explore significant links with other doorways and EDGs**		
9. Biodiversity			
10. Aesthetic and spiritual (arts and appreciation of nature)			

Figure 2.6: Making the vision a reality

During feedback sessions, it's important to identify where the main connections are between the doorways and SDGs; indeed, I've run separate sessions just to consolidate this point. Once this thinking is established, it's actually more difficult to distinguish individual points without making connections to others. This planning tool will be picked up again in Chapter 3, where we will explore how it can influence curriculum content and delivery. The various frameworks featured in Chapter 3 are also good starting points for a whole-school approach to sustainability.

Note: ambitious whole-school sustainability launches are all very well and can fast-track the approach. However, some leaders begin by adopting a drip-feed approach, as I did when starting out. As ever, it depends upon the circumstances of an individual school or groups of schools.

BACK TO THE FUTURE

Although there are many vintage Ofsted case studies of sustainable schools being highly effective on all fronts (Ofsted, 2003, 2008, 2009), the pity is that I've come across few failing schools that used a sustainability ethos to get out of trouble. This is not to say that some schools haven't used other non-mechanistic ways of improving, such as utilising the creative arts and humanities. I'm amazed that many of these schools don't seem to recognise the pedagogical and creative links to sustainability. At a conference organised by the London Environmental Educators Forum (LEEF) in 2020, I shared a panel with Professor Bill Scott. One of the questions posed was: 'How do you see environmental education in 30 years' time?' Bill said (and I paraphrase) that he hoped there wouldn't be the need for it because it would have been assimilated into an education system which was fit for purpose. Stone and Barlow (2005, xi) say: 'All education is environmental education ... by what is included or excluded we teach the young that they are part of or apart from the natural world.' This neatly sums up what I have come to believe: that embedded sustainability in schools should be the natural way of things and not a bolt-on afterthought, luxury accessory or result of leadership lunacy. The same can be said for black history in a decolonised curriculum (see Chapter 3).

What Bill advocates can be achieved right now. Although schools are encumbered by frameworks of accountability (all in the public domain so that schools can be named and shamed), education leaders have far more freedom than they might perceive. If a head teacher wishes to put sustainability as described here into operation, then they can do so. It all depends on how resolved they are to implement it beyond tokenism and greenwash. This is easier said than done, but it's not impossible, and there are many case studies from across the UK and the world to show its worth.[15]

TAKING THE STRESS OUT OF LEADERSHIP

Looking at some current leadership development programmes, I'm concerned that the curriculum for leaders has become as narrowed as that in many schools. Managerialist approaches are more common in schools and this has made leaders more susceptible to top-down diktats, which they in turn push downwards onto their long-suffering staff. The normalising of principles through standards (i.e. getting everyone to believe that valuing narrow, easily measurable outcomes should be the main priority) is a hallmark of the designer leadership mentioned earlier. The rise in staff stress levels might be a key indicator of this. The Teacher Wellbeing Index 2021 – which sampled 3,354 education staff from primary to higher education – reported that 72% 'describe themselves as stressed' and 77% 'experienced behavioural, psychological or physical symptoms due to their work' (Scanlan and Savill-Smith, 2021, p. 6). Most significantly in the context of this chapter, 38% said their organisational culture had a negative effect on their mental health and well-being as opposed to 30% who said it had a positive effect. Although this was an improvement on previous years, it still left a further 32% who said the culture had no effect, or who didn't know (Scanlan and Savill-Smith, 2021, p. 46). This may show that teachers – or leaders, for that matter – had never really considered the nature of their school culture or realised what positive and negative effects it might have on them and their protégés. Leaders for sustainability seek to shield their staff from the worst excesses of external accountability regimes.

I think that commodification has permeated professional relationships within schools, and this has exacerbated the stress felt by staff. Performance-related pay encourages cold transactional relationships. There is a narrow set of measures

15 See, for example: https://www.wwf.org.uk/sites/default/files/2019-02/Case%20Studies%20Steve%20Woodhouse_19.pdf; https://www.isc.co.uk/sector-info/sustainability-for-schools/case-studies; and https://www.greenschoolsproject.org.uk/schools-in-action.

(often based on pupils' test results) and teachers either pass or fail to measure up. This narrows any professional discussions between individual and line manager. It also means that staff are more likely to adhere to their job descriptions and be less emotionally committed to the organisation.[16] While there are always some transactional behaviours in all organisations (bottom up as well as top down), transformational behaviours provide the most impetus for the creation of a sustainable school.

FUTURE LEADERS

I worked in partnership with WWF-UK and Commonwork to develop transformational approaches when running a residential Leading for the Future course, based on wilderness experience methodology (Buckley Sander and Blair, 2011). The course aimed to create more leaders for sustainability in education. By immersing the participants in the natural world and providing physical activities interspersed with philosophical and practical discussions on education and leadership, these interlinked experiences led to a profound change in their beliefs and, eventually, their values. For some, this was down to learning more about ecological science. For others, they were affected emotionally by some of the practical activities (such as milking cows or making butter) and discussions which gave them new insights into their own and others' experiences. Sometimes, a combination of all these effects propelled them towards advocating for sustainability. Perhaps you're reading this book for the very same reasons.

The Leading for the Future participants were also provided with alternative visions of reality to encourage them to analyse their values and realise why they held them. Ultimately, we wanted them to come up with their own visions and break out of the professional acculturation (some might say brainwashing) that can inhibit innovation. We kept in touch with Leading for the Future participants after the course and found that many instigated radical programmes to embed sustainability in their own schools. This shows that leaders for sustainability don't have to be born, and why values can develop from experience and behaviour, as well as being

16 Mehdinezhad and Nouri (2016, pp. 47–48) advocate a more transformational leadership style which relies upon everyone sharing values and helping their collective interests. They argue that this style is better suited to unstable times (due to internal or external instability). Transformational leaders are 'able to unite their followers and change their goals and beliefs. They offer a vision of future prospects ... [and] can provide platforms for creativity.'

the starting point which determines our behaviour. I've witnessed school leaders who have changed course and embraced sustainability – having previously had scant regard for it personally or professionally – usually in a slow-burn way, although I've seen a few have a burning bush moment! This shows leaders that there are many options when it comes to changing the values and actions of others in their school.

But it's not just a matter of converting someone to the cause (or preaching to the converted, for that matter). This rather implies that sustainability is some sort of cult which requires the use of underhanded indoctrination. The Leading for the Future course revealed that, unsurprisingly, most of the participants already valued sustainability factors, but hadn't made sufficient links with their day jobs. They also didn't fully appreciate the moves into sustainability that some schools are already making, in the same way that they didn't fully appreciate what schools can do to undermine sustainability. Most teachers go into the profession to make a positive difference to the lives of their pupils, and this isn't a million miles away from ensuring that future generations survive and thrive. The same couldn't be said if we were dealing with oil company executives whose concept of 'survive and thrive' would likely be very different, as would their take on creating a sustainable future, even if they did advocate the phasing in of renewables.

MAVERICK MAKEOVER

Given that leaders for sustainability have a strong moral imperative, the question is over the extent to which they should compromise this due to national imperatives and external accountability. In the UK, many leaders seem to avoid too much contemplation of this, partly because they want to avoid the label 'maverick', which can have career-threatening possibilities, or they suffer from any of the aforementioned syndromes. After all, 'maverick' can denote that a person is a loose cannon and rather unpredictable, if not unreliable. It can also link to the discredited label 'progressive'. While this can be true in some cases, I would subscribe to the Oxford dictionary definition that says a maverick is 'an unorthodox or independent-minded person'.[17] From this less emotive definition, I would

17 Oxford University Press, maverick, *Lexico.com* (2021). Available at: https://www.lexico.com/definition/maverick.

advocate that all education professionals, especially top leaders, should at least have maverick tendencies. If not, then it isn't surprising if schools are non-thinking, non-learning establishments.

Critical thinking and associated activism are similarly feared by those who wish to preserve business as usual. Michael Gove's 'Blob' springs to mind: 'radical' thought being synonymous with Marxist or hippy ideology (Gove, 2013). The Blob itself was a group of anti-reformist teachers that Gove – who, at that point, was secretary of state for education in England – thought needed to be expelled from the profession.

Having a deeply engrained sustainability ethos also means that such leaders are often at the forefront of other educational developments. For example, in recent years I've worked with the inspirational head teacher Naheeda Maharasingam, who has developed a sophisticated and highly successful approach to using metacognition as a means of improving pedagogy and learning. She's also been a leading light in London for developing social justice education and incorporating this into the SDGs. Her route into ESD has been through the development of social sustainability. I have seen many other examples over the years where pioneers of sustainability have also championed other innovations which emanate from it or are used to enhance it. These leaders are invariably early adopters of home-grown initiatives or of those developed by other innovators which they make their own with adaptations. This also helps them to be 'inside out' and to develop networks of excellence with others.

Tragically, many leaders in education don't want to, as Gandhi says, 'be the change you wish to see in the world'.[18] They may do an excellent job in terms of passing external inspections, delivering good exam results and having career success, but they do little for the causes of sustainability.

Extolling the virtues of maverick tendencies wasn't meant to imply that I think that the education system should be smashed by a green Blob, rather that it should be seriously critiqued and radically adapted to suit our present times and, more crucially, the future. In his 2013 BBC Reith Lectures, artist Grayson Perry, when describing the role of artists in society, said that they should be realistic and realise that most of their work would sooner or later be utilised by the capitalist

---

18 Or not. It appears Gandhi didn't actually say this, although it sums up many of his sentiments. See https://quoteinvestigator.com/2017/10/23/be-change/#note-17089-10.

system.[19] In this context, they should be 'subversively compliant'. I think that this is an apt role for leaders for sustainability, so that societal systems can harmonise with those of the physical planet.

Education leaders need to gird their loins and develop sustainability as a moral imperative which triggers radical actions. Back in 1992, Fullan and Hargreaves asked the question in the title of a book: *What's Worth Fighting For in Your School?* I can think of nothing better than sustainability as discussed here. If this isn't forthcoming, I fear that Gaia won't give us much more wriggle room to once again live in harmony with ourselves and the planet.

The next chapter shows how sustainability in the curriculum can break glass ceilings of attainment and provide motivational activities that will help children thrive today and into a sustainable future.

LEADERSHIP FOR SUSTAINABILITY RECOMMENDATIONS

- What are your values? How many tie in with sustainability as presented here? Write them down – you might be surprised!

- Which style(s) of leadership do you employ? To what extent do you use Machiavellian tactics? Are they fit for purpose for sustainability?

- Examine the sort of professional language that you and others use (especially jargon). What does this say about you and your organisation? Question whether it needs to be modified and how this might link to change and the feelings people have about you and the organisation.

- Create sufficient time for others to debate and formulate new ideas for school improvement. Their opportunity to do this is the mark of authentic distributed leadership. Would circle meetings help?

- Look for more holistic strategies for addressing wicked problems. Pose pertinent questions to colleagues rather than providing answers, see relationships rather than structures or single issues and reflect on, rather than merely react to, issues. These behaviours relate very well to ecological thinking as described here and, therefore, would be the mark of a leader for

19 Grayson Perry's Reith Lectures can be heard at: https://www.bbc.co.uk/programmes/b03969vt.

sustainability. Remember, some wicked problems – such as issues children bring into school from home – have to be lived with, but they can't be allowed to dominate. Look for wicked solutions.

- Pin down the barriers to your professional well-being and that of others. Work collegially to overcome them – or, at the very least, find ways to live with them more comfortably.

- Revolution or evolution or a bit of both? Re-evaluate what you do in these terms. Ask yourself whether you should concentrate on maintaining the status quo (and what this actually is) or what changes might be needed over time (and how much time) in your personal and professional life. Share these thoughts with your team and get their take.

- Consider how you could build upon existing sustainability strengths, rather than always looking for weaknesses or shortfalls. Remember that most schools do various aspects of sustainability really well just by being schools.

- Seek out other leaders for sustainability and sustainable school support networks. Be inside out – you aren't alone!

- Consider how the hidden curriculum affects children's learning capacity. How much of this can you influence for the better?

- Staff and pupil stress is a big issue. Consider how a leader's behaviour affects this. A stress-filled school isn't a sustainable school.

- Do you need more transformational approaches and fewer transactional ones? Discuss.

Chapter 3

CURRICULUM

To young children ... nature is full of doors ... and they swing open at every step. A hollow in a tree is the gateway to a castle. An ant hole in dry soil leads to the other side of the world. A stick den is a palace. A puddle is the portal to the other side of the world.

Robert Macfarlane (2015, p. 315)

The curriculum as taught in the classroom is at the heart of what children are supposed to learn when in school. The origin of the word is from the Latin for 'race' – as in competitive running – which morphed into the term used to denote a fixed course of study. The ghosts of the etymological past still haunt the way the curriculum is thought of and delivered today. By this I mean that, through a knowledge-based curriculum, schools are generally expected to produce individuals who are adept at achieving economic success and the accompanying kudos as part of a successful GDP-based growth economy. The declining status of the arts and sports in schools in England is another symptom of this, and illustrates a narrowing curriculum with a summative assessment bias.[1] Unfortunately, in this race there are winners and losers, adding to generational inequality and poor life chances. It's part of the larger system outlined in Chapter 1 which is overexploiting people and planet.

I pose this in polemical terms to encourage readers to stand back and take a critical look at the philosophy behind the curriculum, as defined by national imperatives, and how it's interpreted and operated at a school level. Despite the challenges, this chapter shows practical ways of utilising sustainability to produce

---

1   See Cooper (2018) who highlights the decline of the arts in primary schools.

an enriched and meaningful curriculum, more suited to our overall needs now and in the future.

ENVIRONMENT IS EVERYTHING

When I was training to be a teacher in the late 1970s, one of the most useful reference books was entitled: *The Teacher's Handbook to Environmental Studies*. It was first published in 1968 and gives a warning which is eerily prescient today:

> [the] demand for specialist knowledge, guided by syllabuses for external examinations, tends to filter further and further downwards through the school. The dangers of this are oft-repeated and obvious – especially the risk that the true meaning of education may be lost in a welter of isolated 'subjects'. (Hammersley et al., 1968, p. 7)

The three authors of this book were heads of geography, science and rural studies, respectively, at teacher training colleges. Their book is full of practical activities encouraging teachers to take their classes outside the classroom – in rural and urban settings – for real-life learning experiences. It also extolled the value of pupils being in a 'learning partnership' with teachers. One aim of the book was to prevent pupils from being frightened of the environment and to instead embrace and value their locality before moving on to a wider understanding of the world (a type of local to global). As befits its vintage, it didn't cover global threats to the environment or encouraging pupils to improve an aspect of their environment through activism. It did, however, encourage the identification of local problems which might emerge from observations and discussions. These limitations aside, you can't fault it for its practical advice on the role of the teacher, paraphrased below:

- Arouse children's interest in their environment and raise challenging problems connected with it.
- Discuss the approach to problems or topics.
- Organise working groups.
- Arrange visits or expeditions.

- Provide reference material for children to use.

- Provide materials needed for practical work.

- Arrange visits from speakers.

- Discuss and guide the progress of each group.

- Initiate and develop discussion and debate.

- Persuade each group of children to explain their work to the rest of the class.

- Provide facilities for displays or exhibitions of the work carried out.

- Draw together the various aspects of the work and summarise the results.

- Link the work to the wider world.

The role of the child was to:

- Suggest approaches to the topic.

- Work as part of a small group.

- Learn to handle reference material.

- Experiment, investigate and discover for themselves.

- See the relevance of their own work to that of the rest of the group and of the class.

Over 50 years later, there is much in here that is relevant to education today. It describes an appropriate way to deliver real-life, context-based, effective environmental education. Green (2015, p. 5) brought a more contemporary description to environmental education in the form of three interrelated components:

- **Education IN the environment.** Using children's immediate surroundings and the wider world as a learning resource. This can be thought of as the 'hands-on' element.

- **Education ABOUT the environment.** Developing knowledge and understanding about the environment should begin with an awareness of the local environment and then extend to an understanding of global environmental issues.

- **Education FOR the environment.** The development of positive attitudes and behaviours towards the environment. This can only be effective if the other two elements are in place.

She goes on to say that: 'With children and young people spending less of their free time outdoors (due to issues such as technology and safety worries), and budget cuts leading to the closure of outdoor learning centres across the country, environmental education in schools is more important than ever!' (Green, 2015, p. 5).

Another important component is education AS the environment: developing the capacity to consider yourself as a significant factor in the environment and to identify with the natural environment and other people in an emotional and social way. This fits with the indigenous perspective of humans being an integral part of nature, as does the 'think global, act local' perspective. All this is encapsulated within the 'I, we, planet' concept developed by Jane Riddiford's Global Generation. The organisation states: 'This approach provides space for people to increase awareness of self, to connect to each other and to connect to the natural world.'[2]

A phrase I picked up many years ago, but can't recall where from, is that environmental education can 'make the known more knowable'. This view on life has the potential to encourage us to be more curious, aware, joined up and, therefore, more effective learners (and leaders). This belies the stereotype of an environmentalist being some sort of geeky hermit, cut off from the real world of industry and commerce. Local environmental studies are the basis on which, over the last couple of years, I helped a large group of schools in London to revisit and revamp their geography and history work. This entailed developing urban trails and giving a local context for topics covering national and global issues. One of these showed the effects of bombing during the Second World War on the streets the children walk down today through an excellent online mapping resource linked to contemporary accounts.[3]

I still refer to the old Hammersley et al. book for solace as well as for practical ideas. For me, their book is a totem of my education philosophy and why I see environmental education as an essential curriculum ingredient. Not only does it create a

2   See https://www.globalgeneration.org.uk/about-us. For examples of the 'I, we, planet' approach see Jayasena (2017) and Riddiford (2021).
3   See https://bombsite.org.

cohesive cross-curricular strategy, but it also encourages people of all ages to think and act in ways which will help to secure the sustainability of our civilisation. My own environmental education also showed me how this type of ecological perspective is a massive asset when it comes to leadership. Hence this book!

HEAD, HEART, HANDS

Curriculum delivery can be viewed as a type of industrial process in that you have inputs of knowledge and standardised criteria for measuring what the learner retains. This approach works when manufacturing a car, but as the input of teachers and the reactions of learners is multifaceted, the analogy starts to break down. The tensions between traditional vs progressive and neutrality vs advocacy (discussed in more detail later) are all wrapped up in this. In some ways, the polarisation of these often dogmatic arguments gets in the way of determining what actually works best for different learners at varying stages of their lives. I start from the premise that learning needs to be as brain-friendly as possible. This fits with generative approaches in education and has been described as 'relaxed alertness for optimal learning' (Smith, 2010), which is also the basis of permaculture theory and practice, described in Chapter 5. With this in mind, sustainability has much to offer and centres upon head, heart, hands methodology (see Figure 3.1 on page 64).

This model shows a combination of 'objective' knowledge (head), emotional/aesthetic feelings/self-knowledge (heart) and kinaesthetic skills (hands). Together they can create transformational learning, especially if facilitated by skilled educators. We structured the Leading for the Future training featured in Chapter 2 using this methodology.

I include 'place' in this model because it covers local to global links. Also, it helps to set a context for the learning, rather than it being abstract and beyond learners' prior experience. As discussed, local studies are a useful vehicle for this. For example, while working with the group of London schools, I discovered that a Roman road ran near to one of them. We then started to look at old maps to see how it was used through the centuries and found out why it was established in the first place. Realising that we could still walk along the course of some of it, in urban south-east London, had a big impact.

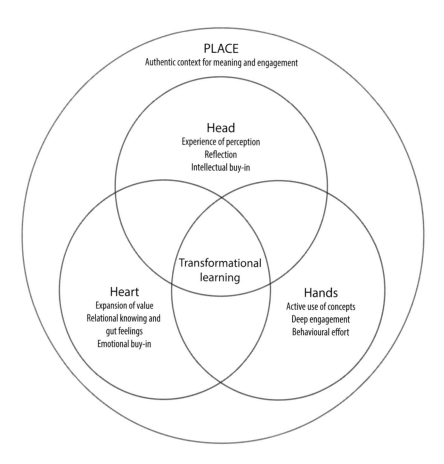

Figure 3.1: Head, heart, hands model of learning

Source: adapted from Singleton (2015)

Head, heart, hands is used in many types of training for people of all ages. Forest school, described later, is a great example of this. The Leading for the Future course (introduced in Chapter 2) provided participants with immersive and sometimes challenging experiences, not endless PowerPoint presentations and information handouts. The element of reflection permeated everything. One of the activities was milking cows at daybreak. Participants had to get their hands dirty, and this visceral activity helped us to illustrate how an organic farm operates. It was experiential learning par excellence and a head, heart, hands activity rolled into one. One participant said that it was the most profound experience they'd ever had and they no longer looked at a carton of milk in the same way.

The hands element had an additional benefit in that these activities, particularly gentle artistic ones, helped the participants to mentally process the previous heart and head engagement, leading to further thoughts and ideas. This works equally well with children, so it pays to have a healthy mix of head, heart, hands activities throughout the day. You only have to think of how a walk in the park or a craft activity can help you to make sense of previous experiences and inspire ideas. All this and more increases the ecological literacy and associated thinking described in Chapter 2.

GREEN LEARNING POWER

In most education systems, hands – and, to a certain extent, heart – activities diminish as a learner gets older, leaving the head to absorb lots of information. You certainly don't get many heart and hands experiences in most leadership training! I was reminded of the value of the head, heart, hands approach as I observed seasoned school leaders on the Leading for the Future course becoming absorbed in various art and investigative activities in the great outdoors. Not only did I see enjoyment and motivation, but also a change of mindset and a boost to creative and critical thought. The same is true in any other educational context, regardless of the ages of the learners. One Leading for the Future participant said, partly in jest, that it was 'like a Montessori for school leaders', which I took as a great compliment.

There is a wide body of literature from writers and researchers on ESD who see the head, heart, hands model as central to learning and of vital importance to the continuation of our civilisation. This is because we need to get away from the idea that the natural world is merely a commodity for us to exploit. It also taps into the 'progressive' movement promoted by John Dewey (2007 [1963]), who advocated a child-centred hands-on approach which fully engaged the child's head and heart. Nature can provide this in abundance through visceral experiences and practical activities, with the proviso that it's conducted with care and respect.

So, this approach is meant to be not just transformative but emancipatory for learners and, by extension, leaders. Singleton (2015) thinks that it helps people to progress 'from knowing to caring to loving to doing'. It takes courage to use the word 'loving' in the context of schools and learning because it could be deemed wishy-washy, subjective and unprofessional. I would say it's important to recognise the value of this in the learning process, because if learners have a positive emotional attachment to their learning, they are more likely to be highly motivated, retain knowledge and develop their understanding of concepts.

ESD recognises that the natural world is an excellent backdrop for learning. As the Leading for the Future example shows, being immersed in nature helps people to re-evaluate their circumstances and/or seek relaxation and recuperation. You can pay for expensive retreats involving yoga, various forms of meditation and treatments. These invariably take place in beautiful natural settings, and often take a large carbon footprint to get there! A Japanese version is called 'forest bathing'. Wild swimming and other 'wild' outdoor pursuits are also in vogue. When I was a child, it was just called 'swimming in the sea/river/lake'. Yet, regardless of the label, we recognise the value of being outdoors and, ideally, being surrounded by some form of greenery, but we don't necessarily need to take a long-haul flight to experience it.[4] Having said that, wild space is less plentiful than it once was due to urban development. Free-range childhoods like mine are increasingly rare; in this more fearful and traffic-clogged age, fewer parents allow their offspring out and about on their own. Being wedded to electronic media also curtails the time people, particularly children, might spend in nature (or outside generally). I suspect the average young person is in more danger on the internet than they ever would be in the local park, fields or woodland.

---

4   Being immersed in nature can help us to be less agitated and more calm, taking us away from the frantic over-stimulation of the modern world. See Killingsworth and Gilbert (2010), who show why it's good to slow down, chill and focus.

THE WORLD IS YOUR CLASSROOM

The Learning Outside the Classroom Manifesto can help schools to evaluate how well they cater for this vital outdoor vehicle for learning and well-being (Department for Education and Skills, 2006). Another organisation with a similar philosophy is Semble, which coordinates Outdoor Classroom Day and has many resources and ideas for making these special and meaningful, which can help schools to kick-start this approach.[5] The London Sustainable Development Commission (2011) conducted a wide-ranging review of studies which showed how being in nature is so beneficial for children.

I found that the children in our London school were particularly noisy and full on, which didn't help their listening or contemplative skills. To help address this, we introduced some meditation/quiet time just after lunch. Through a grant, we obtained a large yurt which was used by classes for circle time and also by Children's Centre parent groups. By changing the physical circumstances alone, we changed the mindset from raucous abandon to quieter reflection.[6]

Richard Louv's (2008) book *Last Child in the Woods* highlighted the steep decline of children's contact with nature. He coined the term 'nature-deficit syndrome' and continues to campaign on the matter through highly informative blog posts.[7] This is part of a similar argument that Palmer (2015) makes in her book *Toxic Childhood*. She shows how modern consumer-orientated lifestyles are taking their toll on humanity, and especially the young. She also highlights the valuable work done by the back to nature movement, exemplified by the National Trust report, *Natural Childhood*, written by Stephen Moss (2012). This document is packed with research showing how isolation from nature is deleterious and what we can do about it. It categorises the beneficial effects accordingly:

- Cognitive Impacts (greater knowledge and understanding).
- Affective Impacts (attitudes, values, beliefs and self-perceptions).
- Interpersonal and Social Impacts (communication skills, leadership and teamwork).

5   See https://outdoorclassroomday.com.
6   See Holt's (2005) account of the 'slow school' for a discussion on how schools in general need to calm down.
7   See https://richardlouv.com/blog.

- Physical and Behavioural Impacts (fitness, personal behaviours and social actions (Moss, 2012, p. 9)

The National Trust also created a list of '50 things to do before you're 11¾'. Here are some random examples:

---

2. Roll down a really big hill

4. Build a den

26. Hunt for fossils and bones

34. Discover wild animal clues

41. Help a plant grow

47. Cook on a campfire[8]

There is also research that suggests that if children don't visit woodlands and green spaces when they're young, they won't use these spaces as adults and will miss out on the physical and emotional benefits of access to nature. This was flagged up as vitally important by the Sustainable Development Commission in 2010 (more on this in Chapter 5).

Pergams and Zaradic (2008) found that people in the United States were visiting the national parks less frequently, and that this was due to an increased use of electronic media. Malone (2007) describes young people as a 'bubble-wrapped generation', who are not allowed out and, if they are, 'helicopter parents' are on hand to stop them taking risks or getting dirty. Recently, I came across the term 'curling parent' (curling as in the ice sport) to denote a mollycoddling adult who smooths the way for their children at every opportunity, so they seldom encounter problems and end up less resilient and creative.

Children with nature-deficit syndrome are exposed to fewer language reference points from the natural world. Robert Macfarlane and Jackie Morris (2017) high-lighted this in their book *The Lost Words*. They were inspired to write it when they discovered that lots of words had been expunged from the *Oxford Junior Dictionary*. Most of these related to nature – such as 'acorn', 'bluebell' and 'conker'. They'd

8   See https://www.nationaltrust.org.uk/features/50-things-to-do-before-youre-11--activity-list.

been replaced with 'analogue', 'broadband' and 'celebrity'. The book and accompanying education pack is now used by many schools to redress the balance.[9] To further combat nature-deficit syndrome, in all my schools we did all we could to make them literally as green as possible by growing lots of plants, inside and out (more on this in Chapter 4).

I was surprised by how much my 6-year-old daughter loves a book called *The Complete Book of Flower Fairies*. Originally written in 1923 by Cicely Mary Barker, it beautifully illustrates the flowers from hundreds of British trees, hedgerows, verges, fields and gardens and allocates each a fairy, illustrated in a style befitting the flower. Sadly, many of these flowers are rarely seen by children today even if they cared to look for them. Nevertheless, my daughter is delighted when she spots one and now has a better knowledge of them than I do. For example:

The Song of the Nightshade Fairy

My name is nightshade, also Bittersweet;

Ah, little folk be wise!

Hide you your hands behind you when we meet,

Turn away your eyes.

My flowers you shall not pick, nor berries eat,

For them poison lies.

This poem also reminds me of the day when I inspected the outdoor area of my London school's nursery and found a large clump of nightshade growing in the corner. Nobody knew how hazardous it was and had left it there because it was 'pretty'.

There's a chicken and egg situation going on here. (Where would we be for metaphors if there were no longer chickens or eggs?!) We are using fewer words from nature because more people are cut off from it and biodiversity is decreasing. This, in turn, makes nature as a metaphor or simile redundant and reinforces the human–nature dichotomy and human obliviousness. Furthermore, it's a symptom of shifting baseline syndrome. Think how the works of Shakespeare would be

---

9   See https://www.sustainablelearning.com/resource/lost-words.

diminished without words and phrases associated with nature.[10] Also check how many place names relate to geographical features and animals. This can aid historical understanding of a place. I live near Penge (of Celtic origin and meaning 'head of wood'), which relates to the Great North Wood that used to occupy most of south London (Pencoed in Wales has a similar origin).[11] Children can find this sort of investigation fascinating as it provides new insights into a locality and how it may have changed.

FOREST SCHOOL

The most tangible link between mainstream education and the natural world comes through the adoption of the forest school programme pioneered in Scandinavia. We introduced it into my last two schools to enrich the ESD curriculum and ensure that children had sufficient experiences in nature. This was of particular importance as they were both in urban areas with limited access to biodiverse green space. An area of the school grounds was designated exclusively for forest school, with several staff, including teachers, receiving training. Without sufficient training, people often fail to appreciate how specialist this form of facilitation is. Although children need to be given lots of freedom, they shouldn't just be left to go 'wild in the jungle'.

'Forest school' is also the name of a pedagogical technique. The methodology is based on the concept that contact with nature and freedom from the classroom supports pupils' development through the head, heart, hands approach described on pages 63–65. Forest school practice involves achievable tasks which are led by the pupils. It encourages learning from instinct and from freedom, as well as understanding the consequences and boundaries that can be present in a natural environment – for example, when climbing trees, you may find it's easier to wear particular shoes. There are also taught skills such as safe fire-lighting, carving wood and using natural materials to make sculptures and other types of art. Teamwork and personal reflection are emphasised, along with respect for the natural world (i.e. not treating it as a plaything and making sure that it's not despoiled

---

10 See De Gex (1999).
11 See https://hidden-london.com/gazetteer/penge.

by the activities). Where wear and tear take place, the area concerned is left to replenish itself.

In extensive research, involving literature review and first-hand observations, O'Brien (2009, p. 50) concluded that forest school boosts children's learning and their overall ability to learn, including improving self-esteem and social, communication and motor skills. She also noticed that the relationships between staff and children deepened and improved, as they did between the children, and this fitted with the findings of other research that looked at outdoor learning generally. Above all, the children were highly curious and motivated to learn (O'Brien, 2009, p. 53).

Some may view this as peripheral and not part of the 'real' work that children do in the classroom. I would argue the opposite, because I've witnessed at first hand the difference it can make to children's capacity to learn. You can never predict how a child will react and perform in forest school. Often, it allowed 'underperforming' children to excel and build confidence, with a positive knock-on effect once back in the classroom. Perhaps a new label would encourage every school to operate a forest school: a semiotic revamp to reset perceptions. If it were called a 'pupil progress outdoor booster programme', it might make more education leaders take notice.[12]

Most schools confine forest school to the early years (3–5-year-olds) because they feel it matches this part of the curriculum. Some schools with a forest school area don't operate it properly because they haven't got adequately trained staff. Such schools seem to think that forest school is just 'mucking about in the woods'. In our schools, we operated forest school in every age group because it related to wider curricular and learning aspirations befitting our sustainability ethos. I drew up Figure 3.2 to show teachers and inspectors the rationale behind running forest school for all year groups within the context of an experiential curriculum.

----

12 It's difficult to do forest school justice in this relatively short summary. If unacquainted, I would recommend visiting: https://www.forestschoolassociation.org/what-is-forest-school.

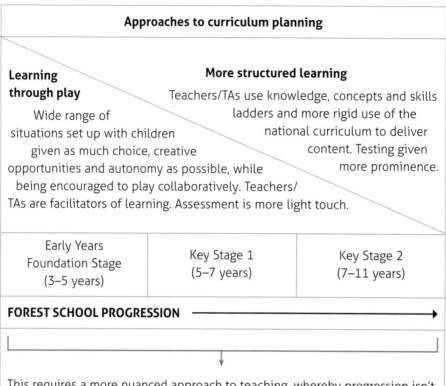

Approaches to curriculum planning

Learning through play

Wide range of situations set up with children given as much choice, creative opportunities and autonomy as possible, while being encouraged to play collaboratively. Teachers/ TAs are facilitators of learning. Assessment is more light touch.

More structured learning

Teachers/TAs use knowledge, concepts and skills ladders and more rigid use of the national curriculum to deliver content. Testing given more prominence.

Early Years Foundation Stage (3–5 years)	Key Stage 1 (5–7 years)	Key Stage 2 (7–11 years)

FOREST SCHOOL PROGRESSION ⟶

This requires a more nuanced approach to teaching, whereby progression isn't just seen as a move away from play-based learning as children get older (secondary pupils and adults also need to play to learn through head, heart, hands activities). This is helped by incorporating forest school into the curriculum for all year groups. Forest school can also help to embed ESD as a central core of knowledge and approaches to learning, with a particular emphasis on knowledge of the natural world and our place in it, plus associated critical thinking and opportunities to take actions for personal and community benefit. This should also include aesthetic appreciation and creativity. This type of enriched curriculum encourages many aspects of speaking and listening, which are prerequisites for the development of vocabulary and the articulation of thought.

Figure 3.2: Forest school for all

By its very nature (pun intended), forest school has sustainability at its core and no discerning leader for sustainability should be without it. The Leading for the Future course was really a forest school for adults, although it wasn't labelled as such. This shows the universality of the positive effects of communing with nature. It's just a matter of getting off the treadmill of mechanistic thinking and desk-based learning.

At first, when older children attended their forest school sessions, their teachers weren't involved and tended to see it as cover to enable them to have non-contact time (known in England as planning, preparation and assessment or PPA time). To remedy this, we made sure that the forest school leader liaised with teachers so that links could be made to what the children were doing back in the classroom. Certain forest school purists would disapprove of this, but I found that it didn't detract from the freedom of the experience and actually gave more added value to the children's learning and credibility in the eyes of external school improvement advisers.

CURRICULUM COUNTS

Ardoin et al. (2020) reported how 'citizen science' made a significant contribution to people's attitude towards the natural world by encouraging them to get outside and find out what was happening. Researchers at Stanford University looked at over 100 environmental education programmes and found four main success criteria. I list them here along with some practical examples from our schools indicated in italics.

- 'Focus on local environmental issues or locally relevant dimensions of global issues.' *Year 6 children traced all the ingredients in a pizza and calculated the number of food miles and associated carbon footprint (see page 96). They discussed whether alternative local ingredients could be used.*

- 'Collaborate with scientists and resource managers.' *Year 5 did a butterfly survey as part of the UK-wide Big Butterfly Count.[13] They later analysed locally produced data and compared it to other regions. In the process they learned how to identify different species. The school eco-team (an elected child from each class in*

---

13 See https://bigbutterflycount.butterfly-conservation.org.

Years 1 to 6) worked with the school site manager to help reduce fuel bills by encouraging people to shut doors, switch off lights and shut down computers. They tracked energy use data to gauge the effects of their campaign (see Chapter 5 for more on this).

- 'Incorporate action elements into programmes.' *The pizza work influenced the school kitchen's food procurement process by encouraging the cook to look for more local sources. In response to the butterfly survey, the children planted more butterfly-friendly flowering plants in the school grounds. The energy reduction project was very successful and led to the school building receiving a much better energy rating. The money saved was ploughed back into the school budget.*

- 'Measure and report programme outcomes.' *Following our drive to save energy in school through behaviour change, the site manager provided data to show the savings in kWh and money, which was presented to the school and governors.*

THE REAL THING

In a central area of our London school stood a magnificent plane tree. It was about 200 years old – it had survived the Blitz and an arson attack on the school in the 1980s – and yet everyone seemed oblivious of it. I couldn't find anyone, staff or children, who even knew its genus. Once the children were made aware of the tree, their appreciation increased enormously and it inspired intense scientific study and artwork. This sort of awareness-raising was linked to other aspects of ESD, which encouraged children to notice what was going on around them and to engage with it.

In 2012, our part of London was host to two main Olympic events: the showjumping and, perhaps unfortunately, the shooting. Local parks were to be used, and when the plans started to emerge, we decided to try an engagement exercise with a group of Year 2 children (6–7-year-olds). We told them that one of the parks near the school might be used as an Olympic venue, which would mean chopping down the trees, relocating play equipment and so on. The children had already studied this park and knew a lot about the flora, fauna and amenity value. As a result, they weren't pleased about the proposed developments and there was much heated discussion about it. Despite their tender years they were able to offer quite sophisticated reasons why the development shouldn't take place. However, some came up with the idea that it could create much-needed jobs; a number of them had parents who were out of work and they made the link. This was a counterargument to the eco-considerations. Never underestimate the debating powers of even very young children!

Older children were taught how to use Aristotelian debating techniques.[14] It's well worth having a whole-school debating policy, which can be another aspect of a metacognitive approach to learning and also covers many important elements of speaking and listening. The Economist Foundation has some attractive resources for developing this.[15]

These examples illustrate that the children were engaged at a cognitive, emotional and physical level (head, heart, hands), with teachers facilitating through the provision of age-appropriate resources and various forms of discussion. Debating was of particular value, helping children to formulate and express ideas and challenge each other in an orderly way. This emulates debating societies which are common in private schools. Giving the curriculum a real context always reaps dividends.

ENVIRONMENTAL EDIFICATION

ESD also resides in the area of development education, which in the UK is more commonly called 'global learning'. I've always felt that some in the global learning fraternity veer too much towards social justice elements at the expense of natural science. However, the methodology of global learning is extremely valuable as a pedagogic and learning process, and has added greatly to the strength of ESD as a whole. Of particular value is its emphasis on critical thinking and innovative and emancipatory pedagogy, as advocated by Bourn (2014, p. 37), although he gives the following warning: 'A key challenge for teachers and educators is ... to ensure that feelings and emotions are connected to knowledge and skills, and lead to reflection and debate. Engagement in development and poverty needs to be more than an emotional reaction.'

As mentioned earlier, emotions within learning are essential, but not in splendid isolation. This is why natural science and geographical and historical knowledge are an important part of the mix. Essentially, global learning methodology

14 For an overview of these see Langston (2016). There are many other online resources and books out there.
15 See https://economistfoundation.org/resources/ks2-debating.

encourages everyone to become a global citizen, as illustrated in Figure 3.3, and also keys into the decolonising agenda.

Global citizenship involves ...	It is not ...
asking questions and critical thinking	telling people what to think and do
exploring local–global connections and our views, values and assumptions	only about far away places and peoples
exploring the complexity of global issues and engaging with multiple perspectives	providing simple solutions to complex problems
exploring issues of social justice locally and globally	focused on charitable fundraising
applying learning to real-world issues and contexts	abstract learning devoid of real-life application and outcomes
opportunities for learners to take informed, reflective action and have their voices heard	tokenistic inclusion of learners in decision-making
all ages	too difficult for young children to understand
all areas of the curriculum	an extra subject
enrichment of everyday teaching and learning	just a focus for a particular day or week
the whole-school environment	limited to the classroom

Figure 3.3: Characteristics of global citizenship

Source: Oxfam (2015, p. 5)[16]

....

16 See second table on p. 5 of *Global Citizenship in the Classroom: A Guide for Teachers* (2015) – adapted by the publisher with the permission of Oxfam, Oxfam House, John Smith Drive, Cowley, Oxford, OX4 2JY, UK (www.oxfam.org.uk). Oxfam does not necessarily endorse any text or activities that accompany the materials, nor has it approved the adapted text.

From this, teachers would need to have a large array of pedagogical techniques and integrated knowledge sets to enable learners to fulfil these criteria.[17] The leadership team would need to value and understand the concept unconditionally.[18]

GLOBAL LEARNING: A HEALTH WARNING

We've got to be careful to avoid an exclusively Western perspective. For instance, this often overlooks that Africa, as a continent, has probably the most diverse range of countries and cultures in the world (ancient and modern), the origins of which predate Western equivalents by many centuries. Many African artists and arts movements lead the world in innovation and originality, and the latest technologies are present in most countries. Children need to appreciate and explore these aspects if they truly are to be global citizens, rather than inquisitive beings from a so-called 'superior' WEIRD culture.

The same warning should be applied to studies of all non-Western cultures. This is decolonising in action (more on this on page 82). By the same token, I wouldn't wish to gloss over the persistent problems of poverty and deprivation in many 'developing' nations where millions of people still need aid for basic survival and suffer terribly from armed conflict and forced migration. The bottom line, however, is that our history and present lifestyles have caused much of this deprivation.

LOCAL TO GLOBAL AND BACK AGAIN

The Global Learning Programme (GLP) ran in the UK from 2013 to 2018, financed by the UK government's now-defunct Department for International Development (DfID). Some 10,000 schools voluntarily took part and many that fully embraced it were praised by Ofsted as it delivered high standards in spiritual, moral, social and cultural (SMSC) education, as well as improving critical thinking skills and subject knowledge, particularly in geography. One of its main reference points was the UN's SDGs. The GLP shifted the perspective on global issues from 'exotic oddities'

17 See Oxfam's (2015) excellent guide entitled *Global Citizenship in the Classroom: A Guide for Teachers.*
18 For a comprehensive Global Learning training programme and motivational resources, see Lyfta's offering: https://www.lyfta.com.

to being integral to all our lives (i.e. appreciating links, consequences and butterfly effects: local to global and I, we, planet). As it dealt with real-life issues, pupils' motivation was very high. Our school in London was one of the expert centres scattered across the country which received funding to deliver GLP workshops for groups of schools. We had varying success because some schools didn't fully embrace the project, meaning that the drop-out rate was quite high – a situation reflected in many other expert centres nationally. Having talked to teachers from some of the participating schools, it was apparent that commitment to the GLP depended on how much it was valued by senior leaders. The schools that did fully embrace it experienced many learning benefits, as highlighted by a comprehensive Geographical Association report (Hopkin, 2018).

You would think that if the GLP was so successful, why bring it to an end? Ultimately, it was a political decision as the funding was controlled by government. It's significant and somewhat ironic that the Department for Education (DfE) played little part in it. The content and methodology were all about creating critical thinkers and certainly pulled no punches when it came to examining dubious social justice and related aspects of lifestyle which damage the planet. The fact that it was discontinued says a lot in itself. The GLP morphed into a new programme run by the British Council, which placed more emphasis on twinning UK schools with schools overseas.[19] Although some of the GLP elements remained, I always felt that this was a somewhat retrograde step, being less likely to influence the curriculum. Time will tell. DfID itself is no more, having been absorbed into the Foreign, Commonwealth and Development Office in 2020. Linking aid with trade is given greater priority under this new incarnation (further development of globalisation, methinks). This also means that global learning has been extracted from a great office of state.

The GLP teaching and learning resources were archived by Global Dimension and still provide comprehensive whole-school and cross-curricular planning and subject-based ideas for primary and secondary pupils.[20] Global Dimension partners with an organisation called Reboot the Future, which operates on the basis of 'treat others and the planet as you would like to be treated' and offers interesting insights into leadership and education.[21] Resources and advice from the Royal Geographical Society are also worth a look.[22]

19 See https://connecting-classrooms.britishcouncil.org/resources/global-learning-resources.
20 See https://globaldimension.org.uk/resources/?query=GLP.
21 See https://www.rebootthefuture.org.
22 See https://www.rgs.org/schools.

A separate independent Global Learning Network was formed by some of the for-mer GLP partners, hosted by the UCL Institute of Education to continue to promote this area of learning. UCL is also the base for the Development Education Research Centre, which is a leading light on global citizenship and learning.[23] See also the related Global Education Network Europe.[24] Further excellent global learning resources can be accessed via the Geographical Association.[25]

The GLP made strong links to the SDGs and showed how they could be embedded into curriculum planning. As an exercise, in our London school, we looked at the 17 goals and mapped out how we were aligning with them, outlined below in brackets.

1   End poverty in all its forms everywhere. (*We help families to reduce their energy and food bills.*)

2   End hunger, achieve food security and improved nutrition, and promote sustainable agriculture. (*We grow fruit and vegetables for the school and families and provide breakfast for all who need it.*)

3   Ensure healthy lives and promote well-being for all at all ages. (*We promote healthy lifestyles across the curriculum and through our Children's Centre.*)

4   Ensure inclusive and equitable quality education and promote lifelong learning opportunities for all. (*We provide study support for all who need it, including out of school hours and during holidays.*)

5   Achieve gender equality and empower all women and girls. (*Everyone is treated equally during all activities.*)

6   Ensure availability and sustainable management of water and sanitation for all. (*Our school eco-team and site manager ensure that we use water sparingly and we capture rainwater in butts.*)

7   Ensure access to affordable, reliable, sustainable and modern energy for all. (*We operate solar panels for a local co-op and help the community to tackle fuel poverty via the children.*)

8   Promote sustained, inclusive and sustainable economic growth, full and productive employment, and decent work for all. (*The children learn about*

---

23 See https://www.ucl.ac.uk/ioe/departments-and-centres/centres/development-education-research-centre.
24 See https://www.gene.eu.
25 See https://www.geography.org.uk/Resources-and-activities.

careers and jobs to which they can aspire and the school hosts skills courses for parents.)

9   Build resilient infrastructure, promote inclusive and sustainable industrialisation, and foster innovation. (*Our solar panels create local investment via the solar co-op.*)

10 Reduce inequality within and among countries. (*There are many nations represented in our school and everyone is given unconditional regard. Global learning reveals inequality and how we can deal with it.*)

11 Make cities and human settlements inclusive, safe, resilient and sustainable. (*Our school models how others can do this through its curriculum, campus and community.*)

12 Ensure sustainable consumption and production patterns. (*Our campus continues to reduce all types of waste.*)

13 Take urgent action to combat climate change and its impacts. (*We campaign to get rid of fossil fuels as part of Keep It in the Ground, and we helped to make a video with the* Guardian *newspaper* (Breuer et al., 2015).)

14 Conserve and sustainably use the oceans, seas and marine resources for sustainable development. (*We learn about our local river – the Thames – and how we can protect it from various kinds of pollution.*)

15 Protect, restore and promote sustainable use of terrestrial ecosystems, sustainably manage forests, combat desertification and halt and reverse land degradation, and halt biodiversity loss. (*We create more biodiversity in our school grounds by planting trees, shrubs and wild flowers and developing a pond.*)

16 Promote peaceful and inclusive societies for sustainable development, provide access to justice for all and build effective, accountable and inclusive institutions at all levels. (*We learn about the UN's Convention on the Rights of the Child.*)

17 Strengthen the means of implementation and revitalise the global partnership for sustainable development. (*We help the WWF-UK to protect the planet by taking part in fundraising events and sponsoring the adoption of tigers.*)

MORAL DILEMMAS

School leaders and teachers start to get jittery when it comes to imparting certain values to the young, particularly when these stray into economic and political territory. When teaching about sustainability, there's a tendency to let the 'facts' speak for themselves. So, if something like the GLP demands more than this through discussions which lead children to develop value judgements and demand actions, some would say an unacceptable line had been crossed (see Ofsted chief Amanda Spielman's views on this in the conclusion). Individual teachers might feel especially vulnerable if senior leadership doesn't support them in encouraging unfettered pupil voice and associated activism. This shouldn't be a situation of indoctrination inflicted on the learner by the teacher, rather a teacher facilitating a situation in which learners can think for themselves and then, if they so wish, take action.

Vare and Scott (2007) developed a two-type classification of ESD activities – ESD 1 and ESD 2, paraphrased below – which can help us to think this through:

- **ESD 1: promoting behaviour change.** Relates to the teaching of predetermined skills and behaviours which are to be adopted as taught. The impact of ESD 1 can be measured in wider environmental terms. The downside of ESD 1 is that it doesn't build our capacity to act as autonomous individuals in the short or long term. An example of this type of learning would be teaching children to pick up litter and put it in the appropriate recycling bin so that it doesn't end up in the sea (plastic waste being a particular hazard). The underlying reasons why the litter exists might not be discussed in much detail.

- **ESD 2: learning for sustainability.** Relates to building learners' capacity to think critically about the behaviours identified as delivering sustainability. There are no predetermined learning or practical outcomes for this approach. The downside of ESD 2 is that it may not lead to effective sustainable behaviour (i.e. we just sit around all day talking).

These approaches are not mutually exclusive and need to be balanced out. I would add 'ecological knowledge' to ESD 1 so that any debate in ESD 2 isn't just based on emotional reaction (see Bourn's point on page 75). This can also extend to ecological ways of thinking (described in Chapter 2). The critical thinking in ESD 2 is needed if we are to nurture future generations who don't just accept things at face value, or at simplistic levels of understanding, or stay within comforting echo chambers. I would also add an ESD 3 (reflected in Doorway 10, described in Chapter 2): covering the aesthetic value of the environment through the arts, which could complement ESD 1 and 2.

The recent concerns about fake news show the value of ESD 2, as it helps us to judge the merits of the vast outpouring of information and opinions churned out by 24/7 media. All news is slightly 'fake' because it contains bias through the editorial process. Children need to be taught to navigate through this, even if it isn't explicitly covered by the national curriculum. If nothing else, this is a safeguarding issue: children can be groomed online by various manipulative individuals and organisations for nefarious purposes.

At our London school we used the WWF-UK's *Pathways* document (Hren and Birney, 2011). The section on the 'characteristics of effective learners' included the development of children who were: inquirers, thinkers, communicators, risk takers, knowledgeable, principled, caring, open-minded, well-balanced, reflective, globally minded and civically engaged (Hren and Birney, 2011, p. 12). We used these characteristics as part of our medium-term planning (described on page 102).

DECOLONISING AND DEBUNKING

An increasingly important issue in the curriculum debate centres around 'decolonising'. The recent discourse on whether or not to take down statues of 19th-century traders and industrialists who earned vast sums on the back of their slave trading links to this, as do the demands that museums return artefacts looted from other countries during war or colonial rule. We have to draw the lines of blame and reparation somewhere, and these lines are constantly shifting (usually back in time) as our moral debates continue. Should I, for instance, being a white male of Anglo-Saxon origin, be held responsible for atrocities against Ancient Britons? Certainly not, as the mists of time make this an irrelevance (although they can give insights into human nature today). Of definite relevance are the antecedents of the transatlantic slave trade, Nazi Holocaust, genocide in Kosovo and colonial mistreatment of Australian Aborigines and its enduring harmful legacy.

The list could go on and should also be seen in the light of continuing discrimination against certain ethnic groups and classes.

Even at a local level, it's important for young people to realise why certain roads are named after Important People who may have a mass of skeletons in their cupboards worthy of investigation. It can also call into question the 'Great Man' view of history (a few 'Great Women' creep in here too), which emphasises the enduring 19th-century view that history is determined by the actions of generals, politicians, inventors and industrialists, most of whom happened to be white and male because this demographic ruled the roost and still does. Another example of the WEIRD society.

ESD in schools can be treated as a bolt-on, rather than as integral to the curriculum. There are similar bolt-ons – such as Black History Month which, although very worthwhile, begs the question of why black history and the content, perceptions and insights it affords isn't part of our wider history in the first place. In a fully decolonised curriculum this wouldn't be an issue, which echoes Bill Scott's views (discussed in Chapter 2). As Olusoga (2017, p. 27) puts it: 'Black history is too often regarded as a segregated, ghettoized narrative that runs in its own shallow channel alongside the mainstream, only very occasionally becoming a tributary into that broader narrative.'

I would argue that sustainability should also feature in the decolonising agenda because we need to debunk aspects of the exploitative system which inflicted centuries of misery on many, most notably black and indigenous people, but also the white working class. We've always taught about terrible conditions in factories and mines, but what we haven't done is link this sufficiently to an overall exploitative system which grew with various forms of capitalism and was turbocharged by industrialisation and globalisation (much of which was founded on wealth derived from slavery). To one extent or another, this system is still exploiting us all and wrecking the planet in the process. It's gone even further than turning people into rampant consumers, as with the onset of the world wide web people are now part of the product, with our 'mined' personal information being traded.

Learners need to develop unbridled critical thinking in order to overcome accusations of bias and brainwashing on the part of the teacher. This allows for criticism of all views, including the green perspective, which has many flaws in the form of greenwash, and some 'entitlement' perspectives on what form society 'should' take. Perhaps the phrase 'decarbonising the curriculum' might come into vogue.

Lobbying museums not to take patronage from fossil fuel companies and campaigning for divestment in all planet-damaging industries is already part of this movement.

MESSAGE IN A COLA BOTTLE

What shouldn't be overlooked in all the angst about 'brainwashing the young' is that children and parents can easily spot it. If children come to certain conclusions themselves, that's all well and good; if these conclusions aren't particularly environmentally friendly, that's still all well and good and the environmentally zealous teacher should back off and wait for other opportunities to change hearts and minds. If the school has a sustainability ethos, then, in my experience, this in itself will influence while not seeking to indoctrinate. (There is more on this in Chapter 5 and the conclusion.)

The other thing to bear in mind is that children are constantly bombarded with messages from consumer capitalism in very blatant ways through highly effective advertising and product placement strategies. This can include greenwash and subverted 'wokism' if companies wish to present a veneer of environmentalism or social responsibility. So, if education doesn't assist children to develop a dispassionate and critical eye, then I feel educators are doing them a disservice. I would be the first to say that capitalism isn't evil per se; it's the current dominant global version that's the problem, compounded by the uncritical and fatalistic way in which most of us respond to it. By the same token, you have to be aware of the biases emanating from the environmental NGOs that often produce educational materials for class teachers. They all have their own agendas, so it's best for schools to use material from more than one in any given topic to compare and contrast the content.

TIME AND TIDE

The related dilemma for the environmentally minded teacher or school leader is that, while not wishing to be seen as green propagandists, the state of the bio-sphere is so precarious that we can't just wait for individuals and governments to act more radically. This points to the need to be proactive, rather than hanging around for a crisis to bring everyone to their senses. If we consider what happened when the UK had its last existential crisis, there was no circumspection as to how to influence the public. I am talking, of course, about the Second World War, when the UK and other governments didn't hesitate to intrude on all aspects of life, including controlling the economy to ensure national survival. A similar situation has arisen when dealing with the COVID-19 pandemic. Why isn't climate change and its associated dangers being treated in the same way? There isn't enough space to go into this issue here, but perhaps it boils down to the climate and bio-diversity crisis, in richer nations at least, still being perceived as a potential rather than an actual existential threat, rather like the Second World War being dismissed as a 'phoney war' (until real bombs started dropping).[26] However, as it stands, if educators add too much fuel to the fire of environmental anxiety, we might end up with a counterproductive response; not just rejection or denial but a leap towards ever-greater hedonistic consumption while the going is good.

I think that teachers are in a similar situation to the BBC. Up until 2014, the BBC retained a 'balanced' and 'unbiased' approach to climate change by making sure that climate change deniers had equal air time to climate change proponents, despite only a tiny minority of the scientific community arguing that human-caused climate change was false. A report by the BBC Trust (2014, p. 2) questioned the wisdom of this and said: 'The BBC has a duty to reflect the weight of scientific agreement ... Audiences should be able to understand from the context and clarity of the BBC's output what weight to give to critical voices.'

Despite my misgivings about being too impartial, there is a fine line between the diminishing returns of promoting sustainability and being so neutral as to inade-quately challenge the prevailing system. On reflection, I think I worry about this too much, because if a school has an embedded sustainability ethos in terms of captaincy, curriculum, campus and community, children pick up sustainability mes-sages by a kind of osmosis, in the same way they subliminally take in the messages

26 See https://www.iwm.org.uk/history/britains-phoney-start-to-the-second-world-war.

of consumerism because they are surrounded by them. We should also remember that schools have always promoted aspects of sustainability through the curriculum and other aspects of school life, although it's not usually labelled as such – for example, growing plants, fundraising for disadvantaged people, anti-racism, anti-bullying, fair play, supporting the weak and being kind to animals. The list could go on.

I would argue that the environmental data and the evidence from our own senses would suggest that educators *should* highlight the dangers, but, just as importantly, highlight solutions and offer opportunities for children to develop their own ideas. When visiting a primary school recently, I saw some impressive whole-school cross-curricular work about global warming (which should now be called global heating). The children had obviously learnt a lot about this subject and had translated their knowledge and emotional responses into some magnificent artwork. However, it was unexpurgated doom and gloom. Nowhere was there evidence that the teachers had done work on hope or aspiration for a better world.

CONVINCING STORIES

Storytelling is another strategy which needs to permeate a curriculum for sustainability. It helps to counter the prevailing narrative of consumerism and the commodification of everything and can share good news to counter the zoom to gloom. Stories can also provoke new perceptions and thoughts and be a force for community cohesion by exposing learners to cultures and experiences they might never otherwise encounter. Literature shouldn't just be seen as a way of improving reading and writing skills, but as a way of improving empathy and knowledge of others. This is reflected in stories contained within the main world religions. Stories were also a mainstay of our ancestors. Stories link indigenous people with their place of living and helped them to understand and appreciate it. Lanese (2017) says: 'Stories give character to local wildlife, voices to trees and spiritual resonance to the sunrise. They connect indigenous people to their environment and guide their interactions with it.'

Much of this has been eradicated by the move to urbanised situations and the decimation of wildernesses, which have caused the isolation of individuals or families and cut people off from the natural world. Shifting baselines are at play here. This also exacerbates our general ignorance of nature and lack of empathy with it (despite the popularity of moving documentaries from David Attenborough and others). Many indigenous stories encourage listeners to respect nature and warn about damaging it; hence, they provide strong moral messages which are passed down the generations. Cruikshank (2019) highlighted this when looking at how these stories can provide further insights into climate change. She says: 'Indigenous stories also suggest a different way of thinking about the natural world, as populated with sentient beings that have as much agency and political standing as humans do.' She also points out that, invariably, indigenous people are affected far more immediately and profoundly than most, which must make their physical and psychological pain all the greater.

These stories can be used today to show the errors of our modern ways. Cruikshank also shows how First Nations Canadians, who preceded European settlers by many centuries, consider that glaciers are part of a 'sentient landscape' that commands respect. For example, there is a cautionary tale about a man who disrespects a glacier by frying food next to it. This sort of cooking was believed to mock the glacier through the crackling sound it made and the melting of fat. The man also disrespected the glacier by saying that it had no nose and hence couldn't smell his cooking. He met a horrible death crossing a bridge when the glacier suddenly blew out a surge of hitherto restrained water, causing him to fall. In the story, this was the man receiving his just desserts! Using these stories in a positive way assists the decolonisation agenda because we are valuing and using indigenous wisdom. This involves a change of perception, giving us another view of 'reality'.

Similarly, we can use modern fables, not necessarily with an overt environmental theme, to facilitate philosophical discussion to reveal messages about our current plight. An example of this is a simple tale for young children called *Who Sank the Boat?* by Pamela Allen. It's about a group of animal friends – a cow, a donkey, a sheep, a pig and a mouse – who decide to go for a sailing trip together on a very small boat. They get in one by one and the boat dips deeper into the water. After each animal boards the question is asked, 'Who sank the boat?' It eventually sinks when the last animal, the mouse, gets in. The allegory can be applied to many metaphorical environmental boats, including the Earth as a whole, and the potential for reaching hazardous tipping points. The book *Who Will Save Us?*, suitable for 6–8-year-olds, by Rebecca Morch and Pen Hadow has a more obvious environmental theme about the plight of penguins on a melting ice sheet, with accompanying teaching and learning suggestions. Dr. Seuss's *The Lorax* is worthy of special mention and, despite being written in 1971, is very thought-provoking and perti-nent. A school could base an entire topic on it! There is an increasing range of new story books and non-fiction linked to integrated ESD themes. Just having them in the school library gives rise to interesting discussions and thoughts. There are also magazines such as *Eco-kids,*[27] a junior version of *National Geographic*[28] and those produced by various environmental charities, such as WWF-UK.[29]

Stories of inspirational leaders can also be used – for example, Wangari Maathai, who in 1977 launched the Green Belt Movement aimed at alleviating poverty through tree planting. In 2004, she received the Nobel Peace Prize for 'her contri-bution to sustainable development, democracy and peace'.[30] Hopkins (2019) advocates the use of inspirational stories about people and communities who run ambitious and successful sustainability projects. As discussed, this helps to shift the narrative around sustainability from negative to positive.

School assemblies can be an excellent vehicle for showing children the value of stories on a regular basis and it's worth planning these out over the year. In both my schools we had a theme of the week, which linked to sustainability issues as well as national events such as Anti-Bullying Week or Black History Month. We launched the theme as part of the Monday morning whole-school assembly and it was followed up in year-group assemblies and class discussions. Not only did this ensure continuity across the school, but it also reinforced the ethos to staff and children. One particularly effective theme was 'random acts of kindness'. This was based upon a website which shares stories of people helping others.[31] We asked the children to look for their own opportunities to offer random acts of kindness, and many did. We also provided training for teachers on how to utilise philosophy linked to literature and topical issues across the curriculum.[32]

---

27 See https://www.ecokidsplanet.co.uk.
28 See https://kids.nationalgeographic.com.
29 See https://support.wwf.org.uk/go-wild.
30 See https://www.nobelprize.org/prizes/peace/2004/maathai/facts.
31 See https://www.randomactsofkindness.org.
32 An example of a provider is Philosophy for Children (P4C): http://www.philosophy4children.co.uk/home/p4c.

ART FOR THE PLANET'S SAKE

Drama and music can also be used to good effect to help children and their parents to address big issues. We put on ambitious productions which presented these in an entertaining way. For example, one was called 'Revenge of the Alien Eco-Warriors', which I co-wrote with another teacher. Each class contributed a scene showing an environmental problem through dance and music. The plot centred around a big show trial in which the aliens accused the human race of damaging planet Earth. Happily, the humans were let off on the condition that they did something to make amends.

Once again, there was a confluence of high-quality cross-curricular provision with an ESD theme. The children learned through ESD 1 and ESD 2 *and* developed dance and drama skills. Parents helped with costumes, scenery and props. Other outcomes which shouldn't be overlooked were confidence-building and pure enjoyment – not so easy to measure but essential in any school, sustainable or otherwise. Parents assimilated green messages along with enjoying the performances. This reinforced the pester power of their children when they shared their other sustainability learning and wanted to make changes at home.

There are many off-the-shelf drama and music packages with a green theme, as an internet search will show. You will have to discriminate because – as with all resources – some are better quality than others, both in terms of content and entertainment value (once again, beware of greenwash). Our London school helped a musician called Jess Gold to develop her 'Planet Earth Rock' music scheme. The content is unapologetically focused on sustainability, but also contains great songs for assemblies and class music.[33]

---

33 See https://www.projectearthrock.com.

KEEPING YOUR COUNCIL

The school council can be utilised to create a debating culture. Although many schools have such councils, some seem to be minimally used to tick the pupil voice Ofsted box, rather than meaningfully in a way that might affect the running of the school. The council of our London school became fervent about the poor quality of school meals to such an extent that the governors agreed to the school taking the catering in-house (more on this in Chapter 4). We had given the councillors coaching and tried to be as open-minded as possible when considering their suggestions. It had a big impact on them when we took them to visit the local council chamber and the London Assembly.

The school council didn't get everything they wanted – such as a new swimming pool – but they came to see that they were taken seriously and were suitably empowered. It wasn't just a case of creating an appointed elite or puppets of the senior leadership team; they were elected by their peers and we allocated time for them to give and receive feedback in their respective classes. This meant that the children realised that everyone in the school could make a positive contribution and improve the way it was run. Later, we combined some of the council meetings with those of the eco-team (described in greater detail in Chapter 4). All this fitted with the government drive to instil fundamental British values, as it showed one of the five values, *democracy*, in action (more on fundamental British values in Chapter 5).

FEELING RESPONSIBLE

In our Nottinghamshire school we introduced a national package developed by the Department for Education and Skills (DfES) – as it was called then – about social and emotional aspects of learning (SEAL). It was a non-statutory whole-school approach for personal, social and health education (PSHE), which some schools still operate today (the E now stands for economics). It helped us to develop the internal social sustainability of the school, as it encouraged children to be more self-aware and empathetic, which could then be applied to the external world. SEAL had five main elements:

1   Self-awareness.

2   Managing feelings.

3   Motivation.

4   Empathy.

5   Social skills.

We wanted to wean children off external rewards and sanctions as the main ways of improving their behaviour towards each other, adults and their learning (see Alfie Kohn's (1999) thought-provoking book *Punished by Rewards*). SEAL can be adopted across a whole school or used as a selective resource to assist when negative interpersonal issues arise, such as bullying. It helped our teachers to see other strategies for learning which could be applied more generally, hence it was another practical way in which we could promote our sustainability ethos. Organisations continue to produce resources, and SEAL – or social and emotional learning (SEL), as it's now called – has the approval of the Education Endowment Foundation.[34]

SWIMMING WITH THE TIDE

When it suits, even hands-off governments issue national 'guidance' which, due to the inspection system, schools ignore at their peril. For example, a statutory requirement introduced to schools in England in 2020 aimed to implement relationships and sex education (RSE) (Department for Education, 2020). For primary schools, RSE can key into sustainability topics and critical thinking as it covers relationships with family and friends, physical and mental well-being, and online safety. Of course, 'sustainability' isn't mentioned as such, but you could easily link RSE to the ethos and practices described throughout this book. It just goes to show that when there is a political will to implement a statutory policy, no effort or expense is spared. Think how marvellous it would be if sustainability was suddenly a statutory imperative of the DfE!

Promoting fundamental British values, as mentioned above, is another case in point where a statutory policy can be harnessed to deliver sustainability. This is described in Chapter 5 in the context of developing a community enrichment strategy.

34 See https://educationendowmentfoundation.org.uk/evidence-summaries/teaching-learning-toolkit/social-and-emotional-learning.

INTERNATIONAL RESCUE

As ever, much innovative ESD work at an international level has gone largely unnoticed in the UK. For example, the United Nations Economic Commission for Europe (UNECE, 2012) produced a concise yet very informative book outlining learning competencies which it believes people will need if we are to have a sustainable future. There are four main themes: 'Learning to know', 'Learning to do', 'Learning to be' and 'Learning to live together' (UNECE, 2012, p. 14).

Within each theme learners would need to acquire the ability to think holistically, envision change and achieve transformation. In other words, to think things through in a joined-up way to co-create ideas for a better world and then have the practical capabilities to make that a reality. The details are well worth reading because they can provide further perspectives on, and ideas for, developing sustainability in schools. Once again, this sort of work speaks of creating more rounded and active learners rather than passive receivers of disconnected chunks of knowledge. It also has messages for learning leaders (as discussed in Chapter 2). It's gratifying to know that despite the challenges and frustrations of developing sustainability in schools, there are many global initiatives to draw upon which can add knowledge, strategies and credibility to the cause.

TOPICAL TIPS

To show the relevance of SDGs as a reference point for the curriculum, Figure 3.4 illustrates how they can be embedded in a theme on food, using the curriculum, campus and community. It also incorporates the 10 Doorways framework (introduced in Chapter 2; see another adapted version from the organisation Sustainability and Environmental Education (SEEd), plus related resources[35]). Attached to each doorway are relevant SDGs (we'll return to the doorways in Chapters 4 and 5). This framework can be used as a planning tool for integrated topics, or as a whole-school audit/planning tool. We will explore other planning frameworks later in the chapter.

---

35 See https://se-ed.co.uk/sustainable-schools-alliance/sustainable-schools-framework.

Doorways	Curriculum	Campus	Community
1. Buildings and grounds SDGs 1, 2, 3, 11, 12, 13, 15	**Coverage: geography, history, health education, art (including aspects of Doorways 8, 9 and 10)** Children are involved in growing and cooking food. They all have a 'seed-to-plate' experience, helping them to understand the biology of plants, food chains and healthy living. Exotic fruit/ vegetables grown in school greenhouse. They learn about the problems of water and food shortages, land degradation and the effects of meat eating and food miles on carbon and water footprints. Also	School vegetable garden and greenhouse created (greenhouse made out of plastic bottles). Each class to have its own plot. Crop rotation established.	Parents help to establish and maintain the garden.
2. Energy and water SDGs 6, 7, 11, 12, 13, 17		Water butts installed to save water.	Parents fundraise to buy water butts for school and are influenced to do this for their own gardens.
3. Travel and traffic SDGs 11, 12		School kitchen uses vegetables and saves food miles.	Parents do the same at home.
4. Purchasing and waste SDGs 11, 12, 13, 16, 17		Fair trade, organic, local food sourced. Vegetable peelings composted.	School sells organic vegetable boxes to parents.

Doorways	Curriculum	Campus	Community
5. Food and drink SDGs 1, 2, 3, 11, 12, 13	explore the benefits of eating locally grown food in season. Should we do more of this at the expense of variety? Children compare and contrast crops in UK with those abroad and explore why there are disparities of diet. They also investigate fair trade and how this lessens the exploitation of poor farmers. Historical perspective on this through learning about the slave trade and sugar production. They learn about the effects of monoculture farming on biodiversity, soil quality and the	School kitchen helps teachers to deliver cookery lessons.	Parents invited in for sessions.
6. Inclusion and participation SDGs 3, 5, 10, 11		Parent participation in topic by helping children to get 'down and dirty' in the garden. Children also encouraged to grow vegetables at home.	
7. Local well-being SDGs 3, 11, 16, 17		Feel-good factor of growing your own and cooking on a budget. Cookery courses for parents run in conjunction with local organisation.	
8. Global dimension SDGs 1, 2, 3, 6, 10, 11, 12, 13, 14, 15, 17		Twin with a school in another country and compare and contrast local food growing.	School raises funds to help a community in Africa to boost their food production (e.g. sinking a well while appreciating the often-superior farming husbandry compared to UK).
9. Biodiversity (science) SDGs 5, 11, 12, 13, 15		Understand that biodiversity in the school grounds helps to control pests without the need	Parents pick up gardening knowledge which benefits their families.

Doorways	Curriculum	Campus	Community
	aesthetic qualities of the landscape.	for chemicals. Identify 'useful' vertebrates and invertebrates. Understand the life cycles of flora and fauna in the garden and importance of pollinating insects.	
10. Aesthetic and spiritual (arts) appreciation of nature SDGs 4, 5		Draw, paint and make models of animals found in the school grounds that help or hinder the garden. Celebrate the harvest. Draw and paint fruit and vegetables and look at famous artists who did the same.	Parents take part in harvest festival celebrations and help to show similarities and differences between UK and other countries.

Figure 3.4: Food topic showing links to sustainable schools doorways and SDGs

The seed-to-plate scenario includes all children, with the school garden fully utilised, meaning that produce can be used either in hands-on cooking sessions or in the school kitchen. This overview doesn't show other curriculum aspects which can be usefully incorporated, particularly maths (measuring, weighing, timing, etc.), English (creative writing, speaking, listening and debate) and science (food webs and chains). These can feature in more specific planning, as illustrated later. The

Royal Horticultural Society has excellent resources, which include strategic advice on establishing a school garden and cross-curricular lesson plans.[36] This ensures that the school garden is used to maximum effect and teachers and learners appreciate its value.

Bear in mind that many members of staff may have little or no gardening experience. We made sure that training took place, while allowing experienced staff free rein. In our London school, one teaching assistant was a particularly skilled and enthusiastic gardener and helped each year group with its plot. It was also essential to bring the site staff on board when plots were being established and a composting system was needed. In addition, we utilised resources from the Food for Life programme and they helped us to take over the school catering service.[37] For further sources of help, several farming and countryside organisations provide advice and wide-ranging resources.[38]

Food is a very wide area and it is best to narrow it down to a food group or even a single food item, such as bread (see page 97) or a specific vegetable or fruit. A range of foods can be covered through small group or individual research followed by whole-class discussion. It's important that research skills are actively taught to avoid endless copying from books or websites. Taking one processed food item and researching its carbon footprint can prove highly interesting and educational for children and adults alike. A simple food carbon footprint calculator can be used for this (see Stylianou et al., 2019). I used the example of a pizza as part of geographical training for London primary teachers:

- Flour to make the base, from North America – 5,400 miles

- Tomatoes from Italy (the home of pizza) – 1,000 miles

- Mozzarella cheese, also from Italy – 1,000 miles

- Tuna fish from Mauritius – 5,600 miles

- Pineapples grown and harvested in Kenya – 4,500 miles

- Peppers grown in the UK (but transported from the growers to supermarkets) – 200 miles

- Black pepper from India – 5,000 miles

36 See https://schoolgardening.rhs.org.uk/resources.
37 See https://www.foodforlife.org.uk.
38 See https://www.countrysideclassroom.org.uk/resources/661; http://www.farmsforschools.org.uk/ffsresources/resources.htm; https://leafuk.org.

So, the pizza that is delivered from 'just around the corner' has in fact travelled an incredible distance of 22,000 miles. How could this be reduced?

When I taught older children, one of our curriculum projects involved propagating fast-growing brassicas from seed to seed in under a month – the plants went through their entire life cycle and produced more seeds. This involved constructing a light box, pollinating the flowers with mock bees on the end of sticks and observing the progress of the plants on a daily basis. All this came in a kit which also covered aspects of primary and secondary science.[39]

One idea I saw at the Chelsea Physic Garden was to grow plants in the processed food packaging they eventually came in – for example, growing a bean plant in a baked bean tin or a maize plant in a cornflake packet.[40] This amply showed the connection between the highly processed and packaged products in the shops and the living plants. In this vein, children can grow wheat, harvest it and grind it to make flour. Having added more shop-bought flour, bread can be baked. Add to this homemade butter (simply churn cream) and the children will never forget the experience. This example illustrates the head, heart, hands process.

Bread fits into many subjects, such as:

- History – how bread-making has changed through the ages and the socio-economic reasons for this (it is funny how rustic wholegrain bread was seen as food for the poor and refined white bread for the rich – a situation now reversed, expedited by industrial methods).

- Geography – why wheat grows in certain areas and not others.

- Science – life cycles and yeast action and the nutritional value of different breads.

- ESD – farming practices through the ages (and how sustainable these are) and the relative health benefits of different types of bread. Global learning could include finding out which people have difficulty accessing bread and why this is the case (e.g. climate-change-induced famine) and what implications various supply chains have. Soil health would also figure in this.

For further inspiration on making links between ourselves and our food, I would recommend Michael Holland's book *I Ate Sunshine for Breakfast*. It's ostensibly for primary-aged children, but suitable for all.

39 See https://www.saps.org.uk/secondary/teaching-resources/126-rapid-cycling-brassica-kits.
40 See https://www.chelseaphysicgarden.co.uk.

People sometimes think that awe has to be instigated by trips to Niagara Falls or by being present at someone's birth. As early years teachers know, it can be created by discovering woodlice under a log. Awe also fits with the Robert Macfarlane quote at the beginning of this chapter, whereby first-hand experience can inspire imagination and creativity.

PLANNING PERSPECTIVES

A whole-school topic can be a great way of introducing a strong ESD approach to the curriculum. The plastic pollution example in Figure 3.6 (see page 101) illustrates an initial way of planning out what and how it might be covered. Notice the prevalence of practical work and the opportunities for discussion, research and making a positive difference at a local level to a wide-ranging global problem. It also looks at a single issue from a more joined-up perspective.

From this, the grid in Figure 3.4 can be used to help break the topic down into manageable chunks, through the use of the 10 Doorways, SDGs, and curriculum, campus and community approach. See Appendix 10 for additional planning guidance.

Differentiation is always an important consideration, in terms of ensuring content and skills progression from one year group to the next and within ability ranges. For example, with the plastic topic, early years could simply classify the different types of rubbish. By Year 6, children could be looking at the different types of plastic as identified by international Resin Identification Codes and deciding whether it could be recycled or not and what the environmental consequences might be.[41] The Waste and Resources Action Programme (WRAP) offers great resources and links to help children understand plastic and other forms of waste.[42]

When planning these whole-school topics, we would allocate different aspects to each year group. The next step was for the teachers to link these to the national curriculum in ways which made the most sense – in terms of subject and age/ability range. For example, in the waste topic, surveys of household waste generated by the children's families would obviously involve maths skills.

----

41 See https://microdyneplastics.com/2015/08/recycling-codes-how-resins-relate-to-the-numerical-symbols.
42 See https://wrap.org.uk.

Source: Jane Genovese, used with permission [42]

Figure 3.5: Topical takes

43 For other curriculum mind maps by Jane Genovese, see https://learningfundamentals.com.au/
go-plastic-free-find-your-strength.

As we became more confident with implementing ESD, there was less need for special days or whole-school topics because we were covering knowledge and issues as a matter of course embedded within the daily curriculum. This entailed having an ESD section on all long-, medium- and short-term planning in each subject area.

TOPIC TIMING

Teachers often complain that they 'don't have the time to fit everything in'. This thinking can be a death knell for ESD if it's seen as a bolt-on or a time-expensive luxury. There are two solutions to this. The first is to prioritise the areas of the topic to be covered. It's always best to do *less better* by having depth of study, rather than skirting over everything in a superficial, rushed manner. An in-depth study of pizza over a week's lessons may be better than a general look at 'where our food comes from'. If the topic is very large, children can be grouped to research different areas and then report back. This in itself promotes valuable skills, including the ability to synthesise and present information. The second is to see where the topic can include core skills from your curriculum subjects, which might otherwise be covered in isolated chunks using disparate stimuli. This overcomes the curse of topic work: contrived links which don't really add much to skills and understanding. For example, should Year 1 make iceberg-shaped meringues because they're doing an Arctic topic? Surely, it would be far better to make something out of ice. Sadly, the meringue-bergs were a real example that I observed recently.

Once the subject links have been established, then it's easier to see what other important day-to-day skills are left that the topic can't effectively cover. From this you can see that astute teachers are in effect working double or even triple time. They integrate as many core skills as possible into the topic, which are made more relevant and enjoyable, and then they have to cover less as separate entities.

When starting to scope out areas of local history and geography for the group of schools in London, we emphasised the need to embed ESD and showed how it can add important critical thinking to the mix. See Figure 3.6 for an overview of this. Notice how it isn't just a brainstorm of content but identifies key skills, learning outcomes and links to other subject areas.

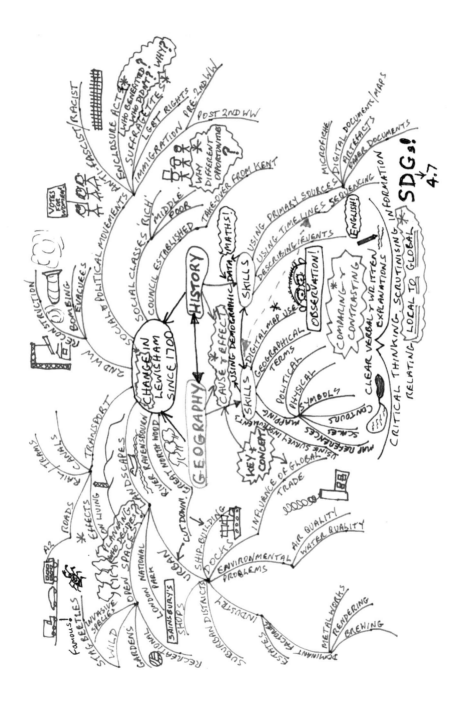

Figure 3.6: Scoping exercise

Following the scoping exercise, we looked at how the topic corresponded to curriculum areas that would then feed into short-term weekly planning. We drew up some guidance for this, as shown in Appendix 10. This was for Key Stages 1 and 2 as the early years foundation stage (EYFS) kept their own integrated planning format. However, we retained the EYFS areas of learning for continuity and to stress the need for integrated planning. It was used as a medium-term planning format to refine the messiness of initial ideas and to help determine which subjects were to be utilised in any given topic. This format also used the previously mentioned WWF-UK's characteristics of effective learners (Hren and Birney, 2011, p. 12) along with the adapted Doorways guidance as outlined on page 49 (we had done an INSET on these). Teachers would then fill in a blank version on an A3 sheet of paper to hone down which areas suited particular subjects the best (see Appendix 9).

This process helped to make the content manageable and relevant, rather than too contrived, and highlighted important skills and links. It was crucial for year teams to work together on this, which meant making sure that their non-contact time coincided. The process was supposed to be messy, until ideas could be pinned down, hence the use of mind mapping. To help embed ESD, some schools include references to the SDGs in their planning, as shown in the food topics in Figure 3.4 (see page 93).

BEST LAID PLANS

Our planning framework was also greatly influenced by the approach used in Chris Quigley's excellent curriculum planning package.[44] Although it isn't an ESD framework, it can be utilised to embed sustainability *and* deliver the knowledge and skills demanded by the national curriculum. It certainly gets away from potentially wishy-washy topic work while utilising the strengths of an integrated approach.

There are other well-established planning frameworks out there that are worth investigating, which means that teachers don't have to start from scratch.

One that we used to good effect was provided by Eco-Schools. In the UK, the programme features 10 interrelated areas: biodiversity, energy, global citizenship, healthy living, litter, marine, school grounds, transport, waste and water.[45] Schools

44 See https://www.chrisquigley.co.uk/product/essentials-full-spectrum-curriculum.
45 See https://www.eco-schools.org.uk/about/how-it-works.

tackle these over time, following a seven-stage process, and are assessed at three ascending levels – Bronze, Silver and Green Flag. The most useful tool within the Eco-Schools framework is the school audit. This provides a baseline from which to work and judge progress. It also helps to show teachers where they can incorporate ESD centrally in the curriculum, rather than it being a bolt-on. One word of warning: it's often the case that the task of leading Eco-Schools is 'given' to a non-teaching member of staff or junior teacher. This can also lead to a degree of tokenism, as it's relatively easy to tick the accreditation boxes without really becoming an all-singing, all-dancing sustainable school. To avoid this situation, you need senior leader buy-in.

The United Nations Educational, Scientific and Cultural Organisation (UNESCO) has created many useful frameworks and resources for ESD, including accredited schemes for social justice through the United Nations Children's Fund (UNICEF). Some of these also include auditing schools and strategies for implementation and inspirational case studies.[46] UNESCO also has a range of curriculum materials to help teach about climate change.[47]

A straightforward auditing tool and advice for developing and implementing a sustainability ethos can be found on the SEEd website.[48] This organisation also runs ESD courses for staff, is networked with similar organisations and is a strong advocate for environmental education. It also disseminates a wealth of resources for leaders and teachers.

The International Primary Curriculum employs a cross-curricular methodology with a very clear progression of skills and concepts, and has a strong emphasis on practical investigation.[49] Teachers can access high-quality training, materials and strategies for learning. A similar offer comes from an organisation called Whole Education.[50]

Independent Thinking provides educators with innovative approaches and resources which fit nicely with an ESD ethos.[51]

---

46 See https://en.unesco.org/themes/education-sustainable-development.
47 See https://aspnet.unesco.org/en-us/climate-education-education.
48 See https://se-ed.co.uk.
49 See https://fieldworkeducation.com/curriculums/primary-years.
50 See https://www.wholeeducation.org.
51 See https://www.independentthinking.co.uk.

The social justice aspect of ESD can be developed through UNICEF's Rights Respecting Schools accreditation. This has a wealth of curriculum resources which can be incorporated into assemblies and topic work.[52]

The Green Schools Project has many interesting case studies and ideas for making schools carbon neutral.[53]

The Ministry of Eco Education is a great one-stop-shop for curriculum resources and links to organisations that can help schools become more sustainable.[54]

The Healthy Schools programme is another cross-curricular framework which taps into many aspects of sustainability, particularly relating to food and exercise.[55] It suffered badly from government funding cuts but has been revived in the last few years. It recently added a sister programme called School Wellbeing.[56] Both these offer many lesson ideas and links to further resources. A straightforward whole-school framework for mental health and well-being in schools has also been developed by the National Children's Bureau (Stirling and Emery, 2016).

One World has a useful package for anyone wishing to establish an eco-club.[57]

The National Association for Environmental Education highlights good practice, helps to develop curriculum resources and funds innovative projects.[58]

LEEF is a 'network of EE [environmental education] practitioners working in schools, parks, museums, community gardens, city farms, botanic gardens and many other spaces'. It aims 'to make London a world-leading city for connecting people to nature and sustainability'.[59] Forest schools also feature in this realm.

A particularly useful site for learning resources and teacher CPD is the Eco Hub.[60]

Most learning platforms, such as the London Grid for Learning, include elements of sustainability, although sometimes these can be found within geography, science or PSHE topics.[61]

---

52 See https://www.unicef.org.uk/rights-respecting-schools.
53 See https://www.greenschoolsproject.org.uk/schools-in-action.
54 See https://ministryofeco.org.
55 See https://www.healthyschools.org.uk.
56 See https://www.schoolwellbeing.co.uk.
57 See https://oneworlduv.com/starter-club-kit-about.
58 See https://naee.org.uk.
59 See https://www.leef.org.uk.
60 See https://www.the-eco-hub.org.
61 See https://www.lgfl.net/default.aspx.

PLUMBING THE DEPTHS?

In England, there has been an increasing concern that schools have been 'gaming' the accountability system by narrowing the curriculum and putting most of their efforts into teaching to the test, therefore achieving 'outstanding' grades from Ofsted. I have witnessed this myself and actively weaned our London school away from this strategy. In belated recognition of this, Ofsted introduced new ways of inspecting, including what they call 'deep dives' (Ofsted, 2019).[62] These consist of a more detailed look at a few subject areas in the context of a school's overall curriculum planning and implementation.

In some quarters this has caused panic because geography, history, design and technology, the creative arts and PE have become 'Cinderella subjects'. Science has also been devalued since it ceased to be a testable subject in primary schools in 2009, and subsequent sample testing by the Standards and Testing Agency (2019) has shown a large decline in results to the point where only 21.2% of children achieve the expected level. This compares to well over 70% when the tests were conducted in our Nottinghamshire school, which was typical. There's nothing new here as similar concerns were voiced about the narrowing of the primary curriculum in the early 2000s, prompting the DfES to produce the *Excellence and Enjoyment* guidance (Department for Education and Skills, 2003), which is still worth a read and promotes a broad, balanced and enjoyable curriculum.

A curriculum with strong cross-curricular sustainability elements is very well suited to deep dives because it can provide a strong rationale, a framework and experiential skills-based learning that would impress any inspector. Worryingly, schools are finding that many early career teachers are ill-equipped to rise to the new challenges of deep dives, both in terms of subject knowledge and pedagogical techniques. There are no quick-fix solutions, but through sustainability it's possible for schools to reorient themselves so that, in tandem with targeted INSETs, they can provide a broad, balanced and meaningful curriculum. Even if a school is at the start of this process, an Ofsted inspection won't be a problem if an aspirational road map linked directly to learning enhancement can be shown. One way of phasing sustainability into the curriculum is to address this when subject policies need to be revised. I give an example for design and technology in Appendix 6.

62 See this in the context of the revised framework (Ofsted, 2021).

I hope this chapter has illustrated that the curriculum is far more than just the content of siloed subjects and that a sustainability ethos can add greatly to the way in which it's constructed and implemented. The frameworks and schemes I've highlighted help to identify sustainability in relation to standard curriculum areas, but once you get an eye for it there's great satisfaction in putting together your own schemes of work based on local and global issues and events that you know will float the children's boat. For example, we fully engaged a group of reluctant learners, many with special needs, by basing a topic on the World Cup football tournament.

The next chapter shows how a fantastic resource known as the school campus can be utilised to help the sustainability cause.

LEADERSHIP FOR SUSTAINABILITY RECOMMENDATIONS

- Audit your curriculum and ascertain what areas of sustainability you cover already. See how these can be supplemented or enhanced. Use the ESD 1, 2 and 3 categories to help this process. Use the 10 Doorways as a starting point.

- Ask yourself to what extent the school curriculum needs to be decolonised and where you might begin with this.

- Check how well any outdoor education is operating in terms of head, heart, hands opportunities and links to national curriculum skills. Remember that heart and hands are often in deficit and make a great difference to learner morale, motivation and competence, regardless of age.

- Global learning needs to be well understood and implemented and should be linked to critical thinking and decolonising the curriculum.

- Local studies are crucial. Make sure this is linked to wider issues (local to global, or start at global and work back to local).

- Staff training needs to match your aspirations for the sustainability curriculum. Training and co-creation need to precede action or you won't get sufficient buy-in or staff expertise. This is best done incrementally. Find your staff sustainability curriculum champions and help them to spread the word.

- Wherever possible, build sustainability into existing planning frameworks or adopt/adapt those of others. You don't always have to reinvent the wheel. With staff workload in mind, think how curriculum planning as a whole can be made less arduous.

- Make sure your sustainability innovations can be explained clearly in terms of school improvement to various audiences (parents, governors and inspectors).

Chapter 4

CAMPUS

We shape our buildings; thereafter, they shape us.

Winston Churchill (1943)

There are numerous campus-related entry points for developing a sustainable school. They can be quite modest rather than revolutionary, but can start a sustainability butterfly effect. Having a sustainable campus is one of the most tangible ways in which a school can show its credentials internally and externally. In other words, it walks the sustainability talk, and all stakeholders and visitors can experience this sustainability through their own senses. It can help to drive curriculum initiatives with experiential learning opportunities and also creates a brain-friendly learning environment. It's essential to demonstrate all this when wishing to convince others (including some blinkered school improvement specialists). You can point to ways in which sustainability is delivering on their beloved easily measurable outcomes, safe in the knowledge that it's delivering so much more.

OPENING THE CAN

When I entered my first headship in Nottinghamshire, I'd inherited a failing school – in all senses of the word – and this perhaps explains why I got the job, as some of the candidates pulled out in disdain and disbelief. However, being young(ish) and ambitious, it seemed an opportunity rather than a lost cause, so I grabbed it with both hands.

The school had 250 juniors (7–11-year-olds) and was housed in army camp build-ings, which dated from the Second World War, at the centre of a run-down, largely local authority, housing estate. When the school opened in 1950, the conversion from military to educational use was meant to be a 'temporary measure', necessi-tated by a steep rise in the number of young families in the area as the estate grew bigger after the war. This expansion continued and a new infant school (for 3–6-year-olds) was opened next door in the 1960s and expanded in the 1970s, but funding still wasn't available to replace the junior school. Many people called it the 'camp school', which caused some mirth to outsiders.

After adaptation from camp to school, in terms of rooms and layout, the only other major 'improvement', which occurred sometime in the 1980s, was the addition of suspended ceilings. The inside walls were painted a dull green colour, as would befit an old-fashioned mental asylum, and, apart from a bare field for football, the rest of the grounds were tarmacked with no landscaping other than some sickly hedging around the perimeter. The heating system was a coke-fired boiler, which belched black smoke for much of the winter, giving the site a Dickensian feel on foggy days. I offer this level of detail because the significance of this school's his-tory to my sustainability story will feature later in this chapter and in the next.

Source: **courtesy of Victor Miller**

Apart from continuing to implement short-term improvements through a change of tactics, as featured in Chapter 2, I was keen to develop a sustainability ethos and to engage staff and governors. But where to begin? I sold the idea on the back of improving the curriculum, initially through the relatively straightforward action of getting the teachers to take their classes on day and residential field trips. These had largely ceased due to the children's poor behaviour. I also encouraged teachers to include aspects of ESD within their lesson planning (this was before I discovered existing frameworks for developing sustainability).

In the end, I found that actions spoke louder than words. My first act of sustainability was to get an aluminium can recycling bin installed in the entrance hall. This was in the days before local authorities recycled this sort of waste. It wasn't an earth-shattering move, but it set the tone for what was to follow. Of course, a single recycling bin doesn't make a sustainable school. In addition, I drip-fed information to the staff and children about aluminium – that it's derived from bauxite ore, which has to be mined and processed causing a lot of environmental damage. Only in later years did I find out that recycling aluminium cans is really greenwash because about 5–10% of the can is lost and so ore is still needed to top this up. This means that it's dubious to use aluminium for any product. However, at the time this modest act got the attention of staff and children and they started to dutifully bring in their cans. The entrance hall smelt of stale beer, but this was a price worth paying. A company took them away and we earned a bit of income from them, which pleased the budget manager.

The next act was to acquire large tractor tyres from a local company to use for growing ornamental shrubs to brighten up the drab playground. This was in tandem with painting murals, designed by the children, on the outside walls. People also noticed that sustainability was an aspect of my lifestyle. I cycled 10 miles each way to work in all seasons and weathers. This was in contrast to my predecessor, who arrived in his Jaguar.

CAMPUS CONUNDRUMS

When looking at how a school campus can run along sustainable lines, it helps to have working definitions of sustainability which can be applied to any action or project. You don't need a doctorate in ESD to do this, just certain thinking habits and the willingness to investigate the matter in terms of the social, economic and environmental impacts of any given action from a local to global perspective. As the aluminium recycling example shows, at first, not all my investigations came before an action.

Around the year 2000, some new-build schools had wind turbines placed on their roofs at considerable expense. Not only did they not work very well in terms of generating electricity, but there were instances of them causing vibrations throughout the building and having to be turned off. The carbon and other environmental footprints of the buildings themselves – both during construction and later operation – were seldom considered. So, eco-bling needs to be avoided! Professor John Whitelegg, who specialises in sustainable transport solutions, concurs. He advocates a staged approach for reducing greenhouse gases from traffic (see Figure 4.1).

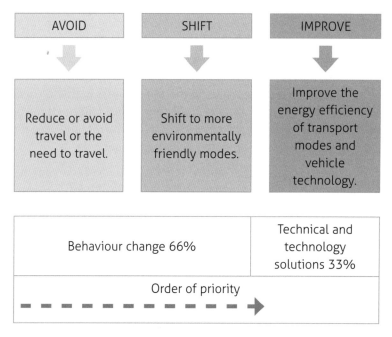

Figure 4.1: Avoid, shift and improve

Source: **adapted from Whitelegg (personal communication, 2021), used with permission**

Notice that behaviour change comes first; proportionately, this is the most important element as it represents the bottom of a hierarchy. Having corresponded with John Whitelegg, he also thinks that this avoid, shift, improve scenario can apply to any change aimed at improving sustainability. This can challenge our deeply engrained attitudes, rather than just aiming to make our behaviours more green (which may well be greenwash). For example, we may think that it is a Good Thing to recycle or repurpose all our waste (anything derived from consumption – for example, packaging, food or electrical goods), but do we think enough about whether we need so many material things in the first place? Bear this in mind as you read the rest of this chapter, as we need to challenge the cultural norms which lead to overconsumption.

This is where the curriculum discussions and transmission of ecological knowledge described in Chapter 3 come into their own. This was sadly lacking in the case of a nameless person who virtue signalled with an impressive array of solar panels on the roof of their house and then spent the saving from the feed-in tariff on a foreign holiday. Their plane flight alone would've wiped out any carbon savings made by the panels. This is known as the 'rebound effect', and many of us can be guilty of it unless we make the effort to fully understand the impact of various kinds of consumption and make the relevant links. Schools can fall into the same greenwash trap by buying more stuff containing vast amounts of embodied carbon upon receiving income from microgeneration projects.

NEEDY PEOPLE

Sustainability is important when considering the basic needs of people who use the school. Learners, staff and visitors need to be physically and psychologically comfortable to function well. These mental and physical aspects are illustrated by Maslow's (1943) well-known hierarchy of needs. If a classroom is too hot or too cold, this will cause physical discomfort, leading to low-level anxiety and inhibiting the children's capacity to learn and the teacher's capacity to teach. This means that not only is energy being wasted, but the school is failing to optimise the children's education. If children, parents and staff frequently associate school with any form of discomfort – physical or psychological – then it's likely they'll feel negatively about it, and this isn't a recipe for sustainable well-being and meaningful learning. A senior leader in our London Children's Centre and I mapped out some of these factors to highlight their importance (see Figure 4.2), and surveyed the centre's services (catering for families with 0–5-year-olds) to see how they matched Maslow's categories of need. This led to more services being created to support the safety and physiological aspects of family life, such as providing more opportunities for swimming, trips to the seaside and local parks, and advice on achieving better sleep.

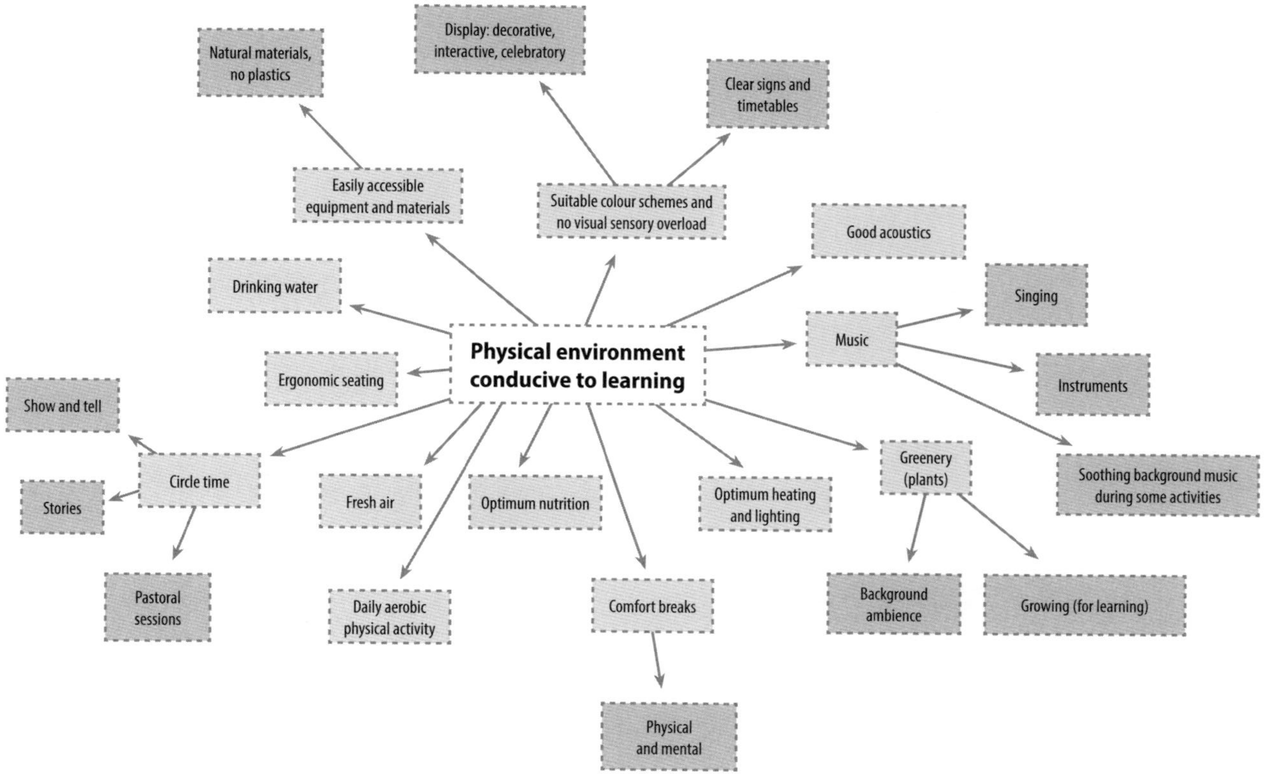

Figure 4.2: Physical environment conducive to learning

Physical environment conducive to learning

- Show and tell
- Stories
- Pastoral sessions
- Circle time
- Drinking water
- Natural materials, no plastics
- Ergonomic seating
- Easily accessible equipment and materials
- Display: decorative, interactive, celebratory
- Fresh air
- Daily aerobic physical activity
- Optimum nutrition
- Suitable colour schemes and no visual sensory overload
- Clear signs and timetables
- Comfort breaks
- Physical and mental
- Optimum heating and lighting
- Music
- Good acoustics
- Background ambience
- Greenery (plants)
- Singing
- Growing (for learning)
- Soothing background music during some activities
- Instruments

Most of the points about the physical environment are stating the obvious, but they are often overlooked or downplayed when teachers and classrooms are being judged on 'effectiveness'. For instance, I've seen many classrooms and playgrounds that are bereft of plants, despite a wide body of research suggesting that having plants in the background is brain-friendly (Daly et al., 2010). Children can be deprived of water for long periods, and I've seen children sitting on a carpet listening to the teacher for far too long.[1] Studies have shown that the best lighting for brain function is as close to natural daylight as possible (Mott et al., 2012). Some schools are now taking this into account during refits.

Notice the elements of Figure 4.2 that relate directly to a sustainability ethos (e.g. use of greenery and natural materials) and those that relate sustainability to the curriculum (e.g. circle time, growing for learning and the use of natural materials). All of the others are either related to the way the campus operates, which can be along sustainability lines, or to the curriculum. For example, a campus with a sustainable catering service can support good nutrition through the provision of local organic food – properly cooked in the school kitchen – and supplemented with fruit and vegetables grown in the grounds. This can form part of the children's health, science, maths and geography learning (more on this later).

Under the guidance of a psychologist, we audited classrooms to gauge the degree of stimulation from walls and displays, particularly regarding the use of colours. This was because we had an increasing number of children on the autistic spectrum, who suffer unduly from overstimulation in the form of bright colours and complex displays. As a result, we calmed down colours, provided more plants and simplified displays. This also benefitted other children because the impact of displays as learning aids is lessened if a classroom is too cluttered.

For many children, just crossing the threshold of the school can be stressful, and stress is the enemy of effective brain function. Think about a test you might have failed just through being nervous. School can be even more alien and stressful to children if their parents had poor experiences of school themselves (hence emphasising the importance of the hidden curriculum and pupil attitudes to self and school in previous chapters).

Poor acoustics can also be hostile factors. In our London school, the echoey hall where children ate lunch was positively frightening for early years children, so we

1   The impact of dehydration on cognition and mood is particularly relevant for those with poor fluid regulation, such as the elderly and children. See Masento et al. (2014).

found another space for them. We couldn't afford to install acoustic panels, so we reduced noise levels by installing a special sensory traffic light which turned red if the children started to talk or behave too noisily. This was one of the many measures we put in place to make the dining experience more civilised and conducive to conversation; others included more free flow to avoid queues, zoning the space to avoid noisy food disposal near tables and having a family dining service (sharing out the food at the table, with older children helping younger ones). To augment this, I incentivised staff to eat with the children by providing them with a free lunch. This encouraged valuable conversations, which in turn improved staff–pupil relationships. After we took over the catering from an outside company, food waste was reduced and the children became less noisy because they were too busy eating (I'll return to catering later).

CAMPUS CATEGORIES

A useful way of planning how the school campus can become as sustainable as possible is to start with the individual child and work outwards (see Figure 4.3). Every aspect of campus operations should be serving the best interests of the child, in the same way as most schools would say that a child's learning is at the centre of all they do, although how many schools are *really* child-centred is another matter! Naturally, a child-centred approach should include both these interrelated aspects.

Figure 4.3 shows six main categories of school campus operations, namely:

1   Procurement (what the school buys in terms of goods, utilities and services).

2   Water (used for drinking, cooking and in heating systems).

3   Energy (gas, electricity, microgeneration).

4   Waste (food, emissions, water, paper, plastic, etc.).

5   Food and catering (breakfasts, lunches, food technology).

6   Travel and deliveries (how staff and children get to school, how goods are delivered).

You'll notice that this model relates to the 10 Doorways described in Chapter 2, isolating the campus elements.

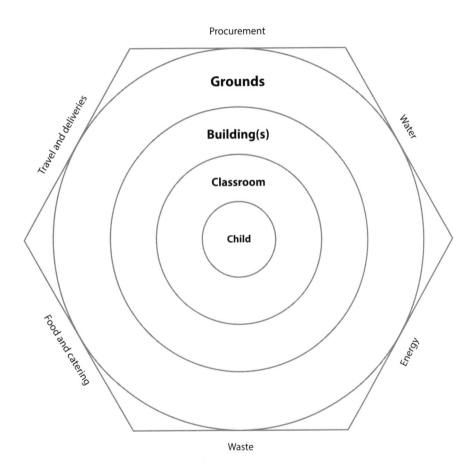

Figure 4.3: Campus considerations

A school leader has many options for running the campus along sustainability lines, making valuable links to the curriculum and community, and saving money. To start this process, each of the six campus operations need to be scrutinised. This is where auditing frameworks – such as Eco-Schools' – can prove useful; a professional energy audit is also recommended. The six operations are listed in no particular order of priority because there are many overlaps and integrations, which we'll explore later. Suffice to say that the campus can be a vehicle and backdrop for physical and psychological harmony and meaningful learning. It can be a 'learning campus', not merely a 'campus of learning'. See the learning charter in Appendix 8.

CARBON COPY

I highlighted the issue of embodied carbon in Chapter 1 because many of schools' detrimental environmental impacts are masked because they're not seen directly by users or measured in money; invariably the consequences of production and consumption are outsourced to the biosphere. Another way of viewing this is through an international accounting tool called the Greenhouse Gas Protocol (GHGP). This encourages organisations to look at their activities in terms of three scopes (see Figure 4.4).

You can see that embodied carbon occurs in Scope 3. In both Scope 2 and 3 there's no direct control of the emissions, but choices about what goods and services are purchased will make a huge difference to the volume of emissions created. Bear this in mind as you read the rest of this chapter, and remember that it's not just emissions linked to climate change that should concern us. As described in Chapter 1, habitat and species destruction is also bound up in our general over-consumption and curtails carbon sequestration on a vast scale.

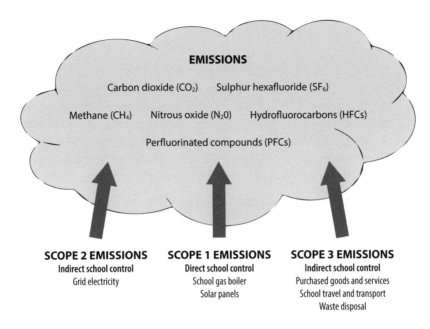

Figure 4.4: Emission scopes

Source: **adapted from Carbon Trust**[2]

The following sections give a more detailed account of the six campus operations and how they interlink to deliver increased levels of sustainability.

....

2   See https://www.carbontrust.com/resources/briefing-what-are-scope-3-emissions.

PROCUREMENT

It can help to develop an ethical procurement policy, which is constantly under review and updated (see Appendix 2), giving guidance to all staff who may be involved in obtaining items for school use. This could outline what is meant by 'product lifetimes' as applied to commonly purchased items and how environmental and social damage could be avoided, diminished or mitigated in their purchase, transport, use and disposal. Related policies can include fair trade, energy and food. I include examples of these from our schools (see Appendices 3, 4 and 5).

The underlying cause of all our sustainability woes is the use of too much stuff and our inability to reduce, recycle, reuse, repair or repurpose enough of what we acquire. The main question a discerning leader for sustainability needs to ask when confronted with a purchase option, whether it is completely new or to replace an existing item, is: do we really need this? Although this seems very obvious, I (along with equally gullible subject leaders) have made numerous mistakes in buying things which the school could do without and have been enticed into some of these purchases by slick presentations from sales reps. The cupboards in most schools bear witness to a swathe of devices, equipment, materials and books which were bought and barely, or never, used. Often this was because a certain educational fad was introduced by a keen member of staff who then departed, leaving the initiative high and dry. For example, one of my schools had a set of 15 plastic dummy computer keyboards with removable keys which were meant to teach the children keyboard skills. Hardly used and then put in a skip! I learnt to curb these excesses by encouraging budget managers to be strict (above all with me) and everyone to be more focused on what the school *really* needed in terms of improving teaching and learning.

It is important to realise that any extra purchase, whether this be a drawing pin, a chair or a new building, puts an added burden on the planet.[3] I always think of the buyerarchy of needs when purchasing anything (see Figure 4.5).

Staff in the London school were greatly amused to see me clamber into the waste skip at the end of the school year to take out items which I considered still useable. In some cases, it was just a matter of passing them on to a different class or making minor repairs. Right to repair legislation is starting to be enacted, meaning

---

3   See https://www.storyofstuff.org.

that appliances must be repairable to counteract built-in obsolescence (see Loughran, 2021).

EYFS seemed particularly wasteful due to the use of plastic items. This greatly diminished when we started to use more natural or scrap items to enhance play opportunities (some linked to the forest school methodology described in Chapter 3). Scrap stores can be a useful source of materials derived from safe, clean industrial waste, which can be used for early years play or more formal science, art, and design and technology further up the school.[4]

Figure 4.5: Buyerarchy of needs

Source: **Sarah Lazarovic,[5] used with permission**

A school I worked with recently wanted to base its early years outdoor learning on sustainability, and after working with the staff we identified different areas for development (see Figure 4.6 on page 123). Not only did this strategy save a lot of

4   See https://childrensscrap.co.uk.
5   See https://www.sarahl.com.

money in terms of not buying expensive commercially produced equipment, but it also improved the quality of the children's learning. Many children lived in flats and were cut off from the sorts of natural materials you might find in a garden, so this made the initiative even more worthwhile. In addition, it meant that the school's embodied carbon footprint was lowered just through buying less new stuff.

This EYFS approach can be replicated across the key stages. It also links to head, heart, hands methodology and can have the added bonus of reducing the need for unnecessary textbooks and facile worksheets. There are many videos and books detailing how natural materials can be utilised for all types of learning, as a quick Google search will reveal (or should I say an 'Ecosia search': an environmentally friendly search engine that, among other things, plants lots of trees[6]).

The durability of items is another important consideration. Unless it's a single-use item, such as a piece of paper, the length of its serviceable life will have a great influence on its environmental impact. For example, if the school buys a cheap toaster for breakfast club which lasts barely a year, then the environmental footprint will be far greater than that of a more expensive toaster which might last 10 years or even longer.

If a purchase *is* necessary, then the next question needs to be: is it ethical? This applies to the way in which the item is made, transported and packaged, including the rights and pay workers in the supply chain receive and what damage may have been caused by the extraction of any raw materials and associated emissions into the air, soil or water. The most damaging aspect might be the transportation. If so, could the item be obtained locally?[7] This relates back to the issue of durability and ease of repair. Is it ethical to buy an item knowing that it won't last very long? Inevitably, a balance has to be struck between how affordable the item is and how much it's needed. Nevertheless, false economy should always be questioned. Fairphone is an example of a provider with good sustainability credentials.[8] They use recycled materials and any new rare metals are sourced from conflict-free mines. The company is socially responsible by ensuring that production workers are paid at least a living wage. The phones are also designed to be easily repaired rather than scrapped. You pay a premium for this, but it emphasises that many of the products we use and abuse are just too cheap.

....

6   See https://www.ecosia.org.
7   Look at sites such as https://www.ethicalsuperstore.com and https://www.ethicalconsumer.org to source low-impact products.
8   See https://shop.fairphone.com.

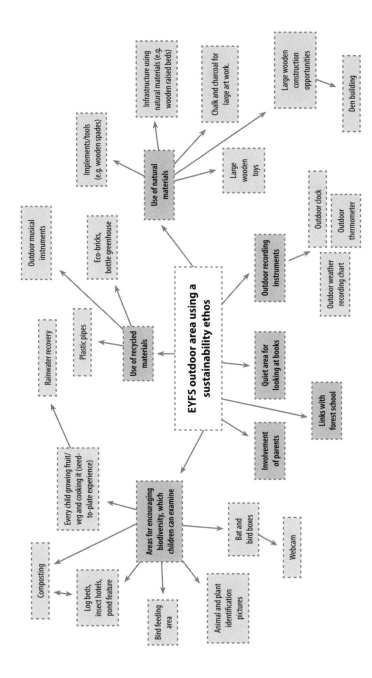

Figure 4.6: Sustainability enriching EYFS

When buying large electrical items – for example, white goods and computers – it literally pays to check their energy rating. Ideally, they should be graded at least an A+ according to the older grading system, which goes up to A+++. Across the UK and EU, a more stringent A to G scale is being phased in.[9]

Other ethical considerations need to be made when obtaining internet services.[10] Many people don't realise that emails have an associated carbon footprint due to the energy consumed by vast server farms. Berners-Lee (2010, p. 15) calculates that each email creates 4 g of CO2e, and an email with an attachment that you open creates 50 g of CO2e. Some providers power these via renewables, but it's unclear which one is the most environmentally friendly. Whatever the case, it gives us an excuse for not opening long attachments! Financial transactions also have a considerable carbon footprint, particularly cryptocurrencies (Purdy, 2021).

Some schools become accredited Fairtrade Schools. The accreditation process helps schools to check the ethical provenance of certain products, but doesn't, for instance, take into account transportation miles – such as fruit and vegetables delivered to us from Africa by plane or other environmentally damaging practices, including the overuse of water for certain crops like pineapples. Similarly, if a school kitchen orders organic food, you might think that all ethical bases are covered, but not if that food has travelled a great distance. The Fairtrade Foundation produces some excellent multimedia educational materials which can help to engage children in the procurement process.[11] Worryingly, certain UK supermarkets are phasing out Fairtrade-branded products because they say that they have their own ethical systems (Vidal, 2017).

Schools use many other products which are potentially harmful. In need of particular scrutiny are cleaning products, including different detergents for washing dishes, hands and various other surfaces. Although there are cost implications, it's well worth looking for the ones that contain non-harmful natural substances rather than synthetic chemicals (Alton, 2017). There are always debates about whether it's better to use paper towels, linen towels on a roll or electric hand driers (Myers, 2016). The jury is still out. There is a similar debate around nappies, which is of relevance to Children's Centres and school nurseries – should they be reusable cloth or disposable (Berners-Lee, 2010, p. 39)? Also paper vs plastic bags (McGrath,

9   For details of the new energy rating system, see West (2021).
10 See an overview of ethical internet at: https://www.ethicalconsumer.org/technology/shopping-guide/
    broadband.
11 See https://schools.fairtrade.org.uk.

2008). Conducting an SDG check can be helpful here, especially considering Goal 12: 'Ensure sustainable consumption and production patterns'.[12] This provides a global perspective and can also add to curriculum resources and ideas for pupil actions.

Reprographics are always a minefield when it comes to sustainability. Photocopiers and printers are all hi-tech and 'intelligent' these days, which means the materials they are made from and the various components within them are highly damaging to the environment. They also use quite a lot of energy, even the ones marketed as 'low energy'. Schools routinely sign up to five-year contracts, some offering new models supplied on an annual basis. Consumables such as ink and paper have highly detrimental effects on the environment. Although paper can come from sustainable sources, the energy taken to make and transport it is considerable. Effluent from paper mills can devastate local water ecologies. Ink can be packaged in tanks rather than smaller cartridges, but it is still a ruinous product. Obviously, some reprographic machines, including laminators, are worse than others and research needs to be done to find the least damaging. This entails scrutinising companies' eco-credentials as, unfortunately, there isn't a totally impartial review organisation. Basically, you need to find out the environmental consequences associated with the lifetime of the machine and balance that against affordability and fixability. Reconditioned machines will reduce the embodied carbon footprint greatly. The most sustainable way of handling this issue is to reduce the need for reprographics in the first place by considering the following:

● Wherever possible, the school office should be paperless.[13]

● Children can get used to having their IT work stored electronically for the most part, with printouts only for display or other special purposes.

● The school can communicate electronically, including sending digital newsletters to parents (although we have to be careful not to contribute to the digital divide, and remember that some parents might not have access to a smartphone, or other device, or reliable internet).

● Only use worksheets where strictly necessary, with teachers given a paper ration.

....

12 See https://www.un.org/sustainabledevelopment/sustainable-consumption-production.
13 Beware of greenwash here. When local authorities went 'paperless', this really meant that they sent resources to schools electronically, with the schools often obliged to make hard copies. A classic case of carbon outsourcing!

The last point needs further thought because, as highlighted earlier, there are vast areas of forest and huge amounts of photocopier energy and ink devoted to school worksheets, and this may indicate that the curriculum has too few experiential learning opportunities and/or children are spoon-fed too much and not expected to record things themselves in their own exercise books or on scrap paper on a clipboard when on a field trip.

Computers, laptops, tablets and various digital hand-held devices are similarly problematic when it comes to what they're made of, how they're made and how they're ultimately disposed of.[14] They are a fact of modern life and so the least damaging options are required.[15] Once again, questions need to be asked about how much time children spend on them and how reliant teachers are on devices such as interactive whiteboards. As useful as they are, if not used with discretion they can dominate the way in which children learn and limit time for experiential learning. During quite a few lesson observations, I've seen teachers in varying states of panic if their interactive whiteboard malfunctioned. They had no plan B, mainly because they had never been expected to teach without this type of aid.

A school uniform shop can help the cause of sustainable clothing manufacture in two main ways. Our Nottinghamshire school sold its own uniforms and gave parents a choice of garments. They could either buy more expensive items made from organic cotton or cheaper ones made from a mix of non-organic and man-made fibres. They were indistinguishable in appearance and the price differential wasn't that great because we only aimed to break even. We found that the majority of parents went for the organic option. A school shop could also stock other environmentally friendly essentials, such as stationery, book bags and water bottles.

We also promoted the sale of second-hand clothing (including shoes), which was very popular. Most used clothing is in good condition because children grow out of it so quickly. It is not shaming to buy second hand and I do this for my own child. This helps to negate the damage caused by the global clothing industry. I wonder how many people still buy fast fashion, oblivious to its deleterious effects on people and planet, as reported by the Environmental Audit Committee (2019, p. 3), which highlighted the forced labour of cotton pickers, production workers on pitifully low wages, excess use of water, pollution of water courses, harmful emissions into the atmosphere and 300,000 tonnes of fabric waste per annum

14 See https://www.ehow.co.uk/info_8354888_advantages-computer-over-manual-typewriter.html.
15 See https://www.greenroundtable.org/7-of-the-latest-eco-friendly-computers.

being incinerated or placed in landfill in the UK alone. The volume of clothing and footwear produced is forecast to increase by 63% to 102,000,000 tonnes per annum by 2030 (Environmental Audit Committee, 2019, p. 8): 'It produces an estimated 1.2 billion tonnes of CO2 equivalent (CO2e) per year – more than international flights and maritime shipping combined.' This extends to 3.3 billion tonnes of CO2e if you take into account the full life cycle of clothing and footwear, including incineration and landfill (Environmental Audit Committee, 2019, p. 28). The report highlights how schools can help by teaching sewing skills (Environmental Audit Committee, 2019, p. 41), thus promoting a make-do and mend philosophy.

Studying the clothing and fashion industry can really help young people to realise what sustainability as a concept looks like and how to achieve it through eco-nomic, social and environmental actions. This can then be applied to any industry and pupils can become adept at following audit trails back from product to source. The human dimension of this is of particular importance and can include learning about modern slavery. The Ethical Trading Initiative is worth checking out as it specialises in promoting workers' rights.[16] Discussions might include why vegans would object to wearing leather. The tanning process to produce leather is notori-ous for producing large amounts of pollution and, of course, it relies upon the slaughter of animals. However, you can always challenge any vegan on the pollu-tion caused by non-animal clothing and footwear. Much of this uses fossil fuels to produce synthetic fibres and plastics. Even when natural fibres are used, there is still a significant environmental footprint due to the way they are grown, pro-cessed, manufactured and disposed of. Ironically, a faux fur jacket may well be more damaging to the planet than one derived from a mink farm. Apart from the manufacturing process, the faux fur will shed microplastics throughout its life. Leaving animal rights to one side (as important as they are), the message is really to buy fewer clothes and, wherever possible, go for second-hand gear.

Some schools have the freedom to choose which bank to use. This can greatly contribute to the sustainability agenda, even though the effects may be well hidden. For example, many banks still invest in fossil fuels or deal with transactions on behalf of fossil fuel companies and other planet wreckers. By switching to a bank that doesn't, a school is helping to add pressure on recalcitrant banks to change their ways. The Good Shopping Guide website ranks banks according to their ethical credentials.[17] School staff may also be interested in this for their

16 See https://www.ethicaltrade.org.
17 See https://thegoodshoppingguide.com/subject/ethical-banks-building-societies.

personal finances. A school can also check the credentials of any company they deal with through websites such as Ethical Consumer.[18]

WATER

Keeping water consumption down is mainly a behavioural issue, which is why it was one of the tasks of our eco-team to monitor and keep its use in check. As in a domestic situation, it's amazing how much water can be saved if taps aren't left running or toilet flushes have limiters. The global issue of water security can be addressed across the curriculum, and if this is linked with the children's own local behaviour, then it's another great example of keeping things experiential (see SDGs 6 and 14).

This means taking conventional learning about the water cycle into the ESD realm, which can include climate change, migration and the overuse of water to produce certain products (water footprints). For example, it takes over 15,000 litres of water to produce 1 kg of beef,[19] 10,000 litres to produce a cotton bed sheet and 52,000–83,000 litres to produce a car (Water Footprint Calculator, 2017). Globally, one in four people don't have access to a safe water source (Ritchie and Roser, 2021). This serves to show that when it comes to our products, it's not just about carbon footprints.[20] There are three categories of water: green (water used and transpired by plants), blue (in bodies of water like lakes and reservoirs) and grey (water which carries pollutants either due to accidents or because of an industrial process).[21] Water conservation – like sustainability generally – is all about not taking more than can be replenished by natural systems. We should always treat it as a precious resource rather than a cheap limitless one.

There's always scope for schools to influence their water footprints. It takes a lot of energy to purify and pump water to consumers, so this is an added

---

18 See https://www.ethicalconsumer.org.
19 See https://waterfootprint.org/en/resources/interactive-tools/product-gallery.
20 For more information on water miles, see https://waterfootprint.org/en/water-footprint/what-is-water-footprint.
21 See Hoekstra et al. (2011) for more details.

consideration. Below are some suggestions for a more sustainable approach to water use through:

- Rainwater harvesting systems which can be fed into toilet flushing. In some areas of the UK, schools get payments or water rate reductions for preventing rainwater from entering drainage systems.

- Installing water-reduction devices to shower heads.

- Installing press-taps.

- Installing water butts for watering the school garden.

- Creating a pond or marshy area, which is great for biodiversity.

- Creating new areas for rainwater to soak through rather than just run off. This might involve replacing tarmac with grass, gravel or a latticed surface, such as Grasscrete.[22] Doing this is very environmentally friendly, particularly during heavy rain when flash floods can inundate the sewage system, causing the run-off of raw sewage into streams and rivers. Astroturf is used by many schools but is extremely damaging to the environment in its manufacture and disposal. During use, it sheds microplastics which end up in the sea (van Rossum, 2017). It also epitomises the rejection of nature in favour of a more sanitised existence. Sustainable schools shouldn't have it.

- Not allowing hazardous chemicals (non-biodegradable cleaning fluids, oil-based paints, etc.) to enter the drainage system, causing grey water to be unnecessarily contaminated and become less easy to purify (more energy implications), plus the danger of contamination of blue water.

- Procuring organic food (or food from any form of less intensive agriculture), the blue water footprint is lowered because this type of growing requires much less irrigation due to better soil management.

Children's appreciation of how much rain actually falls is helped by having a school weather station, including a rain gauge. They are always amazed to discover that 1 mm of rain on a square metre of ground or roof equates to 1 litre (or 1 kg) of water. Older children can do large calculations to find out how much rain has fallen on the school site in a day. This is yet another example of a campus assisting

---

22 See https://www.grasscrete.com/docs/paving/grasscrete.html.

the curriculum. Opportunities for this can be lost if, for example, a school installs a pond for purely aesthetic reasons.

ENERGY

To show the Whitelegg behaviour change premise in action (shown in Figure 4.1 on page 112), the eco-team helped the site manager to monitor utilities consumption (gas, water and electricity) in the school. Subsequently, they developed and implemented a plan for reducing usage. This included launching a campaign across the school and, in some cases, naming and shaming (in a light-hearted way) members of staff who left their classroom lights or interactive whiteboard on. By the end of the first year, we improved the energy efficiency rating of the building from an E to a C just through behaviour change.

The site manager taught the children how to read the meters and showed them read-outs of energy consumption over time. In our Nottinghamshire school, this was part of a European Union energy project, in which schools from seven countries compared and contrasted their energy data and shared how they were trying to reduce their consumption. This included a consideration of the weather (yet another use for a school weather station). It was interesting to see, for example, how our Greek partners used more energy in the spring and summer due to their air conditioning. We also piloted an energy curriculum, which had cross-curricular modules and lesson plans covering many aspects of energy use from transport to space heating and information on fossil fuels and different types of renewables. The UK project was undertaken with our local authority Energy Agency. More recently, most local authorities – like mine in the London Borough of Lewisham – have established sustainability teams (sometimes called climate action teams) and are keen to make links with schools to help with energy saving. They can offer grants for improvements and links to curriculum materials. What's your local authority doing?

We also improved the way in which buildings were heated and ventilated in the winter to avoid opening windows, although this has to be somewhat ignored due to COVID-19 (Anthes, 2021). In our Nottinghamshire school, technical solutions included software that automatically switched off the main computer servers when not needed during the holidays and at weekends. One simple way of saving lots of energy was to alter the heating timer as needed and pay more attention to the local weather forecast, rather than leave things on a mindless time switch.

At our London school, we had a large array of solar panels fitted, which continue to earn about £3,000 per annum for the school. This was achieved through a partnership with a local cooperative company. There are an increasing number of schemes in the UK and elsewhere to install solar panels or retrofit wall insulation and low-energy LED lighting, the cost of which is paid back over time through the savings.[23] Suitably empowered business and site managers can research this and make recommendations; it doesn't have to be the job of the head teacher or principal. Once again, it's educationally valuable for the children to be involved. In our Nottinghamshire school, we installed a large, child-friendly energy monitoring screen, so the children could see how the building was functioning in real-time. The data was from a computerised system that recorded usage, which the older children could analyse as part of maths and science lessons. Geographical work was included when data from the weather station was introduced.

Other types of technology, such as air source and ground source heat pumps, are becoming more feasible for schools to access. These up-and-coming systems are becoming more economical, and are much greener than biomass boilers. (The physics behind this statement would make for an interesting study by older pupils (see e.g. Ravilious, 2020).) Before embarking on eco-bling, I would recommend conducting a thorough energy use assessment. It's often the case that it's more sensible and economical to lag pipes, insulate roofs and walls, and cure draughts before embarking on ambitious microgeneration projects.

Some schools or groups of schools are able to choose their energy providers. If this is possible, then obviously those that provide 100% of their electricity and gas from renewables are to be recommended (although, once again, beware greenwash (see Ambrose, 2021)). If this isn't possible, find out why not and lobby for a change of policy. Beware those that provide 'green energy' which is produced by nuclear power. It may be zero carbon to produce, but a lot of embodied carbon will have been used to construct the power stations and much more will be used to build long-term storage for the highly hazardous waste, not to mention the many other dangerous problems it is setting up for future generations (Piesing, 2020). See Appendix 4 for an example of an energy policy that we developed in one of our schools.

....

23 For an example of integrating retrofitting with the curriculum, see: https://hopes-sustain.org.

WASTE

As my skip foray demonstrated, I was always on the lookout for unnecessary waste in terms of school equipment and materials. Waste is a fact of life and should never be confused with the simplistic concept of 'throwing away'. If we are to achieve a circular economy, there should be no such thing as 'waste' as we commonly perceive it. In nature there is no such thing, as all materials and related energy, in whatever form, are part of a cycle of growth, death, decay and renewal (Webster and Johnson, 2008). Modern humans have tried to buck this trend by making, using and discarding with little thought about where their cast-offs might end up. It's interesting to have discussions with children and ask them where the 'away' is that we throw things to. They soon get the message that whenever anything is discarded there are environmental, social and economic consequences. A topical example is the vast amount of plastic which ends up in the oceans. In contrast, renewable energy can be an example of a human-made circular economy. Fossil fuel usage is simply the burning of hydrocarbons created millions of years ago that will not be replenished any time soon. Simply by utilising microgeneration, our school was contributing to the circular economy (or 'doughnut economy', as described by Raworth (2017)). As we procured this from a not-for-profit cooperative which used local suppliers, this also helped the cause of localism.

Once again, support staff can play an important role. For example, one of our site managers found out how we could dispose of food waste, so that it was broken down and utilised by a biodigester rather than going into landfill, where over time it would add to greenhouse gases via unfettered methane. The behaviour of all school stakeholders needs to be engaged to reduce waste or utilise it safely and usefully. For example, we set up a system on site for collecting non-cooked food waste from the school kitchen and classrooms. This was composted and used in the school garden where the children grew fruit and vegetables. Paper use was monitored and any spare paper in books at the end of the year was saved rather than put in the recycling bin with the rest of the book (those books not taken home, of course). We tried to avoid excess packaging by complaining to suppliers if this was the case and had an ongoing campaign to encourage parents not to include excessively packaged food in packed lunches. At Christmas time, class parties were organised so there wasn't a deluge of paper plates, single-use cups and decorations. It was a good design and technology exercise to come up with ways of having a low-waste party which was still fun. This embraces the concept of 'frugal hedonism' because it shows that you can party like there's no tomorrow, while ensuring that there is a tomorrow![24]

We extended the concept of waste by having assemblies which highlighted how we can waste relationships by treating others badly and waste time on activities which hurt others and the environment, including the unnecessary consumption of stuff. The old adage 'waste not, want not' is certainly appropriate for a sustainable school. Being frugal or thrifty doesn't mean having a diminished quality of life; if anything, just the opposite.

FOOD AND CATERING

Food has great potential for reducing our planetary impact, especially if we can reduce our meat consumption. There are also the potential health benefits of eating better quality local foods rather than overconsuming the fat and sugar associated with highly processed junk food. I've already mentioned food miles in relation to carbon footprints and the need to reduce water footprints. There are many other variables to consider, hence the mind map in Figure 4.7 (see page 134).

Figure 4.7 also shows some of curriculum links described in Chapter 3 (I could've linked the whole mind map to the curriculum). Notice the reference to dining room ambience described earlier. Links with the community through food culture and festivals will feature in Chapter 5.

24 A book of this name by Raser-Rowland and Grubb (2016) explains the carbon footprint of stuff and waste in a very entertaining yet thought-provoking way. Also, the information from WRAP, mentioned in Chapter 3, can be helpful.

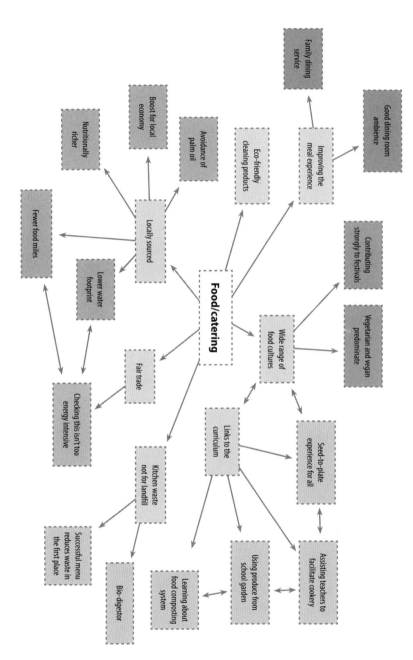

Figure 4.7: Catering for sustainability

One organisation we worked with, which is worth another mention, is Food for Life. Based in the UK, it helps schools and hospitals to develop sustainable high-quality catering. It works in tandem with the Soil Association, which promotes sustainable farming methods and localised food distribution networks and is one of the main organic certification bodies in the UK. Food for Life works with individual schools, local authorities and school catering companies, and has a three-tier accreditation system with sustainability at its core. For example, one of its stipulations is that food should be organic and, wherever possible, locally sourced. Food for Life also keys into the SDGs and gives practical examples of how to develop a school food policy which is linked to the curriculum. Similar to Eco-Schools, it has a very useful auditing tool leading to graded accreditation. It also offers many useful management and curriculum resources and shows how a school which develops this area of work can comply with, and excel against, Ofsted criteria.

In both our Nottinghamshire and London school we amalgamated all the catering under one umbrella. This included food for breakfast club, after-school club, the community and school events. This meant we could control the quality and provenance as well as benefitting from ordering in bulk, which also minimised the carbon footprint of transportation. We were able to spend more money on each meal by cutting out the middle man of a catering company. The whole initiative was instigated by the school council, which, on a weekly basis, had relayed complaints about the quality of food on offer. As a result, we commissioned Greenwich Co-operative Development Agency (GCDA) – a local co-op which, among other things, ran community cafes and cookery classes – to reorganise the catering, including new menus.[25] We had previously made strong links to this organisation through our Children's Centre. GCDA itself has a strong sustainability ethos and was very keen to pioneer a vegetarian menu for us. Children and parents were closely consulted on this through the establishment of a school nutrition action group, and tastings were held to get direct feedback on the proposed dishes. The only concession we made to non-vegetarian food was to include tuna. This was because, without it, the menu couldn't comply with national nutritional standards. Of course, we made sure that the tuna came from a sustainable and ethical source.

By making school lunches more appetising, we persuaded many more children to renounce their unhealthy packed options and drastically reduced food waste. Before this, the children who partook of school lunches felt they were the poor relation and lusted after the sweet and fatty delights that their compatriots had in

25 See https://gcda.coop.

their lunchboxes. To reverse this we had to change the food culture. This involved encouraging parents to try the meals and launching a comprehensive health education programme which dovetailed with growing fruit and vegetables and cooking as part of the curriculum. In our London school we went for a completely vegetarian menu. Not only did the school's carbon footprint plummet, but we no longer needed to provide halal meat (more on this in Chapter 5).[26] See Appendix 5 for an example food policy.

TRAVEL AND DELIVERIES

When schools are on holiday, traffic levels in London fall dramatically. The car insurance firm Admiral (2019) concluded that, during term time, traffic rose by a fifth and there were 43% fewer collisions during the holidays. It also found that, based upon data from Wales, the average distance from home to school was only 1.6 miles (which means that many journeys must be much shorter), yet lots of parents who lived even closer to their child's school chose to drop them off by car. I can vouch for this, knowing as I do fellow parents at my child's school which is less than a mile away. Granted, some parents drop their children off on the way to work, but this begs other questions about why they use a car for commuting in the first place, especially in a city as congested as London.

In many towns and cities in the UK and across the world, the car-free streets movement – also known as Low Traffic Neighbourhoods and School Streets[27] – has taken off (more on this in Chapter 5). This challenges the received wisdom of cars being the ultimate purveyors of travel freedom and high-status lifestyle. People increasingly appreciate that cars place a heavy toll on the environment through the way they're manufactured, their domination of precious space and the detrimental effect of their emissions. Car lovers might say that it's their individual right to use them with impunity, as public transport can be patchy, especially in rural areas. The COVID-19 crisis has added weight to this by giving further justification to why we might want to avoid the train or bus. Nevertheless, cycling and walking, in England at least, are increasing (Department for Transport, 2021) – and you start to feel that we are entering a new societal paradigm in which, in major conurbations

---

26 For more on food miles, see: http://www.foodmiles.com.
27 For more on School Streets, see: http://schoolstreets.org.uk.

such as London, car commuting is starting to be seen as anti-social in the same way as flying.

In the UK, the culture of car drop-off at schools was exacerbated from the late 1980s by the creation of a more market-orientated neoliberal education system, giving parents more 'choice' about where they sent their children to school. This meant that you might not necessarily send your child to the nearest school, hence the need to travel by car. Of course, this 'freedom' only extended to those who could afford it, which is a separate can of worms.

Some would argue that the emissions issue will be solved as more electric vehicles come on stream, but what this thinking doesn't take into account is the *embodied carbon* of the new electric cars (steel, aluminium, plastic, etc.) and the need for rare metals, all of which damages the lithosphere and many rich habitats (which absorb vast amounts of carbon). Apart from the hidden embodied emissions, there are emissions from tyres, brake pads and transmissions, which in the case of tyres have been shown to be 1,200 times more toxic than exhaust emissions (Jupp, 2020). Battery production itself is a very toxic process (Opray, 2017) and the extra nickel needed alone would cause an expansion of damaging mining in ecologically sensitive areas, including possibly the seabed (Heffernan, 2019). Then you still have to build and maintain roads using a nasty hydrocarbon called tar mixed with extracted stone.

The layout of towns and cities is dominated by cars, which makes it more difficult to get around by foot or bike. Overall, this is yet another example of greening the present economy rather than introducing an alternative model. This is where school campaigns for car-free streets can contribute to returning the urban environment to a human scale that is cleaner and more socially amenable. Walking and cycling have significant health benefits, and with so many adults and children being obese – 63% of adults are above a healthy weight and one in three children of primary school leaving age are obese, according to the Department for Health and Social Care (2020) – anything to encourage extra physical activity is to be welcomed.

All this means that a sustainable school has every incentive to encourage parents to get their children to school in a way that doesn't involve a car. Many UK schools have been doing this for some time, using initiatives such as:

● Walking buses. Adults take it in turns to pick up children along a route and escort them to school as a group, helping out those parents who have to be at work or who have other commitments.

● Anti-idling campaigns. Even if parents do use cars, they are encouraged to park in streets further away from the school and to switch off engines when stationary.

● Encouraging staff to use public transport, walk or cycle. In the UK, most schools can access the employer Cycle to Work Scheme, whereby the government offers tax-free incentives for purchasing or hiring bikes and cycling gear through the employee payroll.[28] When we did this in our London school, eight members of staff who had previously come to work by car took it up. It also provided extra business for the local bike shop. To improve uptake further, some schools install staff showers. It has a big impact on parents and children if they observe staff 'biking the talk'.

● Campaigns to make roads next to schools car-free. In the UK, this has been pioneered by a group called Mums for Lungs through their School Streets campaigns.[29] Children are mobilised to help, making posters to display in the neighbourhood, writing letters to lobby councils and using pester power to convince their own parents. They can also help to compile data on traffic volumes and vehicle speeds by borrowing speed guns from the local authority.

● Training children and parents to ride bikes safely. Bikeability is one organisation that helps with this and can offer an accreditation scheme.[30] It also promotes cycling more generally.

● Installing covered bike racks, so there is a secure space to store the children's bikes and scooters.

....

28 See https://www.gov.uk/government/news/cycle-to-work-scheme. See also https://www.bike2workscheme. co.uk.
29 See https://www.mumsforlungs.org.
30 See https://bikeability.org.uk.

- School bike clinics. A partner, such as a local bike shop or voluntary organisation, sends mechanics to offer free bike checks and basic maintenance.[31] In our London school, the local bike shop did very well out of this, attracting many more customers. They also got more staff sales out of the Bike2Work scheme, including from myself! If approached, larger bike sellers and repairers might see such a service as part of their corporate social responsibility.[32]

All this and more can form part of a school travel plan, which is a comprehensive strategy to promote walking, scooting, cycling and the use of public transport.[33] In London, we were fortunate to receive our school travel plan via the local authority, which came with funding for extra cycle racks and a pool of bikes for children to learn on. Some local authorities still do this. The school travel plan provides a template for a baseline audit conducted by teachers and children to ascertain the present situation, and from this targets for improvement can be set. This fits nicely with the travel part of the Eco-Schools accreditation.

As is evident in these examples, there are great curriculum enrichment opportunities to be had, such as:

- Debates on the merits of cars vs other forms of travel. This could extend to more detailed debates about the merits or otherwise of electric vehicles. Pupil voice can be used as the basis for practical actions.

- Mapping out safe local cycle and walking routes.

- Letter writing, using persuasive language.

- Designing posters and other campaign materials using art and computer skills.

- Maths work involving data compiled from traffic surveys.

- Science or geography work looking into the effects of vehicle emissions from localised pollution on global heating and the consequences of vehicle production from raw materials to road.

---

31 For an example of a local voluntary organisation that can work with schools, see: https://lewishamcyclists. org.uk. Many local authority areas in the UK have an equivalent.
32 For an example of this, see: https://www.halfordscompany.com/environment-social-and-governance/ governance/policies/corporate-social-responsibility-policy.
33 For an example from Sustrans Scotland, see: https://www.sustrans.org.uk/media/2767/2767.pdf.

● Looking at the benefits of exercise as part of science or health and well-being.

The deliveries part of this links to earlier points about procurement. Schools can evaluate how they might reduce the number of deliveries and/or the distance products need to travel. This could include rationalising deliveries by joint purchasing with other schools and getting items delivered in bulk, which could also work out cheaper. This would be relatively easy for established groups of schools, such as academy chains. These and other procurement issues can be brought up at meetings by your school budget manager, if they are part of a local network. Some areas already have these self-help groups. School travel and deliveries is another area where there is rich potential for influencing the surrounding community.

CAMPUS COMMUNITY CREDENTIALS

In our Nottinghamshire school, we developed ESD incrementally in all areas. This was given a boost when the school amalgamated with the infant school next door. It had much larger grounds and, with a grant via Groundwork,[34] enabled us to establish a large school garden used by all year groups. This was extended to parents, who were encouraged to help with the class plots. We also released some land to enable parents to grow vegetables for their families. In effect, these were allotments, which have long been used by people who are not fortunate to have large gardens and which are administered by local authorities. Unfortunately, due to the pressure on land use, many allotments have disappeared from towns and cities.

In our London school, we worked with the Black Environment Network and ran gardening workshops for families at weekends, particularly targeted at black, Asian and minority ethnic groups.[35] These proved to be very popular and encouraged people to take seedlings to grow at home, if only in window boxes. This was done in tandem with making the campus more biologically diverse by planting wild flowers and leaving parts of the playing field unmown. We planted indigenous hedging plants and tree whips, which are good for carbon sequestration and

---

34 See https://www.groundwork.org.uk.
35 See https://ben-network.org.uk/about_ben/intro.asp.

biodiversity. All these came free – grown from seeds collected in the neighbour-hood or as donations from the Woodland Trust, which also provides teaching and learning resources.[36]

We installed many bat and bird boxes, one of which had a live camera feed so the children could check on the progress of eggs and chicks.[37] Apart from learning more about life cycles, this was another example of injecting awe and wonder into the curriculum. It's such a powerful thing for a child to be part of scattering wild flower seeds and planting trees, and realising that they are leaving a highly valua-ble legacy for others.

The idea of legacy was used in a project that I recently undertook with a school whose Year 6 prefects wanted to improve an ugly part of the site by creating a quiet area. They also wanted to incorporate sustainability (see Figure 4.8 on page 142).

The original came entirely from the children before I was brought in to help. I spent several sessions facilitating discussions on what form this might take. Finally, it was agreed that a rather unsightly area at one side of the school should be con-verted into a chill-out area for anyone who didn't want to participate in more raucous activities on the main playground. To make it pleasant they wanted lots of greenery, seating, a shelter and to incorporate a mural, which had been one of the most popular stand-alone ideas. I have to admit to trying to influence the project in terms of suggesting that the greenery could provide biodiversity rather than just agreeable background, but this was readily accepted as the school had a strong sustainability ethos. The mural theme was based upon local nature. A professional artist held separate sessions with the children to work up the design. I managed to get a grant of £3,000 from a local charitable trust to fund the main works. It's worthwhile finding out about local trusts because many are little-known but can supply useful pots of money without too much bureaucracy. Most UK local coun-cils collate lists of these trusts, which can save a lot of search time.

---

36 See https://www.woodlandtrust.org.uk.
37 See https://www.seenature.org.uk/taking-part/birdbox.

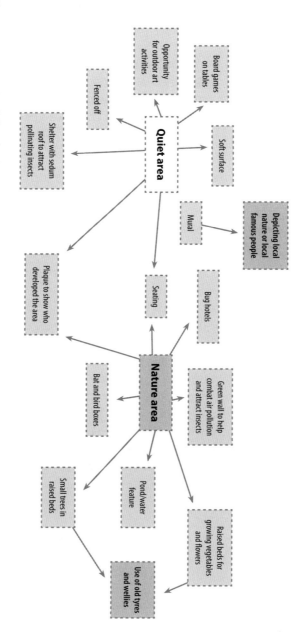

Figure 4.8: Sustainability legacy project

LEARNING BLITZ

As with the school pond example, it's always important to capitalise on learning opportunities within the campus. Another example is conducting a BioBlitz. This is a detailed survey of a part or the whole of the grounds, documenting any wildlife. Each class can be given a survey area and eventually a detailed database emerges. This can be done at different times of the year and used as a baseline for judging the effectiveness of projects aimed at increasing biodiversity. Our London school received a briefing from a scientist from the Natural History Museum, along with resources.[38] Once again, this was an opportunity to involve parents and community volunteers and is an excellent example of the growing trend of citizen science. The Big Butterfly Count (described in Chapter 2) is another of these. Apart from the Natural History Museum, other organisations offer resources – for example, the National Geographic Society[39] and the Royal Society for the Protection of Birds.[40]

Due to late-night working, I discovered that our London school was blessed with many bats. Following this, we involved a local bat enthusiast and organised bat-spotting sessions for various classes, using ultrasonic detectors to hear the clicks of the animals' radar. Each species has its own unique click sequences, which can help with identification. The children were wowed. The Bat Conservation Trust offers more information and learning resources.[41]

LIBRARY LEARNING

Sustainability includes many aspects of culture. Libraries are the conduit for many of these and play an especially vital role in more deprived communities. To this end, we re-established libraries at both schools (one had been converted into an IT suite) by accessing a sizeable grant from the Foyle Foundation.[42] Our Nottinghamshire school had no local library service, despite serving a population of over 9,000. Although there was a large library quite near to the London school, many families didn't use it. Once we started to operate our school library along

38 See https://www.nhm.ac.uk/take-part/citizen-science/bioblitz.html.
39 See https://www.nationalgeographic.org/projects/bioblitz.
40 See https://www.rspb.org.uk/fun-and-learning/for-teachers/schools-wild-challenge/activities/bioblitz.
41 See https://www.bats.org.uk.
42 See https://www.foylefoundation.org.uk.

professional lines, with a computerised check-in and check-out system, the children became very keen to join the council-run library. This was further helped by regular class visits and story times conducted by one of the librarians. Many children came from households with no books, so it was pleasing to see this new enthusiasm for borrowing. It was a change of culture that fitted with the learning community remit. Having a library also assisted sustainability in the curriculum because it exposed the children to more books about the natural world and aspects of global learning. If you don't have the building space for a library, you could think creatively: one school I know used an old double-decker bus to create their library, another used an old London Tube train carriage and yet another an old aeroplane!

BUILDING ON SUCCESS

As the years passed, our camp school gained a reputation for sustainability activities linked to a creative curriculum and extended services via local and national networks. This bore fruit when the local authority was looking for a few schools to host new sports and arts buildings which could also be used by the community. We put in a bid and were successful, which was a massive boost for the school. As well as having a modern facility which could be used as a theatre space, sports hall and computer suite, it was the first addition to the camp for over 50 years. In some ways, virtue had brought its own rewards. If we hadn't established our reputation through a sustainability ethos, we wouldn't have been offered the building.

In the case of our London school, the solar panels and the grounds developments made a big impact on local authority visitors and school improvement advisors because they helped to show clearly our sense of a sustainability ethos. This was embodied in the strong links to an enriched curriculum, the positive effects on children's behaviour and furtherance of community cohesion, and, yes, our continuing success in terms of test results.

In Nottinghamshire, financial capital became available and we were part of an exciting design-and-build project to replace the camp buildings. Unsurprisingly, this included many eco-features, including low carbon embodied materials and low energy usage. We were able to lobby for these features because we had accumulated sufficient knowledge of them. Knowledge is definitely power in these matters! The building incorporated features to make it as brain-friendly as possible. To further develop ideas, we visited various new-build schools locally and some further afield. One excursion included a visit to the Centre for Alternative Technology in Wales, which showcases innovative buildings and building methods, as well as being a centre for permaculture and running a wide variety of sustainability courses.[43] The full story of our new build can be read on my website.[44] But what of the army camp buildings? We retained them: one to house a new dining hall and the rest developed over time for community use. There was another intriguing reason for keeping them, described in the next chapter, which helped us to further develop pride in the locality.

SECOND SIGHT SITE

In both schools, the campus was ever more influential as we introduced further aspects of sustainable operations. As described throughout this chapter, the campus is a tangible entity and people could see the tremendous learning gains and experience the feel-good factors.

The active support of site and budget managers was crucial. The latter didn't take much convincing, simply because we could save and earn substantial amounts of money. The former, in both schools, were soon brought on board because they became interested in the whole area of sustainability. Rather than seeing extra monitoring and helping the eco-team as a burden, they recognised its importance, and it boosted their professional knowledge and self-esteem. As is the case with other support staff, the role of the site manager can be overlooked by others, when in fact they're often the lynchpins of any successfully functioning school, let alone a sustainable one. Our London site manager organised all health and safety training and the schedule for outside contractors. He worked hand in glove with the budget manager and the catering manager on wide-ranging maintenance and development projects and fully understood the principles behind ethical procurement. He wrote reports for the governing body and helped teachers with various curriculum projects, such as growing vegetables, and he was instrumental in setting up a large composting system. At our Nottinghamshire school, we found that

43 See https://www.cat.org.uk.
44 See https://www.drdaviddixon.earth/the-blogs.html.

the site manager was a skilled craftsperson and utilised his talents for quite sophisticated repairs. For example, he could stop window frames from rotting before they needed to be completely replaced. He could also repair classroom equipment. Keeping on top of maintenance is a sustainability consideration in itself because of the saving of energy and materials which would otherwise be needed if something had deteriorated beyond repair.

Site staff need to be sympathetic when classrooms have pets, such as rabbits or any other wildlife, which are so valuable in the primary classroom. These are much rarer nowadays due to health and safety considerations. However, pets and other animals can be managed without too much bother where there's a will. To enhance the curriculum, we brought in caterpillars to observe the life cycle of butterflies and chicken eggs to hatch.[45]

In our Nottinghamshire school, we went one step further and set up a mini farm with chickens (rescued from battery farms) and pigs (Vietnamese pot-bellied). This was made possible with the efforts of an enthusiastic and skilled teaching assistant. The eggs were used in the school kitchen and we fattened up the pigs for slaughter. The learning from all of this was considerable. Many children with quite profound special needs got particular benefit from interacting with and caring for the animals.

The site managers and their team were also crucial in the development of extended services, whereby the school campuses were used extensively out of hours, including weekends and holidays. This leads us to another C factor: community. The next chapter illustrates how, like the campus, this can be a physical and psychological extension of the school, which, if nurtured, can have very positive effects on children's learning. Once again, a sustainability ethos is shown to be the driving force.

---

45 See https://www.spottygreenfrog.co.uk/Butterfly-Life-Cycle-Sets/c-1-180; https://www. thehappychickcompany.co.uk/chick-hatching-at-schools.

POSTSCRIPT

I've just started to engage with the UN's Climate Neutral Now initiative, which provides an auditing tool for schools and individuals to use to ascertain their overall carbon footprint and a mechanism for offsetting this.[46] Although this has cost implications, schools could raise funds through energy saving or special fundraising events. It would also negate the rebound effect. Once again, this would be a demonstration of a local to global response and has the potential to create carbon-negative schools. For an excellent overview of sustainability options for the campus and links to the curriculum and community, see the DfE's (2012) publication, 'Top tips for sustainability in schools'. Its principles and recommendations are still highly relevant.

LEADERSHIP FOR SUSTAINABILITY RECOMMENDATIONS

- Even modest changes to campus operations to improve sustainability can have a big impact on school stakeholders. Involving them at the planning stage can prove highly effective, whether your development involves a new garden plot or a whole new school.

- If a leader has ambitious sustainability aspirations, it's very important to involve all school stakeholders to show them how they can be a part of the development and, indeed, to actively seek their ideas so that the project is genuinely co-created.

- Retain a holistic approach so that the campus is integral to the overall school improvement plan.

- Success breeds success, especially when applying for funding. Remember that although fundraising can be time-consuming and problematic, there are many funding organisations out there that will support a school with a strong ESD ethos. Look for partners who may help and then share the benefits. Some organisations particularly favour those seeking to develop extended services for the community so that the school campus can become

---

46 See https://unfccc.int/climate-action/climate-neutral-now.

dual-use. Sometimes certain admin staff can be developed as effective fundraisers.

- Even if you are not embarking on a large new-build project, consider how a refit might help finances and sustainability through energy saving. Involve the children so that they can benefit from a learning building.

- Nurture site staff and budget managers by involving them in decisions and CPD, and ascertain if any procurement networks can be used or established.

Chapter 5

COMMUNITY

I have never met a bank note that could sew well or a computer system that could sing a baby to sleep. Let's revalue the people resources we have.

Graham Bell (2004, p. 37)

This chapter outlines how a school can push back the frontiers of social sustainability for the benefit of all, while still keying into the conventional school improvement agenda through developing a learning community. I hark back to times when Ofsted gave greater importance to how schools were engaging with and adding value to their communities. This isn't because of some misplaced nostalgia, but because once again I wish to combat boiled frog syndrome. In the same way as some school leaders have – by default or design – narrowed the curriculum, I feel it's a mistake for schools to retract from engagement with their communities, even though the benefits might only be seen in the longer term and be relatively difficult to measure.

Sadly, it's less favourable these days to see schools as the driving force behind the creation of learning communities. This chapter aims to challenge this and sees sustainability as central to the methodology, practices and outcomes that will benefit the whole community in general and individual learners in particular. Specifically, this chapter looks at how a sustainability ethos helps the causes of early intervention and community enrichment in very practical ways, with the emphasis on tapping into communal strengths, rather than just addressing school-centric perceived weaknesses. Once again, a holistic view is central, guided by systems thinking and the principles of permaculture – and considering how schools can utilise these to good effect. Some people equate permaculture simply to land management, when in fact it can apply to much more than this and taps into the wide gamut of sustainability practice described in previous chapters.

COMMUNITY CARE AND HIDDEN HAZARDS

We should never forget that children spend the vast majority of their waking lives in their homes and locality (according to my calculations, about 78%). Of the 22% of time spent at school, about 66% is learning time directly facilitated by a teacher and 34% is where other learning takes place (i.e. the hidden curriculum). This is why, as described in Chapter 4, the campus needs to be a positive place, both physically and psychologically. The same applies to the community, so if schools can influence this in positive ways, everyone wins.

'School community' can be synonymous with 'school stakeholders', such as staff, parents, children, those in positions of governance (internal and external) and in any associated professional networks. However, I've always viewed 'school community' as meaning any individuals and groups within a school's locality, including religious and secular organisations and businesses.

The circumstances of the community also affect the behaviour, well-being and attitudes of a school's families. This includes the socio-economic factors, but also the positive and negative effects of the human-made and natural environment. Some communities are 'poor' in income but rich in terms of social, cultural and environmental capital. The happiest places to live don't always correspond with how monied they are (Maunder, 2021). These aspects – whether dire, beautiful or something in-between – can be rich sources of learning and activism for the children, and this links to the point about making the known more knowable, as discussed in Chapter 3.

ALL FOR ONE AND ONE FOR ALL?

In relationship terms, it's said that 'those who play together, stay together'. I think that this also applies to communities and wider society – it's an aspect of social cohesion, which itself is a prerequisite of sustainable schools and communities. On a practical level, if we all use the same facilities (schools, hospitals, sports centres, libraries, parks, etc.), the most influential of us will lobby for them to be the best they can be. If the more powerful, influential people in society opt out of communal facilities for private or exclusive options, the reverse happens. Our individualistic culture has decimated many aspects of social cohesion. In the absence of established religion, schools can be the last refuges of cohesion and, therefore, are in a unique position to strengthen it for the good of all. Where community cohesion is good, schools can tap into it for mutual benefit through sharing facilities and benefitting from volunteers' efforts – for example, in fundraising, listening to children read, leading gardening projects and so on.

In the UK, there have been various attempts to upscale the successful practice of community-orientated schools and associated education, leisure, social and health services, which has an antecedence in the 1920s (Bird, n.d.). You can look even further back for innovations pioneered by Victorian Quaker industrialists such as Fry, Cadbury and Owen (Angell and Dandelion, 2013) and, in particular, the non-conformist Titus Salt, whom I studied at college.[1] I mention this because it's another example of how my background influenced my desire to develop community links and services.

LEARNING COMMUNITY LEGACY

In Chapter 4, I said that we wanted a learning building rather than just a building of learning. This meant seeing the fabric, layout and operations as opportunities for children and parents to learn about aspects of sustainability by experiencing them at first hand. It wasn't merely creating an empty shell inhabited by teachers who each day would receive children to teach. In a similar vein, a learning community: 'Provide[s] a space and a structure for people to align around a shared goal.

---

1   Salt built a 'model community', Saltaire, near Bradford. See https://saltairevillage.info.

Effective communities are both aspirational and practical. They connect people, organizations, and systems that are eager to learn and work across boundaries.'[2]

There are many and varied definitions of what constitutes a learning community, but I like this one because it describes an ecosystem of learning. The sustainable school can facilitate this and, in turn, be nurtured by it in the same way as a coral reef facilitates and is nurtured by its highly diverse inhabitants. It shouldn't just be a one-way transfer of education, with the school seeing itself as an ivory tower of 'superior' knowing. Yes, the school should provide the professional educators, but they would perceive themselves as part of a wider community rather than being *apart* from it. The only health warning here lies in the word 'progress'. Obviously, for a sustainable community and school, this wouldn't be predicated on economic growth.

By valuing and participating in all these community elements, the school can enrich the learning experiences of all and make a positive contribution to the social fabric with which it interacts. This in itself can send messages much further afield through various types of social and mass media. An example of this might be a school campaigning to save local trees which are due to be felled. Children can take a prominent role in these campaigns, alongside their parents and the school. This sort of real-life experience can be linked to the curriculum in terms of speaking and listening (including formal debates about the merits or otherwise of tree felling), writing campaign materials (posters, blogs, etc.) and researching the scientific and aesthetic value of trees. So, this last sentence has contained elements of English, maths, science, health education, geography, history and IT. It has also included valuable SMSC and offered a contribution to the health and welfare of the locality. The most important thing is that the children are shown that they can make a difference and don't have to accept the status quo. This is 'activism' defined as 'the policy or action of using vigorous campaigning to bring about political or social change'.[3] (See again the discussion on ESD 1 and ESD 2 on page 81.) Schools can swerve political ramifications and complications if they avoid affiliation with certain pressure groups. For example, although I might have personal sympathies with Extinction Rebellion, I would never allow them any involvement in a school environmental campaign.

---

2   See https://developingchild.harvard.edu/collective-change/key-concepts/learning-communities.

3   Oxford University Press, activism, *Lexico.com* (2021). Available at: https://www.lexico.com/definition/activism.

An example of a local to global piece of activism occurred when, as described earlier, our London school contributed to a video which was part of the Keep It in the Ground Campaign, aimed at persuading Bill Gates to disinvest from fossil fuel companies. Rather ominously, however, Gates thinks that divestment is a 'waste of time', as is the 'theory of change' which underpins it (Edgecliffe-Johnson and Nauman, 2019). In his latest book, *How to Avoid a Climate Disaster*, Gates (2021) details how he thinks that hi-tech solutions will solve our environmental woes, which underplays the role of behaviour change as highlighted by Whitelegg (personal communication, 2021). Activists point out that divestment was developed to combat the apartheid system in South Africa and, although we can't know for certain that there is a cause-and-effect relationship between divestment and the demise of segregation, it helped to remove the social licence to operate it. This is a valuable concept to apply to many behaviours which damage the environment. For example, it's becoming less socially acceptable to use single-use plastic or fly short-haul.[4]

VILLAGE PEOPLE

Before compulsory schooling and national imperatives were established, schools were originally set up to cater for the direct needs of their local communities and were responsive to changing needs over time. We can still see the legacy of this in England and Wales, the most obvious being the six-week summer holiday when, historically, children were needed to assist in bringing in the harvest. Up until the 1960s, it was common for most teachers to live nearby, and in country areas a head teacher's house was often built as part of the school. Although this would be largely unthinkable today, those school staff would have first-hand knowledge of their community because they were part of it. I would advise any new head teacher to do detailed research on their school's locality, not just via present-day socio-economic data loaded onto the school's online dashboard, but the history of how and why it is as it is. It's also important to talk to local people from all walks of life, otherwise school professionals can commute in every day and not really get a handle on how a community ticks and, by extension, not be fully cognisant of the social context of parents and children.

---

4   For accounts of flying shame, see https://www.airportwatch.org.uk.

An example of a schism between staff and community culture occurred in our Nottinghamshire school, which served many Travellers. A precocious child arrived in school with a bloodied dead rabbit in a plastic bag and, unannounced, showed it to his teacher, who nearly fainted. He was sent to me for being 'naughty' (as he had been on many other occasions). It transpired that he'd brought in the rabbit for show-and-tell because he was proud that he'd caught it with the help of a ferret. The teacher thought he'd brought it in for devilment. There are many less obvious examples which professionals need to look out for, including how they might be perceived as aloof and judgemental rather than caring. This illustrates the hidden curriculum point again and highlights possible gaps between the culture of schools and their clientele.

Localism itself links to sustainability via the historic notion of the commons. This is a fascinating area to explore because, once again, it shows a shifting baseline which explains many of today's socio-economic and environmental difficulties and conflicts.[5] Localism itself isn't just a matter of parochial solutions remaining at a small and insignificant scale within the greater scheme of things. With today's social media, projects and protests can easily go viral and gain wider audiences and, ultimately, influence decision makers at all levels. Schoolgirl Greta Thunberg's contribution to the climate change movement is a great example of this. The Keep It in the Ground campaign is another case in point.

All this fits with the maxim that 'it takes a village to raise a child', which has its origin as a proverb in the Igbo and Yoruba languages and is present in slightly different forms across Africa (Reference, 2020). It's now known worldwide and alludes to the importance of extended families and kinship, rather than the pursuance of individualistic lifestyles. It links to another proverb that 'the village is the policeman', which stresses that everyone is responsible for good moral standards and behaviour in the community.

In this light, a sustainable school in a deprived area can encourage people to become more aspirational and to value education more highly. A school in a more prosperous area can encourage people to question consumptive lifestyles and selfish individualism and to have a greater appreciation for a school's less easily measurable outcomes. It can also encourage empathy for people in less

5   Guy Standing's (2019) book *Plunder of the Commons* documents how, from the Norman Conquest (1066) onwards, the population in the UK has been systematically relieved of many rights to access land and resources. He cites examples including the Enclosure Acts, clearances of the Scottish Highlands, privatisation of state industries (linked to neoliberalism) and intellectual copyrighting. For a global perspective, see Fred Pearce's (2012) *The Land Grabbers*.

advantaged circumstances at home and abroad. In most schools a balanced mixture of these messages is needed.

COMMUNITY STAKE

This section aims to show how an embedded sustainability ethos can make a positive contribution to the life chances of children when added to conventional early intervention initiatives. My first example features the Sure Start network of Children's Centres for families with children aged up to 5 years, set up in England in 1999. These were established in tandem with the extended schools initiative for school-aged children, which offered after-school and holiday activities 48 weeks a year. These activities included a wide range of sports, arts, IT and study support activities, organised by schools and delivered by school staff and outside providers. Often, breakfast and dinner clubs were included to assist with parents' childcare requirements.

Both Children's Centres and extended schools were part of a broader scheme known as Every Child Matters. This was instigated by a Labour government in response to several high-profile child deaths, which caused scandals when various dysfunctional state services were found to be partially at fault. Every Child Matters covered five main areas, encompassing child development and family support:

- **being healthy:** enjoying good physical health and living a healthy lifestyle

- **staying safe:** being protected from harm and neglect and growing up able to look after themselves

- **enjoying and achieving:** getting the most out of life and developing broad skills for adulthood

- **making a positive contribution:** to the community and to society and not engaging in anti-social or offending behaviour

- **economic well-being:** overcoming socio-economic disadvantages to achieve their full potential. HM Treasury (2003, p. 14)

Every Child Matters is a fine example of some holistic thinking – albeit rather limited in scope and relatively short-lived – as it endorsed an approach which looked at practical support for communities through improving the lot of families. Early intervention through Children's Centres and primary schools can prevent more costly interventions as children get older, particularly if they suffer from adverse childhood experiences (ACEs) and the resultant intergenerational baton-passing associated with varying degrees of physical and psychological neglect, abuse and trauma (see Figure 5.1). The so-called 'toxic trio' – of mental health issues, parental substance abuse and domestic abuse – compromises a child's chances to thrive and is recognised by various agencies in England (see Children's Commissioner, 2018a, 2018b).

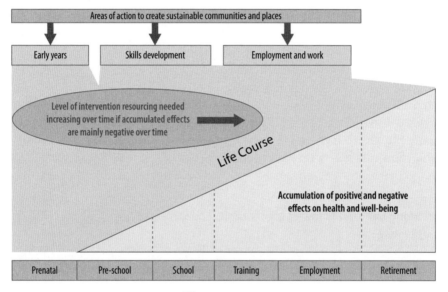

Life course stages

Figure 5.1: Early intervention and added value

LESSONS FROM WALES: JOINED-UP APPROACHES

The Welsh government has been at the forefront of recognising ACEs and looking at ways of countering them through multi-agency approaches. It commissioned a wide-ranging study of ACEs, showing their adverse effects. Here is a selection of the report's headline figures:

Compared with people with no ACEs, those with 4+ ACEs are:

4 times more likely to be high-risk drinkers

6 times more likely to smoke e-cigarettes or tobacco

15 times more likely to have committed violence against another person in the last 12 months

16 times more likely to have used crack cocaine or heroin

20 times more likely to have been incarcerated at any point in their lifetime

Preventing ACEs in future generations could reduce levels of:

High-risk drinking (current) by 35%,

Smoking tobacco or e-cigarettes (current) by 24%

Violence perpetration (past year) by 60%

Heroin/Crack cocaine use (lifetime) by 66%

Incarceration (lifetime) by 65%

(Bellis et al., 2015, p. 5)

This sort of study is highly significant because it's actively seeking to be a catalyst for altering the environmental, social and economic conditions which are putting future lives in jeopardy. In other words, making communities and society as a whole more sustainable.

MORE LESSONS FROM WALES

In 2015, the Welsh devolved government brought in the Well-being of Future Generations (Wales) Act (see Figure 5.2). For the first time, this legislation explicitly linked overall personal well-being with environmental sustainability and the expectation that this would be a thread running through the rest of governance and of social and economic activities. In effect, this means that 44 government bodies, including education, must work towards seven common goals, and these are used as reference points for all other law and decision making.

1 A globally responsible Wales

2 A prosperous Wales

3 A resilient Wales

4 A healthy Wales

5 A more equal Wales

6 A Wales of cohesive communities

7 A Wales of vibrant culture and thriving Welsh language

The public bodies must work on all of the goals not just one or two.

Figure 5.2: Seven goals for Welsh society

Source: **Welsh Government (2019), p. 6**

In 2016, Wales also created a government post entitled future generations commissioner, dubbed minister 'to represent the yet unborn' (Balch, 2019). This was to consolidate the aforementioned Act, making sure that all public bodies made decisions today that don't compromise the Welsh citizens of tomorrow. Haines (2019) reported that the then UN head of sustainable development said: 'We hope that what Wales is doing today, the world will do tomorrow.' The new minister, Sophie Howe, said: 'there is a recognition dawning that the way we have been doing things across the world is no longer fit for purpose – it is damaging the planet and people. I'm proud of what Wales has done' (quoted in Haines, 2019). Wales also created a ministry for climate change in May 2021 (Welsh Government, 2021).

To put it in perspective, Wales could fit into the area of the United States over 400 times, so all this is a minute contribution to global sustainability, and the jury is still out in terms of what impact it's really making. However, it's an example of impressive ecological (joined-up) thinking, which should be applauded and replicated in all walks of life. Hopefully, it will live up to the hype and cause butterfly effects.[6]

UNSURE OUTCOMES

Although Sure Start and associated Children's Centres greatly helped families, it was very much part of the business-as-usual model. This assumed that the work of centres and schools would boost the income and lessen the dysfunction of families, allowing them to add to the overall GDP growth of the economy. Worthy aims, you might think – yes, but not sustainable as defined by this book, being too limited in scope and not sufficiently holistic.

An injection of sustainability into this early intervention mix, providing added value, was highlighted by an extensive European study of early childhood education for sustainability (ECEfS) which concluded that 'it is within ... early years that children present the greatest ability to learn and develop. ECEfS has the potential to foster socio-environmental resilience based on interdependence and critical thinking' (cited by Davies et al., 2009, p. 113).

This fits with good quality early years practice if it incorporates interaction with nature and forest school methodology. It's also a feature of Montessori education.

SON OF EVERY CHILD MATTERS

The *Every Child's Future Matters* report by the Sustainable Development Commission (2010) set out very clearly what additional factors needed to be considered by Every Child Matters and what different perspectives could be employed. A central theme

6 It makes me think of the 1959 film *The Mouse That Roared*, based on the book of the same name by Leonard Wibberley, in which the Duchy of Grand Fenwick declares war on the United States in order to lose and claim foreign aid. They arrive during a nuclear drill and think they've won! Let's hope Wales really does make a global difference.

of the report was the importance of having connections with the natural world, which has the potential to promote robust physical health and mental well-being.

I include some examples of how *Every Child's Future Matters* displayed far more joined-up and expansive thinking than Every Child Matters using the same categories. It just shows what a difference a sustainability perspective has when compared to a largely economic perspective. You can also see how far ahead of its time it was, when looking at issues such as air quality.

Every Child's Future Matters backed up its arguments with references to extensive bodies of research which, although now dated, pre-empted research being done today showing similar results – in particular, the beneficial effects of the natural world on health and well-being. It's ironic that, as part of a 2021 draft strategy for sustainability and climate change (launched at COP26), the DfE called for research into this again to supposedly create 'biophilic' primary schools (Department for Education, 2021, p. 19). They just need to read *Every Child's Future Matters*!

- **Being healthy.** Need to improve air quality. How can children be healthy if they are exposed to air pollution? 'Good parenting' needs to include encouraging children to walk and cycle. Access to green space encourages physical exercise and recovery from mental fatigue and stress.

- **Staying safe.** Need to reduce the hazards of road traffic, which cause many injuries and deaths and lead to many parents in urban settings not letting their children play outside (this links to the green space point above). Green space tends to reduce aggression and violence in neighbourhoods. There is continued evidence for this – for example, Shepley et al. (2019) looked at 40 studies which showed the positive impact of the natural world on aggressive behaviour and associated crime.

- **Enjoying and achieving.** Low-quality environments impact negatively on children's ability to enjoy and achieve. This can include too much noise from road and air traffic. The report quoted studies which suggested that 11-year-olds who were exposed to a consistent level of background noise of 72 decibels did worse in national tests. Enjoyment was also curtailed, whereas it was enhanced when children played in natural surroundings. In fact, they were more likely to play vigorously and better develop their fitness and motor skills.

- **Making a positive contribution.** Once again, playing in natural settings was key. On the basis of 2,000 interviews with urban adults aged between 18 and 90, it was found that playing in natural areas as a child made a significant contribution to knowledge about the environment and led to positive attitudes and behaviours in adulthood. Also, when asked, children have well-formed opinions about the environment and how they would like to improve it. Schools are in an ideal position to harness this through the development of community-based projects – for example, litter picking or creating a community garden.

- **Economic well-being.** *Every Child's Future Matters* highlighted the need for an end to the linear economy, which would limit the future opportunities of today's children, with more emphasis placed on developing new goods, services and markets which wouldn't damage the biosphere. The report cited information from the Stern Review (2006), which warned that climate change 'could lead to a 20% contraction of the global economy, reducing everyone's prosperity and creating mass migrations and catastrophes' (Sustainable Development Commission, 2010, p. 20). In 2021, Nicholas Stern said this situation was even more serious and being compounded by COVID-19 (Stern, 2021, p. 12). Once again, the Sustainable Development Commission advocated more outside exercise and contact with nature to counteract obesity, hyperactivity, poor self-discipline and low concentration, all of which would impact on children's ability to learn and to score well in tests and, ultimately, badly affect their life chances.

Every Child's Future Matters quoted a UNICEF report which could find no obvious relationship between child well-being and national GDP per capita: 'Caution is needed to ensure that national economic growth – by itself – is not assumed to improve children's lives' (Sustainable Development Commission, 2010, p. 21). The assumption that the richer you are, the happier you are has been convincingly challenged by many eminent academics.[7]

Every Child's Future Matters was intended to augment the then government's aim to make every school a sustainable school by 2020, but in practice this didn't happen – not even remotely close. The initiative, launched by the publication of the first

---

7   Layard and Ward (2020) showed that there were diminishing returns over a certain level of comfort. The Children's Society (2018) came to the same conclusion, specifically in the case of child well-being. This is reinforced by Kallis et al. (2018), who advocate the 'degrowth' agenda, leading to a transition to an economy that is smaller and more equitable without diminished well-being and happiness.

edition of the report in 2007, was sidelined and discarded when a new government came to office in 2010.

You have to conclude that if only the recommendations of *Every Child's Future Matters* had been heeded, many of today's escalating societal ills would have been tackled and alleviated in a more holistic way. (These ills are starkly highlighted in the Marmot Review (2010) and its follow-up in 2020.[8])

THE SHOW GOES ON

Despite recent government ambivalence to Every Child Matters and total disregard for *Every Child's Future Matters*, I saw both initiatives as integral to our holistic school improvement strategy, as Figure 5.3 illustrates. Once again this shows that there are no silver bullets.

It underpinned our curriculum and welfare initiatives and helped us to push against the glass ceiling of attainment which can be caused by teaching to the test. I used the diagram when explaining my overall strategy to school governors and inspectors.

Up to 2010, Ofsted explicitly judged how well schools promoted 'community cohesion', before this was removed in the next iteration of the inspection criteria. In effect, this narrowed Ofsted's remit and devalued the role schools might play in community improvement. Some, me included, thought that this was a lost opportunity for schools to prove the value-added element of their activities beyond the classroom. Shepherd (2010) quoted David Blunkett, Tony Blair's former education secretary, as saying that abolishing the requirement was a 'deeply retrograde step'. Blunkett went on to say: 'An emphasis on community cohesion in schools enables pupils to understand the differences between cultures and backgrounds. It also demonstrated the role of schools as key drivers of functioning, safe and vibrant neighbourhoods.'

----

8   Marmot et al. (2020) is a shocking read, showing the devastating effects of poverty in the UK today.

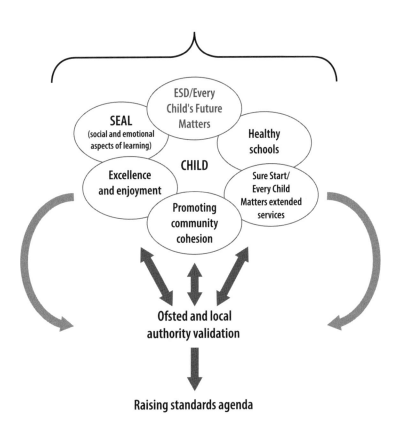

Figure 5.3: Joined-up strategies

Just because Ofsted accountability disappeared, I and like-minded head teachers did not disown the community development imperative (Ofsted also stopped inspecting Children's Centres in 2017). Our values dictated that if these activities were contributing to improving the life chances of our children, they were not about to be jettisoned just because Ofsted weren't going to judge them overtly. Furthermore, you don't have to delve into detailed research to conclude that children who are unfit, hungry, upset and ill-slept will not learn very well. If schools address these basic needs, then who can argue? Having said that, without the Ofsted mandate we had more difficulty in justifying our strategies and could more easily be accused of taking our eyes off the attainment ball.

SWIMMING WITH THE TIDE CONTINUED

Although community cohesion is no longer mentioned explicitly, there are elements of it in various other sections of more recent Ofsted frameworks, notably within SMSC education. Anecdotal evidence suggests that Ofsted teams still show appreciation for work that schools do in this area, if there's proof that it's making a positive contribution to overall standards. Ofsted also appreciate evidence of schools improving the 'cultural capital' of their pupils. This includes the development of critical thinking, being introduced to the influential ideas of others and an overall appreciation of human achievement. What's not to like here, as the only way to achieve this is through a vibrant and enriched curriculum as described in this book. Of course, human achievement can be a two-edged sword if it depends upon unsustainable practices and needs to be critiqued as well as celebrated.

In Chapter 3, we explored utilising statutory measures (in this case RSE) for the sustainability cause. Another example springs to mind here in the form of the government's desire to promote fundamental British values.

Fundamental British values was part of the Prevent strategy (Home Office, 2021 [2015]), which was designed to stop the radicalisation of young people and avoid possible terrorism further down the line. Instilling fundamental British values inferred that there was something *special* about British values that needed to be actively promoted in schools. The same comment I made regarding RSE applies here. There's no point spending time arguing about the merits of these statutory requirements; instead, they can be used as a justification for a school being actively involved in its community via a sustainability ethos. In Chapter 3, we saw how SMSC could be delivered through sustainability in the context of global learning. The fundamental British values agenda can also be utilised in a similar way.

According to the government, there are five fundamental British values, namely: 'democracy, the rule of law, individual liberty, mutual respect and tolerance of those of different faiths and beliefs' (Department for Education, 2014, p. 5). You can quibble about whether there is anything innately 'British' about these principles, and you might suggest that we should go beyond 'tolerance', as this implies putting up with rather than offering unconditional regard. Be that as it may, Ofsted actively look at how fundamental British values are being addressed, so schools that are highly tuned to their communities are likely to do well from this judgement without too much contrivance. (However, I once observed a school that simply put up a British values display – featuring red London buses and postboxes – and had an annual tea party and thought they'd got it covered.)

More interesting than the values themselves are the 'skills and knowledge' that the government guidance suggests should be developed. An example given is: 'include in suitable parts of the curriculum, as appropriate for the age of pupils, material on the strengths, advantages and disadvantages of democracy, and how democracy and the law works in Britain, in contrast to other forms of government in other countries' (Department for Education, 2014, p. 6). If these are addressed through a lens of sustainability values, then who can argue? This could include how sometimes protest is needed to encourage parliament to change laws or introduce new ones that further protect the environment. For example, shouldn't all countries prohibit ecocide? So, there is much room for the use of debate and other forms of pupil voice in order to deliver what the government wants. As shown earlier, a really effective school council can show the democratic process working for the common good.

Another interesting point in relation to fundamental British values is the expectation that they are linked to the Teachers' Standards. As government guidance puts it: 'The Teachers' Standards expect teachers to uphold public trust in the profession and maintain high standards of ethics and behaviour, within and outside school. This includes not undermining fundamental British values' (Department for Education, 2014, p. 5). Although this could be construed as doctrinaire, why not take it at face value and utilise it as a justification for helping to save the planet? I can't think of any worthier or more ethical professional action! The UN Convention on the Rights of the Child[9] and position on environmental rights also links to this professional stance. The UN makes the pertinent point: 'Human rights and the environment are intertwined; human rights cannot be enjoyed without a safe, clean and healthy environment; and sustainable environmental governance cannot exist without the establishment of and respect for human rights.'[10]

CHILDREN CENTRED

As my last two schools had Children's Centres, we were able to integrate these with our extended services. This meant that we were in close touch with many children from before they were even born to when they left us at 11 years old (this sort of all-encompassing provision was typical in areas of particular disadvantage). What follows is a list of our service provision. Notice how many Children's Centre services have direct links to sustainability:

- A wide variety of antenatal and postnatal services in partnership with the health service.

- Distributing food tokens and running a weekly market stall with affordable local fruit and vegetables.

- Basic skills adult education – for example, IT, cooking on a budget, energy awareness to help alleviate fuel poverty, gardening, driving test theory, first aid.

- Citizens Advice Bureau sessions (for advice on debt and other money problems).

- Family/individual therapy sessions.

- Toy and book library.

- Stay and play activities.

- Adult bicycle training.

- Family outings to the seaside.

---

9 See https://www.unicef.org/child-rights-convention/convention-text-childrens-version.
10 See https://www.unep.org/explore-topics/environmental-rights-and-governance/what-we-do/
   advancing-environmental-rights/what.

- Family gardening club.

- Sports and arts after-school and holiday programmes.

- Homework clubs, including access to IT facilities.

- Holiday play schemes and family outings.

- Subsidised breakfasts and evening meals as part of wrap-around care and for those children who lacked sufficient nutrition, particularly in the morning.

- Counselling services for children, parents and staff.

The school and Children's Centre websites and social media presence were used to good effect to keep parents and carers up to date with this and many other aspects of school and community life. Most schools have highly effective communication systems, which can be easily adapted to show sustainability in action across the curriculum and campus, and can also be deployed at home.

MEANINGFUL MEASUREMENT

To help us plan, evaluate and justify the extracurricular provision for 5–11-year-olds, we used the Quality in Study Support and Extended Services framework and accreditation administered through Canterbury Christchurch University.[11] Incidentally, this university has an embedded sustainability ethos and a faculty of education which, unlike many others, actively includes ESD as part of teacher training. This helped us to show Ofsted that we were providing good value for money, particularly in relation to pupil premium funding.

We also had a close partnership with the local authority's adult and child social care services. The effective work of the Children's Centre family support workers meant that many families avoided full-blown intervention from social services, which saved a lot of money but, more importantly, prevented family breakdown. To create more adult learning role models, periodically we would have a grand presentation ceremony as part of an assembly to give parents various certificates of achievement. This had a very positive impact on children and parents because it was an intergenerational celebration of learning success.

11 See https://shop.canterbury.ac.uk/product-catalogue/faculty-of-education/department-of-professional-development/qiss-online-action-planning-tool.

To promote the intergenerational dimension further, our Nottinghamshire school's catering department offered lunches for senior citizens two days a week, which were served by some of the older children. Our school choir went to care homes and sang for them. We established a school radio station that produced news podcasts based on stories from the local press and child newsgatherers. They were edited and read by senior citizens and accessed online.

ENERGISED COMMUNITY

Following discussions with other local head teachers, we formed what we called a 'learning community', which consisted of three schools and a Children's Centre, with additional partners from the local authority housing department, local special needs provision, local church, the aforementioned Energy Agency and a national organisation called the Greening Campaign.[12] After drawing up a charter for partnership (see Appendix 7), we embarked on various projects, one of which aimed to:

- Introduce energy awareness education.

- Help to address fuel poverty (defined as where more than 10% of income is spent on energy).

- Enrich the ESD curriculum and further raise its profile.

- Consolidate and improve partnership working between the learning community and other outside agencies and community groups.

- Deliver these aims through the Greening Campaign initiative.

- Influence the behaviour of 1,000 households.

The Greening Campaign initiative was designed to be an effective community response to global heating. It aimed to show everyone that they could gain significant personal benefit through small, inexpensive actions, which cumulatively made a significant difference at a community level. It was designed to be fun, inclusive and very simple, so that it wasn't too much of a challenge for individuals to cross the barrier from being not interested in tackling climate change to visualising themselves as being green.

12 See https://www.greening-campaign.org.

The project was launched at the local pub. This made an outreach statement in itself because the establishment concerned was often viewed as a den of iniquity to be avoided at all costs. We also used this particular pub for our annual school sports presentation evening. A free buffet was provided – of food from sustainable sources – and this alone attracted a large crowd of all ages. Attendees selected three challenges from a list, which would be marketed to others in the local community in the hope that they would also adopt these behaviours. The scheme was marketed further, and many other activities occurred within a three-stage process (the scheme today has four). This culminated in participants displaying a card with the Greening Campaign logo in their front windows. An adapted list of energy-saving behaviours is shown in Figure 5.4. It can also be extended to other appliances and water savings.

The Greening Campaign founder Terena Plowright (personal communication, 2021) said: 'the greening campaign is a method of gaining community action, and ownership of the campaign is vital to the success – thus the programme of activities they suggest is crucial. Just delivering the cards will not be enough for behaviour change'.

	Small action savings	Annual money saving	Annual CO2 saving
1.	Turn off lights when you leave a room	£4.80	6 kg
2.	Turn off all stand-bys	£124	155 kg
3.	Wash laundry at 30 degrees C	£29	36 kg
4.	Walk if journey is less than one mile one day a week rather than use a petrol or diesel car	£2.50	112 kg
5.	Boil only amount of water needed	£18	22 kg
6.	Turn thermostat down by 1 degree C	£215	268 kg
7.	Heat hot water tank at 60 degrees	£32	40 kg
8.	Put lids on saucepans	£28	38 kg

Figure 5.4: Greening actions

Source: **adapted from our original Greening Campaign (with 2020 updated figures)**[13]

13 See http://www.greening-campaign.org.

Notice how the car is cheap in money but costly in CO2. Also, despite renewables being a significant generator of electricity, in 2020, gas still produced 36% of it in the UK.[14]

After a few weeks, we counted up the displayed cards, enabling us to roughly calculate how much money and carbon had been saved (because everyone was doing the same challenges). This was a version of the long-established Carbon Reduction Action Group used in Energy Transition Communities. One school that served a high-income area came up with a challenge that encouraged families to reduce their energy consumption to 100 kWh a week. The families involved were very competitive, as befitted their image of being high-flying professionals. There are a growing number of organisations which use this pledge format to instigate behaviour change for environmental and community benefit.[15] Celebrating the WWF Earth Hour each March is another way of gently introducing a community approach to energy saving. During a particular hour, people are requested to switch off all non-vital electrical items.[16] Earth Day on 22 April has a wider remit, and there are many linked education resources which might also be of interest to parents.[17] Anything to improve general eco-literacy is to be welcomed.

In our London school, we partnered with a local cooperative company called South East London Community Energy (SELCE).[18] They issued shares, the income from which was used to install solar panels on schools and commercial buildings. The resulting profit from renewable generation was used to help alleviate fuel poverty and to give shareholders a yield of 3–5% per annum. As described in Chapter 4, this produced income for the school, but, just as importantly, it showcased renewable energy to the children and helped fund SELCE to train community energy champions, who then helped others to access lower-cost utilities and to take energy-saving measures. SELCE also helped families with problems such as damp walls and recalcitrant landlords. It's well worth looking for schemes like this run by not-for-profit organisations. Although due diligence is needed, the major burden of a project is taken off the hard-pressed school leader.

Fuel poverty is but one challenge facing disadvantaged families which can adversely affect children coming into school. Another is the digital divide, which still afflicts many (Office for National Statistics, 2019). The Office for National

14 See https://www.jagtapenergy.co.uk/post/uk-s-electricity-generation-mix-for-2020.
15 See https://www.wearedonation.com.
16 See https://www.earthhour.org.
17 See https://www.earthday.org.
18 See https://gcda.coop/selce.

Statistics highlighted the link between this issue and many of the SDGs because it leaves millions of people out of the global loop in terms of communication and access to new technology. In our Nottinghamshire school, in partnership with Microsoft, we set up an e-learning foundation to help supply laptops to families. This was embraced nationally and is now administered through the Birmingham e-Learning Foundation.[19]

All these school–community links combatted what might be termed 'toxic localism', which can include hostility to outsiders, insular attitudes that harbour racism and other forms of intolerance, anti-social behaviour and various kinds of abuse and dysfunction within isolated families. They show that a school can reach out and help its locality in very down-to-earth and practical ways, breaking down barriers of communication and perception. Not only can this approach help to address basic needs, but it can also be a gateway for discussions and collaborations when it comes to helping children to learn at home and at school. Very often 'help your child learn' workshops will have little take-up if relationships between home and school haven't been nurtured in some other shape or form. Enabling families to become more economically yet environmentally sustainable can greatly help this cause.

PERMACULTURE PERSPECTIVES

A way of taking community sustainability even further can be through permaculture methodology. This is a way of thinking and living which incorporates modern life and technology *with* natural systems (see Figure 5.5 on page 172).

Notice that it says there should be 'minimal effort for maximum yield' and the potential for greater educational, social and leisure benefits. Permaculture shouldn't be a painful exercise in abstinence; it can deliver social benefits, enjoyment and fun leisure pursuits which have longer lasting and more fulfilling effects on participants, without having to buy endless amounts of stuff or expensive 'experiences'.

---

19 See https://www.belf.org.uk.

Figure 5.5: Overview of permaculture

Source: **Graham Burnett,**[20] **used with permission**

20 See https://spiralseed.co.uk.

The name 'permaculture' can be misconstrued in that it can be interpreted as the melding of 'permanent' and 'culture', implying a static state. Macnamara (2020, p. 46) offers a useful clarification by saying that permaculture shouldn't be seen as an 'idyllic goal' but as an 'ongoing journey'. I've made the same point regarding the development of a sustainable school. This incorporates 'cultural shifts and emerging new cultures' (Macnamara, 2020, p. 46). She envisages a journey towards fertile, positive and 'regenerative possibilities' and describes three areas of 'regenerative culture' which together create a 'Cultural Emergence' (Macnamara, 2020, p. 46) that is fit for purpose in our challenging times. I paraphrase them here and they all apply directly to sustainable schools. (Notice the similarities between this and the I, we, planet model described in Chapter 3.)

1   **Culture of personal leadership:** this emphasises the need for personal responsibility and the potential for individual actions to make a difference. It requires a constant appraisal of values and a check to see if they align with our thinking and behaviours.

2   **Culture of collective intelligence:** requires that conditions are created which 'encourage individual and collective genius to shine' (Macnamara, 2020, p. 46), so that new narratives for sustainability can emerge.

3   **Culture of planetary care:** having a global perspective on and knowledge about how we as a species are collectively perpetrating ecocide and how we can 'proactively be caring for the fundamental resources of life: namely, water, trees, soil and biodiversity' (Macnamara, 2020, p. 46).

Interlaced with these three aspects, she stresses the importance of an 'Awareness of Culture' (Macnamara, 2020, p. 46) – that is, how our culture individually and collectively ticks so that, where necessary, we can instigate change. She points out that culture is 'a complex, dynamic web of seen and unseen patterns of thinking, feeling, behaving and interacting' (Macnamara, 2020, p. 46). This illustrates that cultural systems are just as complex as ecosystems. It's a vital aspect of ecological intelligence that was discussed in Chapter 2. Without an understanding of prevailing cultures, leaders for sustainability (or any leaders, for that matter) are missing an important trick.

This is yet another way of conceptualising the need for new paradigms of thought and action. These are essential elements of the values-led leader for sustainability models featured in Chapter 2. It moves us from a toxic culture to a nurturing culture which has the resilience and wherewithal to provide a 'good life' for all, now and into the far-distant future. Permaculture shows that it's possible to re-establish ties with nature, which enhance sustainability, rather than degrade it. Ultimately, this creates harmony between all things – living and non-living – needed for a stable and nurturing biosphere and keys into the concept of Gaia, described in Chapter 1.

The reason why I find permaculture to be increasingly relevant to schools is because it harnesses spiritual, ethical and practical elements under one umbrella. It can bamboozle with deep thinking and radical theorising if you want to go down that road, but it also provides a straightforward basis for practical action.[21]

TRANSITION TAKES

A long-standing form of sustainable community is embodied in the transition town and more recent climate action movements. Schools are often part of these initiatives.[22] Rob Hopkins founded the Transition Network in the UK, which is based upon permaculture principles.[23] In his book he says that a central concept is: 'resilience – familiar to ecologists [and] refers to the ability of a system, from individual people to whole economies to hold together and maintain their ability to function in the face of change and shocks from the outside' (Hopkins, 2009, p. 12). This requires not only local security of food and other resources needed for daily living,[24] but, crucially, social cohesion which can withstand adverse changes. Hopkins (2020) sees its relevance to businesses, but all the transition processes he describes can be applied to sustainable schools and how they respond to the needs of their communities.

There are also many big thinkers in the permaculture movement who look beyond the local, while at the same time promoting local solutions. One such person, Starhawk (2016, p. 7), says:

---

21 See David Holmgrem's useful overview of permaculture in practice at: https://www.holmgren.com.au.
22 South Shropshire Climate Action includes schools and colleges in its strategy for change. See https://southshropshireclimateaction.org. See also https://www.dacorum.gov.uk/home/environment-street-care/climate-change/climate-action-network, https://friendsoftheearth.uk/about/climate-action-groups and https://climatenetwork.org.
23 See https://transitionnetwork.org.
24 For more on food security, see https://www.foodsecurity.ac.uk/challenge. Just-in-time supply chains make the UK particularly vulnerable to disruption; perhaps we really are nine meals away from anarchy!

The struggle for social justice is an integral part of permaculture, inseparable from our core ethics of earth care, people care and fair share. We can't effectively care for ecological or human communities unless we address the structures of power that enforce destructive patterns. We must be willing to confront the realities of racism, sexism, classism, heterosexism, ableism, ageism and all other isms that constrain us.

This perspective is needed because most people can't escape to a rural idyll to live in a sustainable way. It echoes the messages of this book, which call for linked thinking across subject disciplines and social and cultural divides. Starhawk also makes the point that diversity is strength, whether it's applied to a woodland or a human community, including a school community. Barkham (2020), interviewing Rob Hopkins, quotes him as saying: 'we are all "frogs in the boiling pan of imaginative decline" and we can and must leap free'. This links to the point made in Chapter 3 about encouraging children to have a creative and optimistic outlook for the future.

You can see that schools have a great opportunity to use and, in turn, contribute to the permaculture approach to sustainability – if their leaders can take that leap. At least they can see that at a local level they will be swimming with the tide. As Hopkins says:

I've never been anywhere where anybody has said: ... 'I was doing all right until I learned to grow my own food.' We are social creatures living in a time that is trying to stop us from being that. There's something good for the heart about being involved in projects with other people. (quoted in Barkham, 2020)

EMBEDDING SOCIAL SUSTAINABILITY: A CASE IN POINT

Our London school catered for children from many nationalities, over 60% of whom had English as an additional language. They also practised a range of religions, the main ones being various forms of Islam and Christianity. When I first arrived, it seemed that the most significant frictions seemed to emanate from the minority of white families, who felt sidelined and undervalued by society in general and, sometimes, by the school in particular. A considerable number were very disadvantaged, and their children tended to badly underperform – their main deficit being language development and the accompanying skills for learning. They weren't overtly racist, but they could talk about others in derogatory ways, which amounted to racism by most objective measures. Once again, ACEs and the toxic trio figured prominently. The most overt racism came from some Eastern European children and families who had encountered few ethnic minorities in their countries of origin and almost certainly none with dark skin.

One complaint I received early on from some white British parents was that the school didn't seem to celebrate Christmas as enthusiastically as other religious festivals and that we never had a sign saying 'Merry Christmas', even though Christmas trees were installed. I realised that this was true. Understandably, we were being careful not to alienate people of other faiths, even so far as having a 'Winter Fair', rather than a 'Christmas Fair', fundraising event in early December. We also had no links with the local church, even though the vicar lived next door. Assemblies were usually of a secular nature, although we would use them to celebrate Eid, Diwali or Chinese New Year. Like many schools, we contravened the English Education Act 1944 in this respect. The Act (which was updated in 1988 and 1994) made it statutory for state schools to conduct a 'daily statutory act of collective worship' (Department for Education, 1994, p. 20) of a 'broadly Christian character' (Department for Education, 1994, p. 21). We had Christmas nativity plays, but these were confined to the youngest age groups. So, what was to be done?

We decided to base all assemblies on sustainability values and to illustrate links between these and morality across the main religions. We gave the celebration of religious festivals an even higher profile and made sure that in religious education lessons each year group studied a world religion properly. This meant that when Christmas came around, we were able to celebrate it even more enthusiastically because everyone could see that all religious festivals had a greater degree of parity. This was helped by inviting parents in to see for themselves and by hosting other events – for example, an international evening, when people brought in an example of their national cuisine to share with others. This strategy had the desired effect because we ended up receiving no complaints from anyone regarding religious matters, and non-Christian children joined in with Christmas activities far better than before, with no parents withdrawing them from things like nativity plays, which were extended further up the school.

One of the advantages we had was that – bar a small disaffected minority (mainly white British but also some Afro-Caribbean) – most parents, regardless of background, were desperate for their children to do well at school. As a result, we had great parental support. This meant that if a child had a behaviour or learning problem, we could usually garner parental action to help tackle it. The inherent aspiration of the parent body helped to overlay a common cause which, on the whole, was above and beyond any other cultural or religious considerations. If anything, we had to moderate this inclination because some parents put too much pressure on their children to achieve academic excellence. This was particularly true when they wanted their children to sit external tests for entry to selective grammar schools. This was a very tall order because these schools were located in other districts, so external candidates would have to reach a higher standard to be selected. Some families made great sacrifices to employ private tutors to help boost their child's chance of success.

Although it was relatively straightforward to go with the grain in terms of parental aspiration, we still had to deal with certain issues sensitively due to cultural divergences. One example was that some parents of Nigerian Yoruba origin expected us to deal with all in-school disciplinary matters because they felt shame if we tried to involve them. There was also a problem that they sometimes instilled discipline through physical chastisement – that is, smacking or other forms of pain. We had the dilemma that because we knew about this corporal punishment, we were required to make referrals to social services due to statutory child protection obligations. In reality, we were able to say to the parent that this kind of discipline was not appropriate and that it needed to cease. Overwhelmingly, this strategy was successful and it also served not to alienate families from the school. Further work was needed to model other forms of behaviour modification, such as positive reinforcement of good behaviour rather than merely admonishing bad behaviour. Through sensitive liaison, therefore, we were able to educate parents, without insulting or discrediting them or stigmatising them unnecessarily by involving social services.

Our strategy was to model a type of behaviour which showed all parents that there was an expectation that school professionals should work in partnership with parents on all aspects of a child's education. Part of this involved showing them how children were taught in classrooms, which was often in a much less formal way than the education they had received. We were fortunate in that our nominated school improvement partner had written a book on Yoruba culture (Olajide, 2012) and was able to offer us valuable insights. Really, we could have done with this sort of knowledge about all of our families' backgrounds, in order to have a sufficiently nuanced approach.

Another culture clash occurred in relation to outdoor learning – particularly forest school activities – and educational visits. Some parents didn't like the fact that their children would get dirty during forest school and didn't understand what the learning outcomes were. We overcame this by inviting them to sessions and explaining how they linked to many areas of the curriculum. In the main we won them over, although there were a significant number who would not allow their children to go on residential trips because of safety or 'modesty' concerns for their daughters.

We always had to be careful not to generalise when dealing with any cultural group and how they related to each other. For example, Bangladeshi Muslims had little understanding of Algerian Muslims, let alone aspects of British culture. Similarly, Nigerian Christians had little in common with Polish Christians, and why should they? Other groups might be refugees from war-torn Somalia or economic migrants from Lithuania. This relates to the point made earlier about the importance of having an awareness of culture in order to pursue the best courses for individual and collective sustainability. Also, culture is more than just religion, and we had to take account of this at the family level regardless of ethnicity or affiliation.

What united most parents was a desire for their children to receive a good education, so they could have a better material life. This in itself provided a basis for social cohesion, although we were keen to make sure that this didn't morph into a message about education being the portal to rampant consumerism. We needn't have worried unduly because the frugality and harmony at the heart of numerous non-Western cultures meant that many religious and social values were already in tune with sustainability. In fact, this informed our version of sustainability in a very positive way and helped wrench us away from the WEIRD mentality. It reminded me that even though I congratulate myself for promoting sustainability, my cultural interpretation of this can still smell of entitlement and greenwash.

A highly successful project, which was universally welcomed, was to take over the school kitchen and make it entirely vegetarian. This meant that we no longer had to use halal meat, which caused friction between those who needed it for religious reasons and those who didn't. Funnily enough, the source of the animosity wasn't the method of slaughter; it was that on some days the non-halal meat ran out and children became resentful that their peers still had some. I was more concerned about bringing down the school's carbon footprint by phasing out meat completely. As discussed in Chapters 2 and 3, this is one of the best ways to reduce CO2 as an individual or institution.

By the time I left the school it had received the first 'good' Ofsted report in its history. Although external accountability had dictated some of the tactics and strategies we employed to stay out of trouble, the learning paradigm promoted through sustainability was certainly more in evidence and the school seemed a much happier place for it.

COMPARE AND CONTRAST

In the Nottinghamshire school, which had a similar demographic in terms of levels of deprivation, I was confronted with very different challenges, or, rather, the same challenges which manifested themselves in different ways. A significant number of parents had experienced deprivation over several generations, which made the task of educating their children all the more challenging. There was poverty due to low income, but just as challenging were the following types of cultural poverty:

- **Poverty of aspiration.** This was a significant problem when we were trying to raise academic standards. Many children came from white British families in which there had been joblessness for several generations and the level of adult education was very low. A significant number came from ex-Traveller backgrounds and did not consider schooling and education a priority. Education was not seen as a means of self-improvement and, for many, school was perceived as merely another agency which caused them hassle – along with the job centre, benefits office or police – but at least it provided childcare for a decent amount of time each week. At the time, in the mid-1990s to early 2000s, the rate of single teenage parenthood in my catchment area was the highest in Western Europe, which in itself meant that school was rather irrelevant for many young people. The boys were particularly hard to engage and continued to perform far below national averages, and although the girls were a bit better, they tended to be passive and just as unmotivated. I once did a survey of Year 5 and 6 children to ask what they would like to be when they grew up. The vast majority of boys wanted to be professional footballers and most of the girls wanted to be hairdressers.

- **Poverty of experience.** Most of the children lived their whole lives on the sprawling council estate which the school served. They weren't taken to many places of culture or exposed to a wide variety of reading matter. Many of their homes were book-free, although invariably they had satellite TV. As mentioned, there was no library service for a population of about 9,000 and the only live entertainment happened at the local public house, all of it unsuitable for children. The estate bordered the countryside, but most of the children didn't visit it. Some Traveller children went out to catch rabbits with ferrets; it can be argued that this was a very rich experience!

- **Poverty of opportunity.** It would be wrong to say that many of the children weren't happy with their lot, but this might be because they knew nothing else and neither did their parents. There was a generational malaise which meant that although the families weren't hungry or lacking proper shelter, they were in a bubble of existence that meant they were passive receivers of help rather than proactive go-getters of knowledge and self-improvement (although, as we've seen, this isn't all it's cracked up to be if wedded to consumerism). They also didn't appreciate different cultures and racism was quite entrenched.

Through our sustainable community development drive – via the Children's Centre, extended services, more open engagement with parents and motivational curriculum – parents were actively trying to get their children into the school from outside the catchment area. This validated our initiatives, but also served to show that a sustainable school delivers more than a narrow form of greenism.

In both schools, there was no friends association or parent–teacher association (PTA). They were considered 'more trouble than they're worth' by previous school leaders. Aside from missing out on regular fundraising events, not having this sort of community involvement sent the message that the school wanted to keep people at arm's length. Once we set them up and actively supported them – rather than leaving parents to get on with it, with the hazard of contentious cliques emerging – they were an excellent way of showing the school's inclusivity. Some participants needed informal coaching to help them in their role and this was undertaken mainly by other parents. One parent in our Nottinghamshire school gained such confidence and skills that they went on to be elected to the town council. We had created a community champion! Wherever possible, the events themselves paid heed to the school's ethical procurement policies. In some instances, it meant that we had certain vociferous and potentially divisive individuals and groups within our metaphorical tent peeing out, but at least they weren't being ostracised and peeing in![25]

COHESION COUNTS: DEALING WITH A 'BLACK SWAN'

The cohesion of the London school community was sorely tested on 22 May 2013 when a soldier called Lee Rigby, from the barracks across the road, was killed in a horrific terrorist attack just outside the school. The school had to go into lockdown and pandemonium reigned outside as the incident unfolded and armed police were mobilised. We had to inform parents by text message that their children were safe and that they should come for them at the usual time, but to a different exit.

I received my first direct experience of 24/7 news media and was deluged with requests to be interviewed on radio and TV. This was very disconcerting and, following advice from the local authority press office, I confined myself to one interview on BBC radio. A news helicopter hovered constantly over the school and the drone of this fuelled the sense of unease felt by everyone. One angle they were interested in was the fact that we had quite a few children from army families and many others from Muslim families. There were false reports of panic within the school, when in fact everything stayed calm and the staff did sterling work to make sure the children were as unaffected as possible.

The whole area was sealed off for a few days while forensic evidence was gathered, but I decided to open the school again the next day because I wanted to send a positive message to the community, which I hoped would calm things rather than prolong anxieties. I'm pleased to say that this worked and we had very little additional absence the next day. I also stuck to my resolve of giving no more interviews or being involved in subsequent discussion panels. It seemed to me that these were part of the media feeding frenzy and I wanted no part of it.

We were very gratified that parents from many different groups, including army families and Muslim families, thanked us for how well the school had coped. Although there were sporadic anti-Islam protests from right-wing groups outside the school, as well as continued media intrusion for all, over the following days and months the school remained a bastion of calm and togetherness, thanks to the

25 I've adapted and made slightly more polite a phrase used by US President Lyndon Johnson regarding FBI Director J. Edgar Hoover, as quoted in the *New York Times* (31 October 1971).

parents and staff. We had recognised the common good and retained our respect for each other, even though others tried to use the incident to foster divisiveness.

Despite having no definitive proof, I feel that we had created a school culture which was resilient enough to come through this sort of incident. This type of resilience is a vital aspect of social sustainability. The prevailing culture went beyond mere 'tolerance' of others. It actively sought to demonstrate in a drip-feed way, as well as through high-profile events, that the concept of 'we' included everyone and there was no room for 'them'. Whenever conflict arose, be it through acts of intentional or unintentional racism or bullying, or any other acts which implied other people were less human than 'me', these were challenged. Sometimes this meant making a big fuss with individuals or groups, but much more often it was a case of having a quiet word or bringing up an issue for discussion in lessons, assemblies or through the school council. As well as clamping down on incidents, large or small, we also highlighted inclusive behaviour at every opportunity.

One example of this was to adopt the random acts of kindness philosophy mentioned in Chapter 3. This complies with the Chinese concept of '*he*', which is the criterion for an honourable and good person who lives in harmony with others and the natural world. Confucius thought that 'Honourable people have harmony even though they may be different from each other. Ignoble people may share a great deal in common, and yet they do not have harmony ... Harmony presupposes the existence of difference' (Chan et al., 2009, p. 39). If you get people from diverse backgrounds together on a regular basis, and a school leader is seen as an honest broker, you tend to get better mutual understanding, leaving less room for prejudice (see again the systems thinking discussion in Chapter 2). It sounds a bit clichéd, but we have far more in common with each other as human beings than we have differences. Children are born without prejudice and 'learn' it through life experiences.[26]

It was important for school staff to show unconditional regard for children and parents regardless of their circumstances. This could be particularly difficult for support staff who lived locally and sometimes brought in preconceived ideas about certain families (which gets back to having cultural awareness). However, it was challenging for everyone and we embedded messages of professional impartiality within our CPD.

Taleb (2008) warns that due to the ever-increasing complexity of human society, it is next to impossible to predict much of the future. He says:

---

26 See The Prince of Wales et al. (2010).

The world in which we live has an increasing number of feedback loops, causing events to be the cause of more events ... thus generating snowballs and arbitrary and unpredictable planet-wide winner-takes-all effects. We live in an environment where information flows too rapidly, accelerating such epidemics. (Taleb, 2008, p. xxvi)

He labels these unexpected and often tragic events 'Black Swans', and the incident in Woolwich was certainly one of these. We can add the COVID-19 pandemic to this ignominious list, it being one of the apocalyptic horsemen described in the introduction. I'm sure there are many more unforeseen accidents waiting to happen. This is why community and individual resilience is so important.

CIVIC PRIDE AND SUSTAINABILITY

In Chapter 4, I mentioned that the old army buildings of my Nottinghamshire school were saved and utilised for community use. This included providing a:

- Second-hand goods shop run by the local church.
- Base for the area special needs coordinator.
- Sensory room for children with high order special needs.
- Base for the town gymnastics club.
- Venue for adult keep-fit classes.
- Base for holiday play schemes.
- Venue for outside agencies, such as Citizens Advice and police.
- Special science/design and technology room (which was externally funded) full of exciting equipment for experiments.

Part of it was demolished and we collaborated with the local child and adolescent mental health services to obtain a grant to build a new facility in the vacated space. This meant that our families didn't have to travel very far to access these services.

We discovered that our army camp was a highly significant site during the Second World War. This was only revealed when we were visited by an ex-Royal Engineer called Victor Miller who trained at the camp in 1944. Although well into his eighties when we first met him, he was able to give us many details about how the camp functioned. It transpired that it had been a massive camp, of which our school buildings were a remnant, which specialised in training Royal Engineers to erect Bailey bridges. These were temporary bridge structures that were needed to replace bombed-out river crossings. The history of the bridge itself was fascinating; it was invented by Donald Bailey, an ex-railway infrastructure designer.[27] This was valuable hidden history, and we based an ambitious Heritage Lottery-funded project on it, involving the whole community. This helped us to transform the area into a learning community which the rest of the town acknowledged as an asset. We were also demonstrating social return on investment – another non-monetary measure of value added to a community.[28]

A CAUSE FOR OPTIMISM

A community-orientated sustainable school can project its ethos and tangible benefits into its local community *and* receive enrichment back. If this is laced with an ESD curriculum, a friendly campus and high-quality social amenities and support, then many positive integrated feedback loops are created which can counteract the negative wicked ones.

This approach also shows that we don't have to wait for Big Government and/or Big Business to take a radical sustainability lead. The onus is on us – individually and collectively – to secure the future, and momentum is building by the day. This in itself, through the butterfly effect, can put pressure on centres of economic and political power to change their damaging ways. As Botsman and Rogers (2011, p. 224) put it: 'We believe we will look back and see this epoch as a time when we took a leap and re-created a sustainable system built to serve.'

As discussed throughout this book, the links between sustainability and other aspects of school life are probably more important than aspects taken in isolation.

27 See https://www.youtube.com/watch?v=aFGh97Bg3cc&t=12s.
28 Social return on investment has been embraced by the Scottish government and is seen as integral to improving the quality of people's lives above and beyond monetary measures. This is part of new economics. See Nicholls et al. (2009).

The leader for sustainability knows this and uses connections to good effect. My thoughts on this are shown in the concluding chapter.

LEADERSHIP FOR SUSTAINABILITY RECOMMENDATIONS

- Get to know your school's locality really well beyond basic demographic data. What makes it tick? What are its strengths as well as its weaknesses? How can the community contribute to the work of the school, and vice versa? See it as an asset and not as a problem.

- Staff need to be tuned into the school community. Some will find this difficult if they come from very different cultural backgrounds. Once again, awareness of the hidden curriculum is needed. Induction of new staff should include providing information about the community and advice on how to navigate some of the challenges it presents (this applies to prosperous as well as disadvantaged areas).

- Discover local community champions and see how they might make a positive contribution to the school. They can be found in local businesses, faith centres and among parents. Nurture the PTA or friends association. Encourage them to stage events with sustainability in mind.

- Revisit *Every Child's Future Matters* and see how its ideals can help a school that wishes to develop sustainability in the community and assist early intervention.

- See if you agree with me that a permaculture philosophy can guide a school to new levels of sustainability. Find out if you have a local transition or climate action organisation.

- Schools can help to create civic pride. Research some of your hidden history or connect to positive local cultural events.

- Above all, don't see involvement with your community as time you haven't got. See it as a social return on investment. Work with local agencies so that their influence can be maximised (particularly in relation to early intervention), so you don't have to do everything.

Conclusion:

CONNECTIONS

Only connect the prose and the passion, and both will be exalted, and human love will be seen at its highest. Live in fragments no longer.

E. M. Forster (1969 [1910], p. 174)

This conclusion expands upon the C-word of connections, which has been a strand running throughout this book. It also ties up some loose ends and suggests more food for thought.

In a workshop that I deliver to conferences and schools, I show a series of pictures and ask participants to think about how they might link issues. One slide has a freshwater dolphin and an electric toaster on it. Most adults are quite poor at even attempting to offer a link. They seem wary about proffering even a speculative answer for fear of being 'wrong'. This says much about their own experience of education. When children see the slide, they'll say things like: 'they both pop up' or 'they're both shiny' (both of which are valid answers). My answer is that this particular freshwater dolphin frequents the Yangtze River in China, and they are almost extinct because of the pollution caused by the electronics industry that produces cheap electric toasters. If we buy these toasters, we are culpable in the demise of the dolphins. The same principle applies to all our modes of consumption if we care to explore the audit trails. Once children learn how to research these trails, they become fascinated by them and soon realise how and why certain products are so damaging in terms of raw material extraction, manufacture, transport, consumption and waste.

As we have seen, sustainability is predicated on the interconnectedness of everything within a circular economy, which recognises and respects planetary limits. The more we understand this, the more we pick up the habit of linked think-ing. Through integrated knowledge and applying critical thinking skills, we can also (hopefully) acquire the wisdom to create a sustainable future through practical actions. Where this occurs in schools, invariably we see harmonious relationships, meaningful learning and a co-created journey. This is the antithesis of what hap-pens in many schools, where stress and unhappiness are caused by overbearing managerialism and educational institutions are seen as cogs in the machine of economic growth. It has been argued that schools are part of the problem, hence the need for more leaders for sustainability to take the reins or, to better fit Chapter 1's ship analogy, the tiller, because it's better that a school is sailed rather than driven!

All schools are different, so some of the narratives in previous chapters won't be replicable in a literal sense and, at the very least, will need to be adapted for con-text. New ideas and opportunities constantly spring up, so if nothing else I hope the stories about my Nottinghamshire and London schools will inspire others to try out this way of working. In the meantime, my journey towards sustainability con-tinues as I seek to lessen my own impact on the planet while encouraging other school leaders to do the same, personally and professionally.

COURAGE OF CONVICTIONS

There's yet another C-word needed here, namely 'courage'. Yes, leaders need the courage to, at times, put their heads above the parapet and do things differently just because they are 'right'. David Orr (2011) puts it another way: he says that this is like 'walking north on a southbound train'. This may sound futile, but if more people do it, the direction of the train itself will be questioned more vociferously and, hopefully, stopped and turned around. A moral compass and sustainability values will be prerequisites to enable people to realise what their direction of thought and travel are in the first place and to judge to what extent this might be changed.

President Obama is just one person to use the quote 'If not us, who? If not now, when?' (Obama, 2010). This is very pertinent in the case of creating a sustainable future. We have already delayed the changes needed to avert civilisation break-down for too long. If we detected a massive asteroid on a collision course with

Earth, the best way to deal with it would be to divert it as early as possible by sending a rocket to gently nudge it a degree or two off-course. Hopefully, this would be enough for its eventual trajectory to miss the Earth. The longer we took debating the issue, the more resources and drastic actions would be needed to divert it. The same is true for achieving sustainability (as we saw in the last chapter, the Stern Review on climate change made this very point back in 2006). We know what the individual and interrelated social, economic and environmental wicked problems are, and we know many of the answers. We now need to act. Schools can be at the forefront of this process (and a few already are), rather than meekly waiting in line for national action and hi-tech solutions.[1]

The latest UK government climate change initiative featured a 10-point plan for action (HM Government, 2020). Most of these actions were based upon making technical improvements to infrastructure, although one involved doing more to nurture the natural world. There was nothing in the strategy about behaviour change or education. This has the potential to be redeemed by the DfE's draft sustainability and climate change strategy, which was launched at COP26 (time will tell, but hopefully not too much time).

I've argued that we require a change of culture more than we need technical wizardry – which can be greenwash or eco-bling anyway – to avert looming disasters. Education is an integral part of this change of cultural paradigm. I've also argued that leaders for sustainability need an entrepreneurial streak and to not be afraid to strike out in different directions. This sometimes means taking risks, disrupting, embracing innovation and being creative.

In England, before sustainability was unceremoniously expunged from Ofsted's remit in 2010, the national inspection body was starting to officially sanction leadership based upon ESD systems thinking, which was seen as being both a valuable process and a product of sustainable schools. Unfortunately, the DfE has employed classic neoliberal outsourcing tactics of distancing itself from sustainable methodology, leaving school leaders to determine their own priorities (once again, I hope this is mitigated by the sustainability and climate change strategy). As we have seen, this light touch isn't really that light because of the coercive tendencies of the standards agenda, relying as it does on testing, national league tables and competition between schools and academy chains. Ofsted (2003, 2008, 2009)

---

1   In a video cited in Hutt (2016), Ian Morris gives a fascinating overview of why civilisations collapse. Many lessons for our civilisation!

even went as far as developing inspection standards for ESD and flagged their value in promoting school improvement more generally in various special reports.

OFSTED OFF-TRACK?

How ironic that, as we enter the climate crisis and mass extinctions of the Anthropocene epoch, Ofsted's defunct views on sustainability are more relevant than ever before. I have argued strongly that schools, and education more widely, should be a significant part of our strategy to alleviate – at the very least, mitigate – global environmental threats, rather than being part of the ugly system that is accelerating them.

I find the comments of Ofsted's chief inspector, Amanda Spielman, quite chilling. When launching the Ofsted 2020 Annual Report, she said that climate change education should lie within the subjects of geography and history and that schools should largely stay out of related social and economic issues (Hazell, 2020). I've argued that this needn't be the case if overtly linked to the nationally accepted school improvement agenda, which Spielman quite rightly promotes. It also fits the Ofsted deep dives agenda (see Chapter 3) and the belief that a narrowed test-based curriculum is the refuge of the underperforming school (Ofsted, 2020).

We're back to gaps here: in this case, a credibility gap between the 2020 Ofsted rhetoric and the reality of raising standards without first narrowing the curriculum. However, in one sense I would heartily agree with Spielman that the science – and geography – of climate change should be taught, but if this isn't related to social sciences, then learners of any age will lack a holistic understanding of the issues and, more importantly, the means to create a sustainable world through practical actions. How else will we develop the individual and collective wisdom to pull back from the brink of annihilation?

BEING PURPOSEFUL

In education, we can fall into the trap of constantly discussing what the best structures are, from whole-system level to individual schools. I hope this book encourages school leaders to give more thought to what the purpose of education should be in highly volatile times. I think it's always important for leaders to periodically rise above the shackles of short-term operational imperatives – as vital as these are – and allow themselves and others to re-examine their purpose. This is particularly vital if a school is to become ever more sustainable. Above all, leaders need to remember that, despite pressures and difficulties, they have it within themselves to make a positive difference, to be proactive rather than reactive and to avoid being sucked into fatalism. With this in mind, being a leader for sustainability can be truly liberating. It isn't a quirkiness reserved for the lunatic fringe; it feeds into a rich tradition of leaders who are values-led and who see their role as vocational rather than self-serving and ruthless.

I've shown how sustainability contributes to less easily measurable outcomes, such as well-being (which, in itself, makes for more successful, less stressed learners and staff). Just as measuring GDP is far from the whole story of a country, measuring narrow academic achievement doesn't reflect a child's whole range of abilities or potential. A sustainable school, therefore, should look for frameworks to help embed well-being and ways of measuring it.[2] Awe and wonder also add to feel-good factors and encourage curiosity and a love of learning.

SACKCLOTH AND ASHES?

Everything is Bad for You is the title of a book by David French (2005) given to me by an anonymous colleague for my Secret Santa present one year. It caused much mirth in the staffroom and gave me pause for thought. It made me realise that good news sustainability narratives are essential. Sustainability certainly shouldn't encompass false notions of Cromwellian frugality, and we proponents need to be careful not to leave this impression. Everything should, as far as possible, be good for you! Of course, this needs to be tempered by one of the permaculture ethics

---

2   See Stirling and Emery (2016) and https://glstaginginternational.education.co.uk/products/pupil-attitudes-to-self-and-school-pass.

of fair shares, meaning that surpluses are shared rather than accumulated. The saying adapted from Gandhi,[3] 'There's enough for all our needs but not all our greed' applies here (Schumacher, 1993 [1973], p. 20). I've shown that a sustainable school can achieve this in microcosm, with the potential to influence further afield, and school leaders shouldn't underestimate their influence to enable people to thrive and flourish now and into the distant future.

GLOBAL GOOD

I've advocated throughout this book that leaders for sustainability should keep a watchful eye on the global dimension while operating at a local level. This emphasises what a crucial role such leaders play in determining a just and sustainable future. It also requires the ability to be dispassionate and to recognise that dominant economic systems just don't cut the mustard. The UN Department of Economic and Social Affairs (2006, pp. 7–8) put it this way:

> Environmental concerns were largely ignored by communist regimes, and are not typically integrated into socialist approaches to the management of human affairs. Capitalist systems tend to 'deify' production and consumption at the expense of balanced, long-term growth. Social justice will only flourish if environmental preservation and sustainable development constitute an integral part of growth strategies now and in the future.

Even this recognition implies that 'growth' is good. How can it be on a finite planet? The only growth which belies this is that of learning and wisdom, both of which need to be present in abundance in a sustainable school. Stuff in the form of manufactured products, be they large or small, always need to be questioned. This was highlighted by Elhacham et al. (2020), who calculated that, at 1.1 teratonnes, global human-made mass now exceeds all living biomass and continues to grow exponentially. Yet another reason to take a critical look at what we really

---

3   Like many sayings attributed to Gandhi, this is difficult to track down. It probably started out as something like, 'Earth provides enough to satisfy every man's need, but not for every man's greed' (quoted in E. F. Schumacher, *Small Is Beautiful: A Study of Economics As If People Mattered* (London: Vintage Books, 1993 [1973]), p. 20). For obvious reasons it was rendered gender neutral.

need in terms of possessions, both personally and professionally. Perhaps this makes my forays into the school skip, described in Chapter 4, look less absurd.

ONWARDS AND UPWARDS?

The English 1952 feature film *The Sound Barrier* fictionalises the ruthless pursuit of a technical solution to get a plane to fly faster than the speed of sound. There are many failed attempts and fatalities, until one of the protagonists thinks in a different way. He decides to counter-intuitively push the joystick instead of pulling it to stop the plane nose-diving when nearing the sound barrier – and it works! Similarly, as a society, should we expect to soar faster and ever upwards, spurred on by Enlightenment thinking and the business-as-usual economic imperative? Post COVID-19, will we simply pick ourselves up, brush ourselves off and get back to unsustainable 'normal', or does there need to be a new normal?

I've spoken of the need to foster hope. I've heard it called, rather dismissively, 'Hopium',[4] suggesting we trust that 'others' (such as Bill Gates?) will come up with scientific and geoengineering solutions to our crisis and, therefore, we can sit back and wait for this to happen. Leaders for sustainability need to disassociate themselves from this idea and instead create the conditions for a genuine and realistic sense of hope, enabling individual and collective actions that make a significant difference *now*. Schumacher's (1973) book *Small is Beautiful* encapsulated this and emphasised that what we all do counts, but especially when we lead on something that creates and channels the energy of others. Once again, butterfly effects can escalate this. To this end, I like the following definition of a leader: 'Leaders are agents of change – persons whose acts affect other people more than other people's acts affect them. Leadership occurs when one group member modifies the motivation or competencies of others in the group' (Bass, 1990, pp. 19–20).

This includes building the capacity of a school community to 'be the change' through creativity and connectivity in the context of high-quality environmental education (see Figure C.1). Connecting to the natural world has been shown to be central to this, and without this connection we are truly lost as a species.

---

4   See https://www.urbandictionary.com/define.php?term=Hopium.

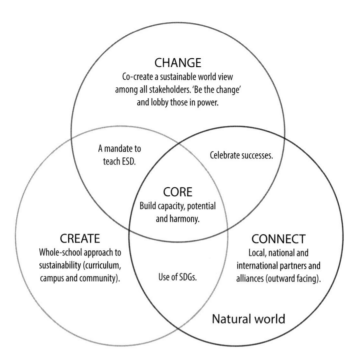

Figure C.1: Changing, creating and connecting

Through selected theory and, more applicably via examples of my own practice, I've shown how making connections through recognising and utilising systems is a vital leadership skill that enables captaincy, curriculum, campus and community to come together in harmony to enhance learning. Furthermore, it connects to the imperative of making a practical contribution to sustainability locally and globally. Throughout, I've highlighted the importance of cross-curricular connections and the related value of critical thinking for all learners (staff, children and other school stakeholders).

At the moment, many visions of the future lack imagination and are either tech-centred or dystopian. Through an 'educated' population, freed of false consciousness created by neoliberalism and other cultural 'isms', we can do much better than this – perhaps not exactly achieving utopia, but a type of sustainability that releases the full potential of our incredible species by enhancing rather than diminishing our experience of life. Only then will we have renounced the age of stupid. Let's all jump aboard that north-bound train by connecting to a sustainable future. After all, as Satish Kumar (2011) says, leadership is:

not about heroic, headline-grabbing actions: true leadership is to live and act with integrity and without fear. Leadership has nothing to do with power, position or office; nor anything to do with birth, class or status ... Leadership is an inner calling to lead ourselves and the world from subjugation to liberation, from falsehood to truth, from control to participation and from greed to gratitude. We can all be leaders. All we have to do is wake up, stand up, live and act.

By this means, leaders for sustainability can definitely save the planet one school at a time.

Appendix 1:

SCHOOL MISSION STATEMENT

Our mission for children, parents, staff and governors is to be:

- A forward-thinking school

  a place of learning for the demands of the 21st century

- A healthy school

  for the mind, body and spirit

- An inclusive school

  where everyone matters

- An environmentally aware school

  where we think globally, act locally and live sustainably

- A place of creative learning

  where everyone is motivated to achieve

- A friendly, secure school

  which helps to build positive relationships

- A learning organisation

  where everyone is a learner

- A constantly improving school

  for the benefit of all

- Instrumental in creating a learning community

  for the benefit of all school stakeholders

Our mission will be delivered through:

- A creative curriculum, incorporating education for sustainable development.
- Enjoyable, brain-friendly learning.
- Innovative computer use.
- Teachers involving children in their own assessment and setting targets for continuous improvement.
- Comprehensive spiritual, moral, social and cultural and personal, social, health and economic programmes.
- Developing close home–school links.
- A well-being approach for children and staff.
- Encouraging, and providing opportunities for, the continuing professional development of all staff.
- Programmes of adult learning for the wider community.
- Offering quality study support opportunities.
- Being a self-evaluative school at all levels.
- Becoming a full-service extended school.
- Nurturing unconditional regard between all adults and children.

Enabling *all* learners to:

- Be critical and linked thinkers with a local to global perspective.
- Be effective communicators and sensitive listeners.
- Be literate and numerate.
- Have sound general knowledge and the ability to use it wisely and effectively.
- Have high aspirations and the motivation to learn.
- Be independent and collaborative learners, who know how they learn (metacognition).
- Be self-evaluative.

- Seek creative solutions, seeing challenges not problems.

- Be confident with computers and other technology.

- Experience a wide range of creative opportunities and develop aesthetic appreciation.

- Make informed choices about their health.

- Value themselves as unique.

- Realise the benefits of cooperation and empathy.

- Understand how rights relate to responsibilities.

- Relate and respond to the needs of others, including those of different religions and cultures.

- Care for the world and its people.

- Appreciate and assist biodiversity.

- Celebrate their own and others' achievements.

Appendix 2:

ETHICAL PROCUREMENT POLICY

INTRODUCTION

This policy has been drawn up in the light of the school aiming for high levels of social, economic and environmental sustainability within all its curriculum, campus and community operations. It outlines general areas for consideration when the school purchases a product or service. Its reference points include the United Nations Declaration of Human Rights, Rights of the Child and Sustainable Development Goals (SDGs).

At all times, procurement processes should be conducted in a transparent and honest way.

The school should always be satisfied that suppliers have systems in place to ensure high standards of propriety in line with the remit of this policy, as outlined below.

Staff directly involved in procurement will have appropriate in-house and external training to enable them to fulfil the requirements of the policy to their best ability.

The motto 'think globally, act locally' (from the school mission statement) is a constant consideration, as are the SDGs.

When procuring a product or service, the following should be avoided:

Social

- Use of child labour.
- Use of forced labour.

- Discrimination (employment, occupation, sexual orientation, ethnic background).

- Excessive work hours.

- Poor and/or dangerous working conditions.

- No maternity provision.

- Little or no manufacturing safety standards or no monitoring and enforcement.

- Any additional circumstances which compromise the health, safety and well-being of employees.

- Poor or no worker representation.

Economic

- Poverty level wages (including consideration of workers on zero-hours contracts and whether employers pay the London Living Wage).

- Abuse of trade through monopolies and cartels.

- Supply chains causing excessive environmental damage and/or employment and conditions abuses as outlined above.

Environmental

Manufactured product or raw materials causing irreparable damage to the bio-sphere through unregulated and harmful:

- Outsourcing of solid and liquid waste.

- Emissions (liquids and gases).

- Non-recyclable materials.

- Large carbon and other footprints in manufacture and/or transportation.

- Wildlife habitats destroyed or despoiled.

- Exploitation of wildlife.

- Inhumane treatment of wildlife.

ADDITIONAL NOTES

Wherever possible, non-meat products are to be used in meals.

In line with the desire for the school to have as little impact on the Earth as possible, all staff need to consider the 5Rs before purchase:

- **Reduce**: can we do without something by cutting down on what we use?
- **Recycle**: how easy will this be?
- **Reuse**: can we reuse rather than buying again?
- **Repair**: how easy will it be to mend?
- **Repurpose**: similar to reusing, can we adapt something that we already have?

Other considerations:

- How will the purchase of a new product feed through to improved teaching and learning? Could it be borrowed or rented?
- Beware of greenwash. Just because a product comes from a 'recycled source', doesn't make it 'environmentally friendly'.

Always bear in mind the buyerarchy of needs:

Source: Sarah Lazarovic,[1] **used with permission**

1 See https://www.sarahl.com.

MONITORING, RESPONSIBILITIES AND REVIEW

The senior leadership team (including the school budget manger and site manager) and the governors will continue to monitor procurement to ensure consistent and improving ethical and environmental standards in all areas. Staff will be briefed in the policy's main aims and there will be active involvement of the children through the school council and the education for sustainable development curriculum.

This policy should be read in conjunction with the fair trade policy and also the school mission, sustainability policy, energy policy and food policy.

Appendix 3:

FAIR TRADE POLICY

INTRODUCTION

The Fairtrade Foundation says:

Fairtrade means fairer pay and more power in the hands of farmers, so that they can create change for us all, from investing in climate friendly farming techniques and clean water for their community, to nurturing women leaders and making sure children get an education. When you choose Fairtrade, you're choosing the world you want to see.[1]

With fair trade you have the power to change the world every day. With simple shopping choices you can get farmers a better deal. And that means they can make their own decisions, control their future and lead the dignified life everyone deserves.

Overall, the school aims to abide by the 5Rs, namely recycle, reduce, reuse, repair and repurpose (see the ethical procurement policy). Within this, the motto 'think globally, act locally' from the school mission statement is a constant consideration, as are the United Nations Sustainable Development Goals (SDGs).

The school is committed to supporting the principles of fair trade wherever possible by:

● Ensuring that fair trade is included in the school development plan.

1 See https://stories.fairtrade.org.uk/what-is-fairtrade/index.html.

- Using fair trade products whenever possible – for example, tea, coffee, sugar and biscuits in the staffroom and at meetings.
- Using fair trade products in the school kitchen and in other cookery activities.
- Purchasing fair trade sports balls when buying new ones.
- Offering fair trade cotton school uniform in the school shop.
- Ensuring that learning about fair trade happens in lessons and whole-school activities.
- Discussing fair trade at school council meetings.
- Promoting fair trade products within the school and wider community.
- Making sure the benefits of fair trade are assessed in relation to carbon emissions and other environmental consequences (i.e. not all fair-trading equates to planet-friendly practices in production and transport).
- Recognising that not all products are covered by fair trade schemes, and that during the procurement process checks should be made on the origins and provenance of potential purchases.
- Incorporating fair trade into the curriculum.
- Whole-school celebration of Fairtrade Fortnight.

MONITORING, RESPONSIBILITIES AND REVIEW

Day-to-day implementation of the fair trade policy to be undertaken by the budget manager and the site manager, reporting to the head teacher, who in turn will update the governing body. This policy is to be reviewed annually by designated governors. The policy will be formally reviewed annually, but may be altered in the light of experience according to the changing circumstances of procurement.

This policy should be read in conjunction with the ethical procurement policy and the school mission, sustainability policy, energy policy and food policy.

Appendix 4:

ENERGY POLICY

INTRODUCTION

The governors and head teacher believe strongly that the school should be as energy efficient as possible, and this should go beyond merely operating utilities (gas, water and electricity) prudently.

The school is basing a lot of its work on education for sustainable development (ESD). This is driving the desire for the school community as a whole to create as low an environmental footprint as possible (in terms of carbon emissions and other pollutants associated with transport, manufacture and waste). Having a low water footprint is another important consideration. Children have a first-hand understanding of energy through observing how it's used in the school.

Using energy efficiently can be seen as 33% a technical solution and 66% a cultural solution (i.e. getting people to change their behaviour is the biggest challenge). A large part of this policy is, therefore, devoted to addressing this necessary cultural change.

This policy aims to define the constituents of the school's environmental footprint and how school leadership and management should seek to minimise the effects. Much of this will be done through the school's system of distributive leadership, whereby everyone is encouraged to take individual and collective responsibility for the implementation of the energy policy in their particular area of work.

Overall, the school aims to abide by the 5Rs, namely recycle, reduce, reuse, repair and repurpose (see the ethical procurement policy). All these activities reduce energy usage. Within this, the motto 'think globally, act locally' from the mission statement is a constant consideration, as are the United Nations Sustainable Development Goals (SDGs).

ELECTRICITY, GAS AND WATER

These utilities are monitored by the site manager and the budget manager. They, in consultation with the head teacher and the local authority monitoring team, look for patterns of usage to target areas for increased efficiency. The Energy Certification scheme assists with this monitoring process.

The school sources electricity from a green source.

The school operates an eco-team in all classes from Year 2 onwards. Children take turns to be in this team and assist with energy monitoring and encourage adults and children not to waste energy within the school buildings. They also lobby for environmental improvements on the school campus and more widely in the community. They work in partnership with the school council.

The school will continue to investigate the use of more renewables and the retro-fitting of energy efficient lighting. Appliances such as dishwashers and all powered kitchen appliances should have at least an A+ rating.

PROCUREMENT

The head teacher, budget manager and site manager will ensure that, whenever possible, any school procurement adheres to the following principles to avoid energy wastage:

- Items should come from a sustainable source (e.g. recycled paper).
- Items should have minimal packaging.
- Items should be sourced locally to cut down on lorry miles (e.g. locally grown food for the kitchen).
- Items should be ethically produced in terms of human rights (e.g. fair trade beverages).
- Where applicable, electrical appliances should have an A+ rating.
- Items should have a long life (i.e. not be disposable).
- Where disposal is necessary, items should be recyclable.

- Items should contain as few synthetic compounds as possible to avoid environmental contamination on use or at disposal (particularly important for food and clothing).

- Items should use the minimal amount of energy during manufacture (e.g. cotton and wool rather than nylon, wood from a sustainable source rather than plastic).

RECYCLING

Given that the school aims to reduce waste and reuse items to save energy, where this is not feasible, recycling takes place. The following items are recycled:

- Aluminium cans.

- Plastic (where possible).

- Printer cartridges.

- Mobile telephones.

- Clothes.

- Paper (including Christmas cards) and cardboard.

- Food waste (either taken away by a commercial firm or composted on site).

- Plastic pens.

These are monitored and organised by the site manager and the budget manager. The eco-team helps with recycling in each class and parents are encouraged to bring items such as printer cartridges into school for recycling.

Important note: embodied carbon is present within every product. This is the carbon (or equivalent) created from the extraction of raw materials, production process and transportation of anything from a drawing pin to a building. This means that, as a school, we need to use the minimum amount of stuff!

COMMUNITY

The activities mentioned in this policy have a positive influence on the community surrounding the school. Messages about using energy efficiently are passed on to adults by the children. This is particularly important as many families are in fuel poverty (i.e. 10%+ of family income is spent on energy).

SCHOOL TRAVEL PLAN

This runs in partnership with the local authority and aims to reduce vehicle road miles. It encourages the children to walk or cycle to school and the school to decrease lorry mileage. The healthy school coordinator and the head teacher lead on this initiative.

MONITORING, RESPONSIBILITY AND REVIEW

The senior leadership team (including school budget manger and site manager) and the governors will continue to monitor school energy usage. The policy will be formally reviewed annually, but may be altered in the light of experience according to changing circumstances.

This policy should be read in conjunction with the school mission, ethical procurement policy, fair trade policy and food policy.

Appendix 5:

FOOD POLICY

INTRODUCTION

This policy aims to ensure that all aspects of food and nutrition in school promote the health and well-being of pupils, staff, visitors and the wider community. This means that all stakeholders have access to good quality food and nutrition at breakfast club, dinnertimes, school events and through other extended services where catering is required.

Good food and nutrition are provided in the context of the school's sustainability ethos (i.e. through ethical/fair trade and local procurement of food). This also aims to reduce waste and incorporate the United Nations Sustainable Development Goals (SDGs).

OBJECTIVES

- Implement Food for Life initiative for the good of all, aiming for Gold accreditation (working from an ongoing action plan).
- Work closely with the school catering manager.
- Operate a parent/governor/staff school nutrition action group (SNAG) to oversee Food for Life and to liaise with the school council and governing body.

- Food and nutrition embedded in the school curriculum and extracurricular activities.

IMPORTANT ACTIONS

School catering will include:

- Teachers and SNAG working together to ensure food-based curriculum topics at each key stage and with the catering manager to develop menu options for breakfast, lunch and dinner (provided for after-school club) at reasonable prices.
- Highlighting catering activities using the school newsletter, special catering newsletter, posters and website.
- Special events promoting good food and nutrition for all.
- Providing water bottles for all children and drinking water in classrooms and communal areas.
- Providing a designated area and equipment for cookery club.
- Arranging basic food hygiene courses in school.
- Encouraging healthy packed lunches by recognition slips in sandwich boxes and through the publicity described above.
- Budget manager working closely with catering manager to source local and, wherever possible, organic food.

MONITORING, RESPONSIBILITY AND REVIEW

- Head teacher to receive report on food-based topics audit and to observe sample lessons.
- Catering manager to provide senior leadership team with numbers of children having school breakfasts and dinners each month.
- Budget manager to give termly reports on food procurement.

- SNAG meetings every half-term to report Food for Life progress.
- School council to feed back any catering issues to head teacher/SNAG.
- Cookery club recipe book to be produced, photographs of club on website and in newsletter.
- Staff to acquire basic food hygiene certificates.
- School gaining Food for Life accreditation and keeping Healthy Schools Gold award up to date.

The policy will be formally reviewed annually, but may be altered in the light of experience according to the changing circumstances and feedback from stakeholders.

This policy should be read in conjunction with the school mission, ethical procurement policy, fair trade policy and energy policy.

Appendix 6:

DESIGN AND TECHNOLOGY CURRICULUM POLICY

INTRODUCTION

The design and technology curriculum links with the school's broader curriculum aims, in terms of giving children the powerful cultural and social capital they need in order to understand the world and shape the future through the promotion of sustainable development. This includes incorporating the United Nations Sustainable Development Goals (SDGs).

Design and technology is a hands-on area of learning through which metacognition, practical skills (e.g. using tools and equipment) and technical knowledge (e.g. using electrical systems and interfaces with IT) can be developed.

Design and technology also has the potential to be a very creative area of the curriculum, allowing children to realise their ideas in three dimensions, either as small-scale models, toys or full-scale projects. Within this, they will appreciate the need to adapt designs and constructions as they go along and share their work for critical appraisal and celebration.

ESSENTIAL SKILLS AND CONCEPTS

The study of design and technology is essential for children to begin to understand and question the impact of technologies and products on people and the environment. The design and technology curriculum is underpinned by the school's Rights Respecting and global learning frameworks, with the aim of developing ecologically literate designers. Throughout the design process and during everyday conversations, the vocabulary of sustainability is promoted through the 5Rs.

Design and technology also promotes critical thinking skills. Through engaging and open-ended starting points, children will come up with multiple ideas and approaches. Children develop an ability to make judgements and critique different ideas, as well as beginning to identify unintended consequences of their projects (e.g. for the environment).

Design and technology is an excellent vehicle for collaborative learning and shows children that ideas and constructions are often better realised when undertaken in partnership with others.

Design and technology enables children to develop an understanding of significant global design achievements. This cultural capital is augmented through looking at existing design products and, where relevant, through visits to regional institutions such as the V&A, Design Museum and Fashion and Textile Museum.

All design and technology learning is underpinned by rich opportunities for communication and language development. Design and technology also provides multiple cross-curricular learning opportunities. Teachers capitalise on significant cross-curricular opportunities by planning for design and technology projects to take part alongside related learning in other subjects (e.g. science, maths, humanities or computing).

Due to the nature of design and constant technological change, design and technology is dynamic and must develop in the light of these changes.

MONITORING, RESPONSIBILITY AND REVIEW

The design and technology coordinator will report directly to the head teacher and liaise with a designated governor. They will also assist planning to ensure that cross-curricular opportunities are maximised (this means liaising with other curriculum leaders). A skills ladder will be developed which ensures that each year group builds upon their competencies as they move up the school, so that by the time they reach Year 6, they are capable of quite complex projects.

This policy should be read in conjunction with the school mission, ethical procurement policy, fair trade policy, energy policy and food policy.

Appendix 7:

LEARNING COMMUNITY CHARTER

INTRODUCTION

The learning community is an inclusive organisation for the promotion and delivery of lifelong learning opportunities for all stakeholders. These include young people (0–19 years), parents, staff and adults who live on the local housing estate. The overall aim is to create a sustainable community in terms of environmental integrity, economic security and social cohesion, thus providing conditions wherein everyone really does matter.

OBJECTIVES

- A commitment to partnership working between all stakeholders facilitated by fully integrated Children's Centres and extended services.

- Management committee to encourage the active involvement of local parents in determining community needs and in policy/decision making.

- Building and maintaining strong networking systems between learning community partners and outside agencies.

- The core offer is made available to all who need it.

- Adult learning, volunteering and employment opportunities created to meet the needs of local people.

- Enabling children and young people to access play and study support outside school hours.

- Promotion of intergenerational working for mutual benefit.

- Contributing to the creation of effective transition arrangements between school phases, particularly from primary to secondary.

- Creating effective means of communication to promote the services and to receive stakeholder feedback.

- Reference made to the United Nations Sustainable Development Goals (SDGs).

Appendix 8:

PRIMARY LEARNING CHARTER

INTRODUCTION

This charter has emerged from the school mission statement and defines the learning entitlement of each child as they move through the school. Many of the points are linked and work from the premise that all children are capable of making significant progress regardless of circumstances. This means that all staff need to have high expectations of each child in their care and actively look for strengths on which to build, rather than just weaknesses to be addressed. Unconditional regard also needs to be embedded, requiring objective professional reflection and practice. These elements also reflect a holistic approach to school improvement which feeds into the learning development of each child. Our Education for Sustainable Development (ESD) ethos is central to all this, as are the United Nations Sustainable Development Goals (SDGs).

OBJECTIVES

To enable all children to be effective lifelong learners, the following elements need to be in place (not in any particular order of priority):

- Each child needs to be happy at school – an anxious child with stress hormones circulating through their body and brain will not learn very well.

- Adults to see each stage of childhood as valuable in itself, rather than merely a stage to 'get through'.

- A physical learning environment which is comfortable (i.e. has correct temperature/humidity, lots of natural light, ergonomic seating, access to drinking water, sufficient freedom of movement).

- Daily physical activity to provide wake-up and feel-good factors.

- A learning environment in which children feel emotionally safe and able to experiment and take risks without fear of destructive criticism from adults or other children. Each child to be treated with unconditional regard.

- Lessons to inspire curiosity, active engagement and emotional attachment – appropriate motivational stimuli is the key.

- Each child to have had enough food at the beginning of the day and at lunchtime in order to satisfy their basic needs.

- Each child to have frequent access to the natural world and to outdoor PE activities. These are to include forest school, horticulture, field studies (urban and rural) and outdoor pursuit challenges where risk taking is to be encouraged!

- Dance, drama and singing to be constantly available as a curricular and extracurricular opportunity.

- Regular comfort breaks built into periods of learning.

- Children to be active participants rather than passive learners – thus, the role of the teacher and teaching assistant to be more of a 'guide on the side' rather than a 'sage on the stage'. Use of carpet time to be rationed to avoid passivity.

- Children need to develop metacognition (i.e. learning how to learn).

- Staff to have high expectations at all times and create learning opportunities that they would desire for their own children.

- Literate environment created and celebrated.

- Resilience built up by offering coping strategies when things go wrong.

- A range of learning opportunities provided to encourage knowledge, concepts and skills development appropriate for each child's needs at any given time.

- Regular access to arts and crafts activities.

- Language development through high-quality speaking and listening opportunities to be at the heart of all learning to improve vocabulary, thinking, expression and, ultimately, writing.

- Mathematical development, wherever possible, to be based upon real-life experiences.

- Cross-curricular links used constantly to provide additional reference points for learning. ESD to be integral to this so that children appreciate relationships and links.

- Opportunities for enterprise activities included in topic work led by the subjects of design and technology, maths and computing.

- History and geography used to provide children with a 'sense of place', an appreciation of different cultures – past and present – and an understanding of global issues and social justice (strong links with ESD). All this to be based on local studies as a reference point. This approach ties in with the 'think global, act local' philosophy and previously mentioned SDGs.

- All children to sow, grow, harvest, cook and eat a vegetable/fruit every year (seed-to-plate experience). Food for Life scheme fully utilised by each class teacher.

- Computers and other technology available whenever this is the most effective vehicle for learning. Each child to have their own work folder and able to access appropriate online resources.

- Parents to be actively involved in their children's learning, progress and targets at very regular intervals.

- Motivational home learning opportunities provided each week. Where these cannot take place at home, children targeted for after-school provision.

- Teacher and teaching assistant assessment is ongoing and rigorous to ensure that children are working at the correct level and are in appropriate groups.

- All children to develop the school's handwriting style.

- Groups to be suitably flexible and fluid according to the activity, rather than set in stone, which may lead to stigmatisation.

- A residential opportunity to be provided for all children from Year 2 onwards.

- Each class/year group to have a field trip at least each half-term.

- Philosophy for Children to be taught across the school.

- Food provided by school to conform to national nutritional standards and, wherever possible, sourced locally.

- All work to be based on real-life situations in order to tap into cultural resources and to provide strong stimulus for curiosity.

- Children to be constantly challenged to problem solve to develop thinking skills (particularly through science, maths and design and technology). This should include problems requiring manual dexterity and those requiring philosophical insight (which can be covered in any subject because it explores meaning).

- Each child to be involved with regular pupil voice activities (including school council, self-assessment, pupil interviews about the curriculum and giving informal views on their school experiences). Debating skills to be promoted, linked to critical thinking.

- Through spiritual, moral, social and cultural education, each child to be encouraged to explore spirituality through the aesthetic appreciation of the arts (including music) and nature, the lives of significant people, and secular and religious ceremonies (showing the relationship with culture).

- Personal, social, health and economic education to be seen as a strand running through the interactions of all people in the school, as well as being delivered as distinct lessons through social and emotional aspects of learning, assemblies or part of an integrated topic. This is to include specific safeguarding education (i.e. stranger danger, internet use and personal risk management during physical activities to improve a child's safety awareness). Also, to include inputs on anti-bullying and anti-discrimination on the grounds of gender, race or sexual orientation and fundamental British values as part of the Prevent programme.

- Relationships and sex education to be covered, in accordance with a child's stage of development, in each class as they move up the school. Again, opportunities should be sought to integrate this into topics and relate it to mental well-being and safeguarding.

- Each child to be given responsibilities in the classroom on a very regular basis.

- Weather recording undertaken by all children.

- Each child to have access to day and residential field trips in urban and rural settings.

Appendix 9:

CURRICULUM STATEMENT

[Briefly describe the circumstances of your school in terms of catchment area, demograph-ics, physical environment and the state of general learning opportunities inside and outside school.]

The curriculum at ____ School aims to give children the powerful cultural and social capital they need in order to understand the world and shape the future to promote sustainable development. Therefore, we provide our children with a broad, balanced and experiential curriculum in which they will be encouraged to develop critical thinking skills, enabling them to consider questions of social jus-tice, inequality and environmental integrity, which are prerequisites for sustainable living, both locally and globally.

This will require the acquisition of study skills and key knowledge and concepts in the arts and sciences, as well as practical opportunities to improve aspects of their locality or the situation of others. This local to global approach, therefore, pro-motes active rather than passive learning and fits with the overall school ethos, which uses metacognition, Rights Respecting and global learning principles. Individual responsibility and wisdom are at the heart of this, although it is also linked to the importance of collaboration, positive group identity and empathy for others.

An aesthetic appreciation of the world is also vital, so that nature and human cul-tures are valued and nurtured rather than overlooked or dismissed. This contributes to personal well-being and positive attitudes to learning.

The curriculum will be delivered through sensitive and effective pedagogy, taking into account the stages of development and personality of each child.

Appendix 10:

INTEGRATED TOPIC PLANNING GUIDANCE

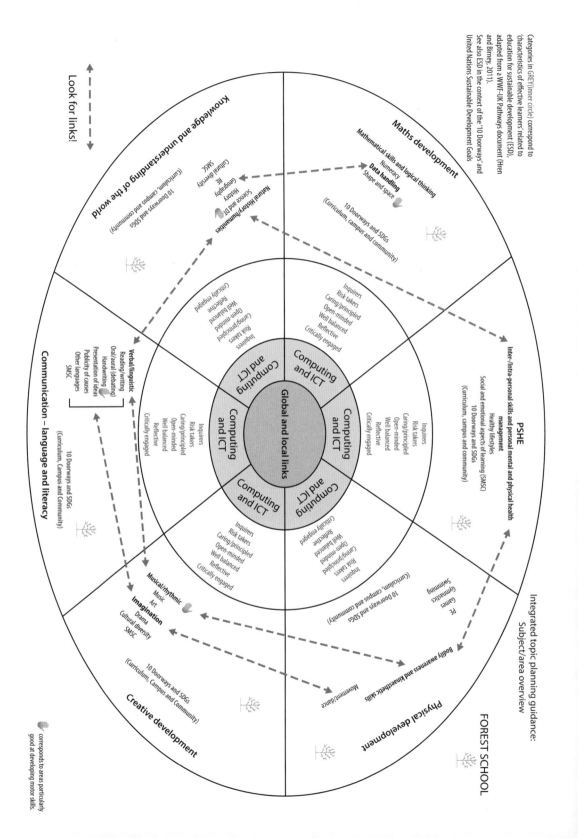

Categories in GREY (inner circle) correspond to 'characteristics of effective learners' related to education for sustainable development (ESD), adapted from a WWF-UK Pathways document (H'ren and Birney, 2011).
See also ESD in the context of the '10 Doorways' and United Nations Sustainable Development Goals

Look for links!

Integrated topic planning guidance: Subject/area overview

FOREST SCHOOL

corresponds to areas particularly good at developing motor skills.

Knowledge and understanding of the world

SMSC
Cultural diversity
RE
Geography
History
Science and DT
Natural History/humanities
(Curriculum, campus and community)
10 Doorways and SDGs

Maths development

Mathematical skills and logical thinking
Numeracy
Data handling
Shape and space
10 Doorways and SDGs
(Curriculum, campus and community)

Inquirers
Risk takers
Caring/principled
Open-minded
Well balanced
Reflective
Critically engaged

PSHE
Inter-/Intra-personal skills and personal mental and physical health management
Social and emotional aspects of learning (SMSC)
Healthy lifestyles
10 Doorways and SDGs
(Curriculum, campus and community)

Inquirers
Risk takers
Caring/principled
Open-minded
Well balanced
Reflective
Critically engaged

Communication – language and literacy

Verbal/linguistic
Reading/writing
Oral/aural (debating)
Handwriting
Presentation of ideas
Publicity of causes
Other languages
SMSC
10 Doorways and SDGs
(Curriculum, Campus and Community)

Computing and ICT
Computing and ICT
Computing and ICT
Global and local links
Computing and ICT
Computing and ICT
Computing and ICT

Inquirers
Risk takers
Caring/principled
Open-minded
Well balanced
Reflective
Critically engaged

Inquirers
Risk takers
Caring/principled
Open-minded
Well balanced
Reflective
Critically engaged

Physical development

PE
Games
Gymnastics
Swimming
Bodily awareness and kinaesthetic skills
Movement/dance
10 Doorways and SDGs
(Curriculum, campus and community)

Creative development

Musical/rhythmic
Music
Art
Imagination
Drama
Cultural diversity
SMSC
10 Doorways and SDGs
(Curriculum, Campus and Community)

Appendix 11:

INTEGRATED TOPIC PLANNING SHEET

The following figure is available to download and print from https://www.crownhouse.co.uk/leadership-for-sustainability.

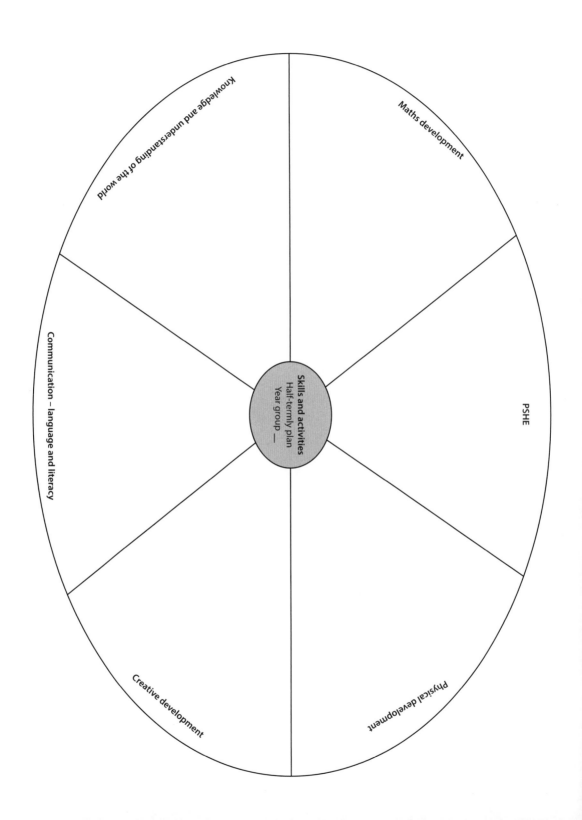

Skills and activities
Half-termly plan
Year group —

Maths development

PSHE

Physical development

Creative development

Communication - language and literacy

Knowledge and understanding of the world

REFERENCES

Admiral (2019). School crawl: drop off adds 22 minutes to daily commute [press release] (July). Available at: https://www.admiral.com/pdf-control?file=sites/default/files/press-office/2019-07/Admiral%20-%20School%20Crawl%20-%20FINAL.

Alexander, R. J. (ed.) (2010). *Children, Their World, Their Education: Final Report and Recommendations of the Cambridge Primary Review.* Abingdon and New York: Routledge.

Allen, P. (2017 [1982]). *Who Sank the Boat?* London: Puffin.

Alton, L. (2017). How exactly do cleaning supplies affect the environment? *Blue & Green Tomorrow* (9 November). Available at: https://blueandgreentomorrow.com/environment/how-exactly-cleaning-supplies-affect-environment.

Ambrose, J. (2021). How green is your 'green' energy tariff? *The Guardian* (2 April). Available at: https://www.theguardian.com/business/2021/apr/02/green-energy-tariff-renewable-deals.

Angell, S. W. and Dandelion, P. (eds) (2013). *The Oxford Handbook of Quaker Studies.* Oxford: Oxford University Press.

Anthes, E. (2021). Ventilation and surveillance testing can help keep US schools open in the fall new studies suggest. *New York Times* (21 May). Available at: https://www.nytimes.com/2021/05/21/health/aerosol-covid-testing-school-reopening.html.

Ardoin, N. M., Bowers, A. W. and Gaillard, E. (2020). Environmental education outcomes for conservation: a systematic review. *Biological Conservation*, 241. Available at: https://www.sciencedirect.com/science/article/pii/S0006320719307116.

Badaracco, J. L. (2002). *Leading Quietly: An Unorthodox Guide to Doing the Right Thing.* Boston, MA: Harvard Business School Press.

Balch, O. (2019). Meet the world's first 'minister for future generations'. *The Guardian* (2 March). Available at: https://www.theguardian.com/world/2019/mar/02/meet-the-worlds-first-future-generations-commissioner.

Barker, C. M. (2016 [1923]). *The Complete Book of Flower Fairies.* London: Penguin Random House Children's.

Barkham, P. (2020). Going local: how to make a big difference in small ways. *The Guardian* (13 January). Available at: https://www.theguardian.com/books/2020/jan/13/going-local-how-to-make-a-big-difference-in-small-ways.

Bass, B. (1990). *Bass and Stogdill's Handbook of Leadership: Theory, Research and Managerial Applications*, 3rd edn. New York: Free Press.

BBC Trust (2014). *Trust Conclusions on the Executive Report on Science Impartiality Review Actions.* Available at: http://downloads.bbc.co.uk/bbctrust/assets/files/pdf/our_work/science_impartiality/trust_conclusions.pdf.

Beaudry, F. (2019). Ski resorts and their impact on the environment. *Treehugger* (3 November). Available at: https://www.treehugger.com/ski-resorts-and-the-environment-1203969.

Bell, G. (2004). *The Permaculture Way: Practical Steps to Create a Self-Sustaining World*, 2nd edn. East Meon: Permanent Publications.

Bellis, M. A., Ashton, K., Hughes, K., Ford, K., Bishop, J. and Paranjothy, S. (2015). *Adverse Childhood Experiences and Their Impact on Health-Harming Behaviours in the Welsh Adult Population.* Cardiff: Public

Health Wales. Available at: https://www2.nphs.wales.nhs.uk/PRIDDocs. nsf/7c21215d6d0c613e80256f490030c05a/d488a3852491bc1d80257f370038919e/$FILE/ ACE%20Report%20FINAL%20(E).pdf.

Berners-Lee, M. (2010). *How Bad Are Bananas? The Carbon Footprint of Everything.* London: Profile Books.

Berry, W. (1971). *The Unforeseen Wilderness: An Essay on Kentucky's Red River.* Lexington, KY: University Press of Kentucky.

Bird, R. (n.d.). Extended schools and the community schools movement. *Teaching Expertise.* Available at: https://www.teachingexpertise.com/articles/extended-schools-and-the-community-schools-movement.

Botsman, R. and Rogers, R. (2011). *What's Mine Is Yours: How Collaborative Consumption Is Changing the Way We Live.* London: HarperCollins.

Bottery, M. (2016). *Educational Leadership for a More Sustainable World.* London: Bloomsbury.

Bourn, D. (2014). *The Theory and Practice of Global Learning.* Research Paper No. 11 for the Global Learning Programme. London: UCL Institute of Education. Available at: https://discovery.ucl.ac.uk/id/ eprint/1492723/1/DERC_ResearchPaper11-TheTheoryAndPracticeOfGlobalLearning[2].pdf.

Brahic, C. (2021). The other environmental emergency: loss of biodiversity poses as great a risk to humanity as climate change. *The Economist Technology Quarterly*, 3–4. Available at: https://www. economist.com/technology-quarterly/2021/06/15/loss-of-biodiversity-poses-as-great-a-risk-to-humanity-as-climate-change.

Breuer, A., Roper, N., Sudhakar, S. and Randerson, J. (2015). Keep it in the ground: Bill Gates, help stop climate change – video. *The Guardian* (30 April). Available at: https://www.theguardian.com/ environment/video/2015/apr/30/hi-bill-keep-it-in-the-ground-campaign.

Buckley Sander, J. and Blair, F. (2011). *Leading for the Future: A Collaborative Project to Support, Inspire and Engage School Leaders for Positive Change in Education.* Available at: http://assets.wwf.org.uk/downloads/ leadingforthefuture_finalreport.pdf.

Chan, B., Choy, G. and Lee, A. (2009). Harmony as the basis for education for sustainable development: a case example of Yew Chung International Schools. *International Journal of Early Childhood*, 41(2): 35–48.

Children's Commissioner (2018a). *'Are They Shouting Because of Me?' Voices of Children Living in Households with Domestic Abuse, Parental Substance Misuse and Mental Health Issues* (July). Available at: https://www. childrenscommissioner.gov.uk/wp-content/uploads/2018/08/Are-they-shouting-because-of-me.pdf.

Children's Commissioner (2018b). *Estimating the Prevalence of the 'Toxic Trio': Evidence from the Adult Psychiatric Morbidity Survey – Vulnerability Technical Report 2* (July). Available at: https://www. childrenscommissioner.gov.uk/wp-content/uploads/2018/07/Vulnerability-Technical-Report-2-Estimating-the-prevalence-of-the-toxic-trio.pdf.

Children's Society (2018). *The Good Childhood Report 2018.* Available at: https://www.basw.co.uk/system/ files/resources/thegood_childhood_report_2018_0.pdf.

Churchill, W. L. S. (1943). House of Commons Rebuilding. Hansard, HC vol. 393, cols 403–473 (28 October). Available at: https://api.parliament.uk/historic-hansard/commons/1943/oct/28/ house-of-commons-rebuilding.

Climate Assembly UK (2020). *The Path to Net Zero: Climate Assembly UK Full Report.* London: House of Commons. Available at: https://www.climateassembly.uk/report.

Cooper, B. (2018). *Primary Colours: The Decline of Arts Education in Primary Schools and How It Can Be Reversed.* London: The Fabian Society. Available at: https://fabians.org.uk/wp-content/uploads/2019/ 01/FS-Primary-Colours-Report-WEB-FINAL.pdf.

Cooper, L. (2017). Jane Goodall's chilling message: 'We have stolen our children's future'. *HuffPost* (19 June). Available at: https://www.huffpost.com/archive/au/entry/jane-goodalls-chilling-message-we-have-stolen-our-childrens_a_22489375.

Critchley, P. (2019). *The Economics of Flourishing* [e-book] (n. p.). Available at: https://www.academia. edu/41227587/The_Economics_of_Flourishing.

Cruikshank, J. (2019). To understand the climate crisis, look to Indigenous stories. *rabble.ca* (18 April). Available at: https://rabble.ca/news/2019/04/understand-climate-crisis-look-indigenous-stories.

Daly, J., Burchett, M. and Torpy, F. (2010). Plants in the classroom can improve student performance (29 October). Available at: http://www.ieqindoorplants.com.au/wp-content/uploads/2012/01/Effects-of-indoor-plants-on-school-performance-2010-V1.pdf.

Davies, J., Engdahl, I., Otieno, L., Pramling-Samuelson, I., Siraj-Blatchford, J. and Vallabh, P. (2009). Early childhood education for sustainability: recommendations for development. *International Journal of Childhood*, 41(2): 113–117.

De Gex, J. (1999). *Shakespeare's Flora and Fauna*. London: Pavilion.

Department of Economic and Social Affairs (2006). *Social Justice in an Open World: The Role of the United Nations*. Ref: ST/ESA/305. New York: United Nations. Available at: https://www.un.org/esa/socdev/documents/ifsd/SocialJustice.pdf.

Department for Education (1994). *Religious Education and Collective Worship,* Circular number 1/94 (31 January). Available at: https://assets.publishing.service.gov.uk/government/uploads/system/uploads/attachment_data/file/281929/Collective_worship_in_schools.pdf.

Department for Education (2012). Top Tips for Sustainability in Schools. Ref: DFE-32056-2012 (1 February). Available at: https://assets.publishing.service.gov.uk/government/uploads/system/uploads/attachment_data/file/187037/DFE-32056-2012.pdf.

Department for Education (2014). *Promoting Fundamental British Values as Part of SMSC in Schools: Departmental Advice for Maintained Schools*. Ref: DFE-00679-2014 (November). Available at: https://assets.publishing.service.gov.uk/government/uploads/system/uploads/attachment_data/file/380595/SMSC_Guidance_Maintained_Schools.pdf.

Department for Education (2020). *Relationships Education, Relationships and Sex Education (RSE) and Health Education: Statutory Guidance for Governing Bodies, Proprietors, Head Teachers, Principals, Senior Leadership Teams, Teachers*. Available at: https://assets.publishing.service.gov.uk/government/uploads/system/uploads/attachment_data/file/1019542/Relationships_Education__Relationships_and_Sex_Education__RSE__and_Health_Education.pdf.

Department for Education (2021). *Sustainability and Climate Change: A Draft Strategy for the Education and Children's Services System* (November). Available at: https://assets.publishing.service.gov.uk/government/uploads/system/uploads/attachment_data/file/1031454/SCC_DRAFT_Strategy.pdf.

Department for Education and Skills (2003). *Excellence and Enjoyment: A Strategy for Primary Schools*. Ref: DfES/0377/2003. Available at: https://webarchive.nationalarchives.gov.uk/ukgwa/20040722022638/http:/www.dfes.gov.uk/primarydocument.

Department for Education and Skills (2006). *Learning Outside the Classroom: Manifesto*. Nottingham: DfES. Available at: https://www.lotc.org.uk/wp-content/uploads/2011/03/G1.-LOtC-Manifesto.pdf.

Department for Environment and Rural Affairs (Defra) (2020). Enabling a Natural Capital Approach: Guidance (4 August). Available at: https://www.gov.uk/government/publications/enabling-a-natural-capital-approach-enca-guidance/enabling-a-natural-capital-approach-guidance.

Department for Health and Social Care (2020). Tackling obesity: empowering adults and children to live healthier lives [policy paper]. Available at: https://www.gov.uk/government/publications/tackling-obesity-government-strategy.

Department for Transport (2021). Walking and cycling statistics, England: 2020 [official statistics] (22 September). Available at: https://www.gov.uk/government/statistics/walking-and-cycling-statistics-england-2020/walking-and-cycling-statistics-england-2020.

Dewey, J. (2007 [1963]). *Experience and Learning*. New York: Free Press.

Edgecliffe-Johnson, A. and Nauman, B. (2019). Fossil fuel divestment has 'zero' climate impact, says Bill Gates. *Financial Times* (17 September). Available at: https://www.ft.com/content/21009e1c-d8c9-11e9-8f9b-77216ebe1f17.

Elhacham, E., Ben-Uri, L., Grozovski, J., Bar-On, Y. M. and Milo, R. (2020). Global human-made mass exceeds all living biomass. *Nature*, 588: 442–444.

Environmental Audit Committee (2019). *Fixing Fashion: Clothing Consumption and Sustainability*. London: House of Commons. Available at: https://publications.parliament.uk/pa/cm201719/cmselect/cmenvaud/1952/1952.pdf.

Forster, E. M. (1969 [1910]). *Howards End.* London: Penguin Modern Classics.

French, D. (2005). *Everything Is Bad for You: An A–Z Guide to What You Never Knew Could Kill You.* Naperville, IL: Sourcebooks.

Fullan, M. (2004). *Systems Thinkers in Action: Moving Beyond the Standards Plateau.* Nottingham: Department for Education and Skills. Available at: http://www.michaelfullan.ca/wp-content/uploads/2016/06/13396063090.pdf.

Fullan, M. and Hargreaves, A. (1992). *What's Worth Fighting For in Your School?* Maidenhead: Open University Press.

Gardener, N. J. L. and Bainbridge, J. A. (2006). Corporate Memory Loss – A Quality Cure? Symposium series number 151. *IChemE.* Available at: https://www.icheme.org/media/9833/xix-paper-46.pdf.

Gates, B. (2021). *How to Avoid a Climate Disaster: The Solutions We Have and the Breakthroughs We Need.* London: Allen Lane.

Gove, M. (2013). I refuse to surrender to the Marxist teachers hell-bent on destroying our schools: education secretary berates 'the new enemies of promise' for opposing his plans. *Daily Mail* (23 March). Available at: https://www.dailymail.co.uk/debate/article-2298146/I-refuse-surrender-Marxist-teachers-hell-bent-destroying-schools-Education-Secretary-berates-new-enemies-promise-opposing-plans.html.

Green, J. (2015). *The Environmental Curriculum: Opportunities for Environmental Education across the National Curriculum – Early Years Foundation Stage and Primary.* Wolverhampton: University of Wolverhampton and National Environmental Education Association. Available at: https://naee.org.uk/wp-content/uploads/2015/06/NAEE_The_Environmental_Curriculum.pdf.

Greenleaf, R. K. (2002 [1977]). *Servant Leadership: A Journey into the Nature of Legitimate Power and Greatness,* 25th anniversary edn. Mahwah, NJ: Paulist Press.

Green Schools Project and NUS (2019). *Schools Sustainability Survey: Research into Pupils' Views on Environmental Sustainability* (March). Available at: https://uploads-ssl.webflow.com/6008334066c47be740656954/606f16921cb6409cf72f5032_20190306_NUS%20GSP_Schools%20sustainability%20survey_Report_FINAL.pdf.

Gretton, J. and Jackson, M. (1976). *William Tyndale: Collapse of a School – or a System?* London: George Allen & Unwin.

Guardian, The (2020). Hilary Mantel: 'Being a novelist is no fun. But fun isn't on my list' (4 October). Available at: https://www.theguardian.com/books/2020/oct/04/hilary-mantel-wolf-hall-mantel-pieces.

Haines, G. (2019). The world's first minister for future generations. *Positive News* (5 July). Available at: https://www.positive.news/uk/the-worlds-first-minister-for-future-generations.

Halberstam, D. (1971). Vantage Point. *New York Times* (31 October). Available at: https://www.nytimes.com/1971/10/31/archives/the-vantage-point-perspectives-of-the-presidency-19631969-by-lyndon.html?searchResultPosition=2.

Hammersley, A., Jones, E. and Perry, G. A. (1968). *The Teacher's Handbook to Environmental Studies.* London: Blandford Press.

Hannon, V., with Peterson, A. (2017). *Thrive: Schools Reinvented for the Real Challenges We Face.* London: Innovation Unit Press.

Hanson, D. and Middleton, S. (2000). The challenges of eco-leadership: green Machiavellianism. *Greener Management International,* 29 (spring): 95–107.

Harland, M. (2018). Redefining the third permaculture ethic: future care. *Permaculture Magazine,* 95 (spring): 6–7.

Harvey, D. (2005). *A Brief History of Neoliberalism.* Oxford: Oxford University Press.

Harvey, F. (2020). Half UK's true carbon footprint created abroad, research finds. *The Guardian* (16 April). Available at: https://www.theguardian.com/environment/2020/apr/16/britain-climate-efforts-undermined-failure-imports-carbon.

Hazell, W. (2020). Teach the science behind climate change not a 'morality tale', says Ofsted chief Amanda Spielman. *iNews* (1 December). Available at: https://inews.co.uk/news/education/teach-science-climate-change-morality-ofsted-chief-amanda-spielman-778882.

Heffernan, O. (2019). Scientists track damage from controversial deep-sea mining method. *Nature*, 567(7748) (March): 294.

Henrich, J. (2021). *The Weirdest People in the World: How the West Became Psychologically Peculiar and Particularly Prosperous.* London: Penguin.

Higgins, P. (2015). *Eradicating Ecocide: Laws and Governance to Stop the Destruction of the Planet*, 2nd edn. London: Shepheard-Walwyn.

HM Government (2020). *The Ten Point Plan for a Green Industrial Revolution: Building Back Better, Supporting Green Jobs, and Accelerating Our Path to Net Zero* [policy paper] (18 November). Available at: https://assets.publishing.service.gov.uk/government/uploads/system/uploads/attachment_data/file/936567/10_POINT_PLAN_BOOKLET.pdf.

HM Treasury (2003). *Every Child Matters: Presented to Parliament by the Chief Secretary to the Treasury by Command of Her Majesty September 2003.* Cm 5860. Norwich: TSO. Available at: https://assets.publishing.service.gov.uk/government/uploads/system/uploads/attachment_data/file/272064/5860.pdf.

Hoekstra, A. Y., Chapagain, A. K., Aldaya, M. M. and Mekonnen, M. M. (2011). *The Water Footprint Assessment Manual: Setting the Global Standard.* London and Washington, DC: Earthscan.

Holland, M. (2020). *I Ate Sunshine for Breakfast: A Celebration of Plants Around the World.* London: Flying Eye Books.

Holt, M. (2005). The slow school: an idea whose time has come. In M. K. Stone and Z. Barlow (eds), *Ecological Literacy: Educating Our Children for a Sustainable World.* San Francisco, CA: Sierra Club Books, pp. 23–31.

Home Office (2021 [2015]). Revised Prevent Duty Guidance: for England and Wales. Available at: https://www.gov.uk/government/publications/prevent-duty-guidance/revised-prevent-duty-guidance-for-england-and-wales.

Hopkin, J. (2018). *Geography and Global Learning: A National Research Report by the Geographical Association.* Sheffield: Geography Association. Available at: www.geography.org.uk/write/mediauploads/projects/ga_global_learning_report_2018.pdf.

Hopkins, R. (2009). *The Transition Handbook: From Oil Dependency to Local Resilience.* Cambridge: Green Books.

Hopkins, R. (2019). *From What Is to What If: Unleashing the Power of Imagination to Create the Future We Want.* London: Chelsea Green Publishing.

Hopkins, R. (2020). Applying the design principles in business. *Permaculture Principles.* Available at: https://permacultureprinciples.com/post/principles-in-business.

Hren, B. and Birney, A. (2011). *Pathways: To Education for Sustainable Development – a Practical Tool for Planning a Whole School Approach.* Woking: WWF-UK. Available at: http://assets.wwf.org.uk/downloads/pathways_2011.pdf.

Hutt, R. (2016). Why do civilizations collapse? *World Economic Forum* (17 March). Available at: https://www.weforum.org/agenda/2016/03/why-do-civilizations-collapse.

Illich, I. (1995). *Deschooling Society*, new edn. London: Marion Boyars Publishers.

Jayasena, S. (2017). Sustainability means to me... By Sonal, 16. *Global Generation* (31 July). Available at: https://www.globalgeneration.org.uk/blog/2017/7/28/sustainability-to-me-means-by-sonal-16.

Jones, B. (2015). A challenged democracy: wicked problems and political failures. *The Conversation* (3 April). Available at: https://theconversation.com/a-challenged-democracy-wicked-problems-and-political-failures-39040.

Jupp, E. (2020). Tyre pollution could be 1,200 times WORSE than exhaust emissions. *Motoring Research* (12 March). Available at: https://www.motoringresearch.com/car-news/tyre-pollution-worse-exhaust-emissions.

Kallis, G., Kostakis, V., Lange, S., Muraca, B., Paulson, S. and Schmelzer, M. (2018). Research on degrowth. *Annual Review of Environment and Resources*, 43: 291–316.

Killingsworth, M. A. and Gilbert, D. T. (2010). A wandering mind is an unhappy mind. *Science*, 330(6006): 932.

Klimek, K. J., Ritzenhein, E. and Sullivan, K. D. (2008). *Generative Leadership: Shaping New Futures for Today's Schools.* Thousand Oaks, CA: Corwin.

Kohn, A. (1999). *Punished by Rewards.* Boston, MA: Houghton Mifflin.

Kumar, S. (2011). We are all leaders. *Resurgence,* 264. Available at: https://www.resurgence.org/magazine/article3272-we-are-all-leaders.html.

Lanese, N. (2017). Storytelling empowers indigenous people to conserve their environments. *Mongabay* (27 November). Available at: https://news.mongabay.com/2017/11/storytelling-empowers-indigenous-people-to-conserve-their-environments.

Langston, C. A. (2016). How to use rhetoric to get what you want [video]. *TED-Ed* (20 September). Available at: https://www.youtube.com/watch?v=3klMM9BkW5o.

Layard, R. and Ward, G. (2020). *Can We Be Happier? Evidence and Ethics.* London: Pelican Books.

London Sustainable Development Commission (2011). *Children and Nature: A Quasi-Systemic Review of the Empirical Evidence.* London: Greater London Authority. Available at: https://www.london.gov.uk/sites/default/files/lsdc_-_sowing_the_seeds_-_literature_review_2011.pdf.

Loughran, J. (2021). EU introduces 'right to repair' rules for electrical goods. *Engineering and Technology* (2 March). Available at: https://eandt.theiet.org/content/articles/2021/03/eu-introduces-right-to-repair-rules-for-electrical-goods.

Louv, R. (2008). *Last Child in the Woods: Saving Our Children from Nature-Deficit Disorder.* Chapel Hill, NC: Algonquin Books of Chapel Hill.

Lovelock, J. E. (2007). *The Revenge of Gaia: Earth's Climate Crisis and the Fate of Humanity.* London: Penguin.

Lovelock, J. E. (2000 [1979]). *Gaia: A New Look at Life on Earth.* Oxford: Oxford University Press.

McClenachan, L. (2009). Documenting loss of large trophy fish from the Florida Keys with historical photographs. *Conservation Biology,* 23(3): 636–643.

Macfarlane, R. (2015). *Landmarks.* London: Penguin Random House.

Macfarlane, R. and Morris, J. (2017). *The Lost Words.* London: Penguin Random House.

McGrath, J. (2008). Which is more environmentally friendly: paper or plastic? *How Stuff Works* (20 August). Available at: https://science.howstuffworks.com/environmental/green-science/paper-plastic.htm.

Macnamara, L. (2020). How to create a culture of collective intelligence. *Permaculture,* 103 (spring): 45–50.

Malone, K. (2007). The bubble-wrap generation: children growing up in walled gardens. *Environmental Research,* 13(4): 513–527.

Marmot, M., Allen, J., Boyce, T., Goldblatt, P. and Morrison, J. (2020). *Health Equality in England: The Marmot Review 10 Years On.* London: Institute of Health Equality. Available at: https://www.health.org.uk/sites/default/files/upload/publications/2020/Health%20Equity%20in%20England_The%20Marmot%20Review%2010%20Years%20On_full%20report.pdf.

Marmot, M., Allen, J., Goldblatt, P., Boyce, T., McNeish, D., Grady, M. and Geddes, I. (2010). *Fair Society, Healthy Lives: Strategic Review of Health Inequalities in England Post-2010* [Marmot Review]. Available at: https://www.instituteofhealthequity.org/resources-reports/fair-society-healthy-lives-the-marmot-review/fair-society-healthy-lives-full-report-pdf.pdf.

Masento, N. A., Golightly, M., Field, D. T., Butler, L. T. and van Reekum, C. M. (2014). Effects of hydration status on cognitive performance and mood. *British Journal of Nutrition,* 111(10): 1841–1852. Available at: https://www.cambridge.org/core/journals/british-journal-of-nutrition/article/effects-of-hydration-status-on-cognitive-performance-and-mood/1210B6BE585E03C71A299C52B51B22F7#.

Maslow, A. H. (1943). A theory of human motivation. *Psychological Review,* 50(4): 370–396.

Maunder, S. (2021). Revealed: the happiest places to live in Great Britain in 2021. *Which?* (28 November). Available at: https://www.which.co.uk/news/2021/11/revealed-the-happiest-places-to-live-in-great-britain-in-2021.

Meadows, H., Meadows, D. L. and Randers, J. (1992). *Beyond the Limits: Confronting Global Collapse, Envisioning a Sustainable Future.* White River Junction, VT: Chelsea Green.

Mehdinezhad, V. and Nouri, F. (2016). The relationship between elementary school principals' transformational leadership and spiritual well-being. *Management in Education*, 30(2): 42–49.

Monbiot, G. (2016). Neoliberalism – the ideology at the root of all our problems. *The Guardian* (15 April). Available at: https://www.theguardian.com/books/2016/apr/15/neoliberalism-ideology-problem-george-monbiot.

Morch, R. and Hadow, P. (2007). *Who Will Save Us?* Callington: Rebecca Morch Publishing.

Moss, S. (2012). *Natural Childhood.* Rotherham: National Trust. Available at: https://nt.global.ssl.fastly.net/documents/read-our-natural-childhood-report.pdf.

Mott, S. M., Robinson, D. H., Walden, A., Burnette, J. and Rutherford, A. S. (2012). Illuminating the effects of dynamic lighting on student learning. *Sage Open*: 1–9. Available at: https://journals.sagepub.com/doi/pdf/10.1177/2158244012445585.

Moyes, S. (2020). How fracking in America makes Scotland the home of plastic production. *Friends of the Earth Scotland* (7 July). Available at: https://foe.scot/how-fracking-in-america-makes-scotland-the-home-of-plastic-production.

Myers, R. (2016). Hand dryers vs. paper towels: which has a larger environmental impact? *Green Schools Alliance* (16 November). Available at: https://www.greenschoolsalliance.org/blogs/16/394#.

Newberry, M., Gallant, A. and Riley, P. (eds) (2013). *Emotion and School: Understanding How the Hidden Curriculum Influences Relationships, Leadership, Teaching, and Learning.* Bingley: Emerald Group Publishing.

Nicholls, J., Lawlor, E., Neitzert, E. and Goodspeed, T. (2009). *A Guide to Social Return on Investment.* New Economics Foundation and Scottish Government. Available at: https://neweconomics.org/uploads/files/aff3779953c5b88d53_cpm6v3v71.pdf.

Norgaard, K. M. (2011). *Living in Denial: Climate Change, Emotions and Everyday Life.* Cambridge, MA: MIT Press.

O'Brien, L. (2009). Learning outdoors: the forest school approach. *Education 3–13*, 37(1): 45–60.

Obama, Barack (2010). Remarks by the president on health insurance reform. Speech delivered at Arcadia University, Pennsylvania, 8 March. Available at: https://obamawhitehouse.archives.gov/realitycheck/the-press-office/remarks-president-health-insurance-reform-arcadia-university.

Office for National Statistics (2019). Exploring the UK's digital divide [statistical release] (4 March). Available at: https://www.ons.gov.uk/peoplepopulationandcommunity/householdcharacteristics/homeinternetandsocialmediausage/articles/exploringtheuksdigitaldivide/2019-03-04.

Office for National Statistics (2019). The decoupling of economic growth from carbon emissions: UK evidence (21 October). Available at: https://www.ons.gov.uk/economy/nationalaccounts/uksectoraccounts/compendium/economicreview/october2019/thedecouplingofeconomicgrowthfromcarbonemissionsukevidence.

Ofsted (2003). *Taking the First Step Forward – Towards an Education for Sustainable Development: Good Practice in Primary and Secondary Schools.* London: Ofsted. Available at: https://dera.ioe.ac.uk/4778/1/Taking_the_first_step_forward_towards_an_education_for_sustainable_development.pdf.

Ofsted (2008). *Schools and Sustainability: A Climate for Change?* Ref: 070173 (May). Available at: http://esd.escalate.ac.uk/downloads/1768.pdf.

Ofsted (2009). *Education for Sustainable Development: Improving Schools – Improving Lives.* Ref: 090004 (May). Available at: https://dera.ioe.ac.uk/1089/1/Education%20for%20sustainable%20development.pdf.

Ofsted (2019). Inspecting the Curriculum: Revising Inspection Methodology to Support the Education Inspection Framework. Ref: 190024 (14 May). Available at: https://assets.publishing.service.gov.uk/government/uploads/system/uploads/attachment_data/file/814685/Inspecting_the_curriculum.pdf.

Ofsted (2020). *The Annual Report of Her Majesty's Chief Inspector of Education, Children's Services and Skills 2019/20.* Ref: HC 972 2020-21. Available at: https://assets.publishing.service.gov.uk/government/uploads/system/uploads/attachment_data/file/939834/Ofsted_Annual_Report_2019-2020.pdf.

Ofsted (2021). Education Inspection Framework (updated 23 July). Available at: https://www.gov.uk/government/publications/education-inspection-framework.

Olajide, F. (2012). *My Culture: Yoruba.* Leicester: Matador.

Olusoga, D. (2017). *Black and British: A Forgotten History*. London: Pan Macmillan.

Opray, M. (2017). Nickel mining: the hidden environmental cost of electric cars. *The Guardian* (24 August). Available at: https://www.theguardian.com/sustainable-business/2017/aug/24/nickel-mining-hidden-environmental-cost-electric-cars-batteries.

Orr, D. W. (2005). Recollection. In M. K. Stone and Z. Barlow (eds), *Ecological Literacy: Educating Our Children for a Sustainable World*. San Francisco, CA: Sierra Club Books, pp. 96–110.

Orr, D. W. (2011). Walking north on a southbound train. In D. W. Orr, *Hope is an Imperative: The Essential David Orr*. Washington, DC: Island Press, pp. 57–65.

Oxfam (2015). *Global Citizenship in the Classroom: A Guide for Teachers*. Oxford: Oxfam. Available at: https://oxfamilibrary.openrepository.com/bitstream/handle/10546/620105/edu-global-citizenship-teacher-guide-091115-en.pdf.

Palmer, S. (2015). *Toxic Childhood: How the Modern World Is Damaging Our Children and What We Can Do About It*. London: Orion.

Pauly, D. (1995). Anecdotes and the shifting baseline syndrome of fisheries. *Trends in Ecology and Evolution*, 10(10): 430. DOI: 10.1016/s0169-5347(00)89171-5

Pearce, F. (2012). *The Land Grabbers: The New Fight Over Who Owns the Earth*. London: Eden Project Books.

Pergams, O. R. W. and Zaradic, P. A. (2008). Evidence for a fundamental and pervasive shift from nature-based recreation. *Proceedings of the National Academy of Sciences*, 105(7): 2295–2300.

Piesing, M. (2020). How to build a nuclear warning for 10,000 years' time. *BBC Future* (3 August). Available at: https://www.bbc.com/future/article/20200731-how-to-build-a-nuclear-warning-for-10000-years-time.

Plowden, B. (1967). *Children and their Primary Schools: A Report of the Central Advisory Council for Education (England)* [Plowden Report]. London: HMSO. Available at: http://www.educationengland.org.uk/documents/plowden/plowden1967-1.html.

Pope Francis (2015). *Encyclical Letter 'Laudato Si' of the Holy Father Francis on Care for Our Common Home*. Vatican City: Vatican Press. Available at: https://www.vatican.va/content/dam/francesco/pdf/encyclicals/documents/papa-francesco_20150524_enciclica-laudato-si_en.pdf.

The Prince of Wales, with Juniper, T. and Skelly, I. (2010). *Harmony: A New Way of Looking at the World*. London: Blue Door.

Purdy, D. (2021). Cryptocurrency mining has a huge carbon footprint. Here's what experts think we should do about it. *Climate News 360* (5 August). Available at: https://climate360news.lmu.edu/cryptocurrency-mining-has-a-huge-carbon-footprint-heres-what-experts-think-we-should-do-about-it.

Raser-Rowland, A. and Grubb, A. (2016). *The Art of Frugal Hedonism: A Guide to Spending Less While Enjoying Everything More*. Hepburn: Melliodora.

Ravilious, K. (2020). Biomass energy: green or dirty? *Physics World* (8 January). Available at: https://physicsworld.com/a/biomass-energy-green-or-dirty.

Raworth, K. (2017). *Doughnut Economics: Seven Ways to Think Like a 21st-Century Economist*. London: Penguin Random House.

Rees, J. (2017). Wellbeing and School Improvement. In D. Price (ed.), *Education Forward: Moving Schools into the Future*. Horley: Crux Publishing, pp. 123–130.

Reference (2020). What is the origin of the phrase 'it takes a village to raise a child?' (15 April). Available at: https://www.reference.com/world-view/origin-phrase-takes-village-raise-child-3e375ce098113bb4.

Reich, C. (1970). *The Greening of America*. New York: Random House.

Reuters (2020). One in five UK children report nightmares about climate change (3 March). Available at: https://www.reuters.com/article/climate-change-children-idUSL1N2AV1FF.

Riddiford, J. (2021). *Learning to Lead Together an Ecological and Community Approach*, Abingdon: Routledge.

Ritchie, H. and Roser, M. (2021). Clean water. *Our World in Data* (June). Available at: https://ourworldindata.org/water-access#access-to-safe-drinking-water.

Ryan, W. (2008). *Leadership with a Moral Purpose: Turning Your School Inside Out*. Carmarthen: Crown House Publishing.

Scanlan, D. and Savill-Smith, C. (2021). *Teacher Wellbeing Index 2021*. London: Education Support. Available at: https://www.educationsupport.org.uk/media/qzna4gxb/twix-2021.pdf.

Schleicher, A. (2021). Green at fifteen – what schools can do to support the climate. *OECD Education and Skills Today* (25 January). Available at: https://oecdedutoday.com/green-at-fifteen-schools-support-climate.

Schumacher, E. F. (1993 [1973]). *Small Is Beautiful: A Study of Economics As If People Mattered*. London: Vintage Books.

Scott, B. (2019). What ELSA said to Ofsted. *University of Bath* [blog] (16 April). Available at: https://blogs.bath.ac.uk/edswahs/2019/04/16/what-elsa-said-to-ofsted.

Seuss, Dr. (1971). *The Lorax*. London: HarperCollins.

Shepherd, J. (2010). Community cohesion slips off Ofsted's agenda. *The Guardian* (20 October). Available at: https://www.theguardian.com/education/2010/oct/20/community-cohesion-off-ofsteds-agenda.

Shepley, M., Sachs, N., Sadatsafavi, H., Fournier, C. and Peditto, K. (2019). The impact of green space on violent crime in urban environments: an evidence synthesis. *International Journal of Environmental Research and Public Health*, 16(24): 5119. Available at: https://doi.org/10.3390/ijerph16245119.

Singleton, J. (2015). Head, heart and hands model for transformative learning: place as context for changing sustainability values. *Journal of Sustainability Education* (16 March). Available at: http://www.susted.com/wordpress/content/head-heart-and-hands-model-for-transformative-learning-place-as-context-for-changing-sustainability-values_2015_03.

Smith, C. (2010). Relaxed alertness: getting the right balance between a caring environment and high expectations. *Charlotte Mason Institute* (1 August). Available at: https://charlottemasoninstitute.org/2010/08/01/relaxed-alertness-getting-the-right-balance-between-a-caring-environment-and-high-expectations-by-carroll-smith.

Soga, M. and Gaston, K. J. (2018). Shifting baseline syndrome: causes, consequences and implications. *Frontiers in Ecology and the Environment*, 16(4): 222–230.

Standards and Testing Agency (2019). *Key Stage 2 Science Sampling 2018: Methodology Note and Outcomes*. Ref: STA/19/8346/e. Available at: https://assets.publishing.service.gov.uk/government/uploads/system/uploads/attachment_data/file/818678/Key_stage_2_science_sampling_2018_methodology_note_and_outcomes.pdf.

Standing, G. (2019). *Plunder of the Commons: A Manifesto for Sharing Public Wealth*. London: Pelican Books.

Starhawk (2016). Why diversity is important in permaculture. *International Permaculture*, 90 (winter): 7–9.

Sterling, S. (2004). *Sustainable Education: Re-visioning Learning and Change*. Bristol: Green Books.

Stern, N. (2006). *The Economics of Climate Change: The Stern Review*. Cambridge: Cambridge University Press.

Stern, N. (2021). A time for action on climate change and a time for change in economics. Centre for Climate Change Economics and Policy Working Paper 397/Grantham Research Institute on Climate Change and the Environment Working Paper 370. London: London School of Economics and Political Science. Available at: https://www.lse.ac.uk/granthaminstitute/wp-content/uploads/2021/10/working-paper-370-Stern.pdf.

Stirling, S. and Emery, H. (2016). *A Whole School Framework for Emotional Well Being and Mental Health: A Self-Assessment and Improvement Tool for School Leaders*. London: National Children's Bureau. Available at: https://www.ncb.org.uk/sites/default/files/uploads/files/NCB%20School%20Well%20Being%20Framework%20Leaders%20Tool%20FINAL.pdf.

Stone, M. K. and Barlow, Z. (eds) (2005). *Ecological Literacy: Educating Our Children for a Sustainable World*. San Francisco, CA: Sierra Club Books.

Stylianou, N., Guibourg, C. and Briggs, H. (2019). Climate change food calculator: what's your diet's carbon footprint? *BBC News* (9 August). Available at: https://www.bbc.co.uk/news/science-environment-46459714.

Sustainable Development Commission (2010). *Every Child's Future Matters*. London: Sustainable Development Commission. Available at: http://www.sd-commission.org.uk/data/files/publications/ecfm3_report_w.pdf.

Taleb, N. N. (2008). *The Black Swan: The Impact of the Highly Improbable*. London: Penguin.

Tilbury, D. (1997). A head, heart and hand approach to learning about environmental problems. *New Horizons in Education*, 38: 13–30.

Tudge, C. (1996). *The Time Before History: 5 million Years of Human Impact*. New York: Scribner.

United Nations (UN) (1987). *Report of the World Commission on Environment and Development: Our Common Future* [Brundtland Report]. Oxford: Oxford University Press. Available at: https://sustainabledevelopment.un.org/content/documents/5987our-common-future.pdf.

United Nations Economic Commission for Europe (UNECE) (2012). *Learning for the Future: Competencies in Education for Sustainable Development*. Utrecht: UNECE. Available at: https://www.unece.org/fileadmin/DAM/env/esd/ESD_Publications/Competences_Publication.pdf.

van Rossum, M. K. (2017). 3 dangers of artificial turf. *Huff Post* [blog] (6 December). Available at: https://www.huffpost.com/entry/3-dangers-of-artificial-t_b_1661499.

Vare, P. and Scott, W. (2007). Learning for a change: exploring the relationship between education and sustainable development. *Journal of Education for Sustainable Development*, 1(2): 191–198.

Vidal, J. (2017). Move by UK supermarkets threatens to bring Fairtrade crashing down. *The Guardian* (25 June). Available at: https://www.theguardian.com/global-development/2017/jun/24/fairtrade-crashing-down-sainsburys-tesco-tea-growers-nairobi.

Voiland, A. (2016). Methane matters. *NASA Earth Observatory* (8 March). Available at: https://earthobservatory.nasa.gov/features/MethaneMatters.

Watson, B. (2016). The troubling evolution of corporate greenwashing. *The Guardian* (20 August). Available at: https://www.theguardian.com/sustainable-business/2016/aug/20/greenwashing-environmentalism-lies-companies.

Water Footprint Calculator (2017). The hidden water in everyday products (7 February). Available at: https://www.watercalculator.org/footprint/the-hidden-water-in-everyday-products.

Webster, K. and Johnson, C. (2008). *Sense and Sustainability: Educating for a Low Carbon World*. Leeds: TerraPreta.

Wells, H. G. (1942). *The Outlook for Homo Sapiens*. London: Readers Union & Secker & Warburg.

Welsh Government (2019). A Guide to the Wellbeing of Future Generations Act. Available at: https://gov.wales/sites/default/files/publications/2019-06/easy-read-a-guide-to-the-wellbeing-of-future-generations-act.pdf.

Welsh Government (2021). New top team to lead Wales into a brighter future [press release] (13 May). Available at: https://gov.wales/new-top-team-to-lead-wales-into-a-brighter-future.

West, Aaron (2021). What does the new energy label mean for you and your home? *Which?* (10 March). Available at: https://www.which.co.uk/news/2021/03/what-does-the-new-energy-label-mean-for-you-and-your-home.

Wibberley, L. (1959). *The Mouse That Roared*. London: Corgi.

Wilson E. O. (1990). *Biophilia: The Human Bond with Other Species*. Cambridge, MA: Harvard University Press.

Wynes, S. and Nicholas, K. A. (2017). The climate mitigation gap: education and government recommendations miss the most effective individual actions. *Environmental Research Letters*, 12(7): 074024. Available at: https://iopscience.iop.org/article/10.1088/1748-9326/aa7541.

INDEX